CULTURE, HEALTH, AND RELIGION AT THE MILLENNIUM

Culture, Health, and Religion at the Millennium

Sweden Unparadised

Edited by

Marie Demker, Yvonne Leffler, and Ola Sigurdson

First published in 2014 by PALGRAVE MACMILLAN® in the United States—a division of St. Martin's Press LLC, 175 Fifth Avenue, New York, NY 10010.

Where this book is distributed in the UK, Europe and the rest of the world, this is by Palgrave Macmillan, a division of Macmillan Publishers Limited, registered in England, company number 785998, of Houndmills, Basingstoke, Hampshire RG21 6XS.

Palgrave Macmillan is the global academic imprint of the above companies and has companies and representatives throughout the world.

Palgrave® and Macmillan® are registered trademarks in the United States, the United Kingdom, Europe and other countries.

ISBN: 978-1-137-47222-9

Library of Congress Cataloging-in-Publication Data is available from the Library of Congress.

A catalogue record of the book is available from the British Library.

Design by Scribe Inc.

First edition: November 2014

10 9 8 7 6 5 4 3 2 1

CONTENTS

INTRODUCTION

HOW GLOOMY IS SWEDEN
AT THE MILLENNIUM?

MARIE DEMKER, YVONNE LEFFLER,
AND OLA SIGURDSON

HOW GLOOMY IS SWEDEN TODAY? WHATEVER HAPPENED to the "Swedish sin"? And what about social equality? English-speaking readers of Stieg Larsson's blockbuster Millennium trilogy—or those who have seen the movies based on these books—might ask with some astonishment, Is this what is happening in Sweden? With its stories of corruption, sexual violence, bureaucracy in the service of corrupt powers, and revenge, the reader or cinephile who has long associated Sweden with images of an affluent, complacent, and homogeneous society—as communicated by the internationally renowned idea of the "Swedish model"—must wonder what has happened to the state of Sweden.

Culture, Health, and Religion at the Millennium: Sweden Unparadised is an attempt by six Swedish scholars to present some answers to such questions, as the image of Sweden has undergone a transformation from that of a well-functioning but existentially bland economic wonder into a more pluralistic, fragmented, and—perhaps—gloomy society. Through interpretations of Swedish cinema, literature, health, politics, and religion today, we offer an understanding of the contemporary cultural and fictional representation of Sweden in media, debate, and popular culture. Coming from such diverse academic fields as comparative literature, film studies, political science, religious studies, and theology, it is our belief that a multidisciplinary approach is needed to capture some of the changes that Sweden has undergone in recent decades, as these have touched on different areas of Swedish society. As a background to the individual chapters, this introduction briefly tracks some of the major historical happenings, not covered by the chapters as such, that have formed what Sweden is today—especially regarding culture, economy, politics, religion, and social cohesion.

THE SWEDISH MODEL AT THE MILLENNIUM

In the 1950s, just after World War II, it was common to refer to Sweden internationally as a model of a successful welfare state. This "Swedish model" had several components, and among the most prominent were progress, consensus, social equality, and centralism. Of course, the attractiveness of this model depended on one's vantage point, but nevertheless, it was undeniable that Sweden had gone from an agrarian nation to an industrial state in a very short time and with very little societal unrest. Sweden championed the United Nations and strove for peace in conflicts the world over. At the same time, art, popular fiction, and cultural resources—perhaps especially its cinematic tradition—were celebrated internationally. In terms of religion, Sweden was increasingly seen as the most secular country in the world—with its strange amalgamation of private religion and a Lutheran state church—and it prided itself on its tolerant attitude.

Today, the image of Sweden abroad is in flux. Gone are the days of the movie director Ingmar Bergman and his existential *angst*, and gone too are the days of Vilgot Sjöman, who challenged the boundaries of what could be shown in a movie. The particular "Swedish model" of progress, consensus, social equality, and centralism has been less successful in meeting the challenges of a multicultural society, and it has lost much of its attractiveness internationally. At the same time, in the current economic crisis in the European Union, Sweden is still considered to be a model for a sound economy and a strong state, but now in a more neoliberal way. The Swedish standard of living has risen and material circumstances have improved substantially for all social groups since the 1950s, and they are still among the highest in the world. In a complex way, then, in Sweden there is today a sense of a gradual loosening of its typical welfare model at the same time as the image of Sweden abroad oscillates between that of a successful economic model and the more sinister one of a culture and a welfare system that have yet to come to grips with their own dark side.

As a model of Swedish culture today, we need look no further than the Swedish journalist and author Stieg Larsson's bestselling novels of the Millennium trilogy (2005–7) about the sleuthing reporter hero Mikael Blomkvist and the researcher and computer hacker Lisbeth Salander. Although our book will not contribute yet another study on the Millennium trilogy, Larsson's story is an illuminating example of the impact of today's popular crime stories set in what the audience recognizes as their own time and in an authentic social and geographic milieu—that is, contemporary Sweden. Even if Larsson and his protagonists retain something of the values that have been an important part of the Swedish self-image during the last century, the trilogy nevertheless paints a picture of gloom and deeper shadows among all the brightness of that image. And if Stieg Larsson's trilogy and its subsequent Swedish and American screen versions are not enough, a vast number of Swedish novels and films can be found on the shelves of any passable bookstore or media store in the Scandinavian crime fiction section. Further building the momentum around Nordic noir, Henning Mankell's bestselling novels and the Wallander mysteries (1987–2004) about police officer Kurt Wallander have resulted in a 1994 Swedish television series (starring Rolf Lassgård and later Krister Henriksson) and a 2008 BBC series (starring Kenneth Branagh) about an eponymous loner detective. In all versions, the Wallander mysteries investigate social tensions, both local to the region of Skåne in Sweden and imported from other parts of the world. Another police series, *The Bridge* (2011), a Danish/Swedish procedural coproduction about cooperation and discord between the two Nordic countries, also gives a very dark picture of the current state of the Nordic welfare states. However, the impact of the worldwide phenomenon of Stieg Larsson's immensely popular Millennium trilogy, and the films based on it, is even more widespread and powerful. As a commercial success in the first decade of the twenty-first century, Larsson was rivaled only by American writer Dan Brown and his *Da Vinci Code*.

The stories contained in Larsson's trilogy, although fictitious, add to the ambiguous picture of the Swedish welfare model. Like all blockbusters with a social message, these stories have become the means by which audiences, wearied by health reforms, banking crashes, and environmental crises, formulate their views about the world and the life lived in it. Weeks—maybe even months and years—of immersion in the present-day Sweden depicted by Stieg Larsson in the course of his three 600-page novels and the films based on them may restore the faith in and the power of fictional stories to keep audiences engaged in a believable fantasy that expresses a coherent view of the world. By compelling audiences to become absorbed in the narrative and inviting them to identify with a range of protagonists, the Millennium trilogy opens up space for reflection and discussion about real-world practices and standards—in this case about contemporary Sweden.

Larsson's leftist views prompted him to create a bleak image of present-day Sweden characterized by disillusion, societal strife, and the dismantling of the key features of the welfare state, such as its collectivism, institutionalized universal social rights, and social security system. Sweden and the Nordic countries are known for their egalitarian values, strong feminist movements, and high level of gender equality. Still, the sexually abused, repeatedly assaulted, autistic-seeming, girlish Lisbeth Salander conveys another story, where Sweden's hidden secrets are unearthed and its schisms are magnified to melodramatic dimensions. It is a story about a cynical neoliberal society where those who possess money hold the power, high-minded political neutrality is an illusion, and civil servants in the welfare state of Sweden are just as evil and corrupt as elsewhere. More than anything else, Larsson depicts a Sweden where men in power—fathers, guardians, physicians, policemen—hate women, which is reflected in the Swedish title of the first volume, *Män som hatar kvinnor* (Men Who Hate Women, 2005). Although Salander is a victim of several sadistic male pedophiles, she is also a feminist icon modeled on Astrid Lindgren's children's books about the defiant child heroine Pippi Longstocking. She becomes an avenging angel by fighting back and destroying her male abusers.

A comparison between the Swedish and the American film versions of the first book makes the specific Swedish cultural context very noticeable. In Niels Arden Oplev's 2009 film, the Swedish actor Michael Nyqvist as Blomkvist is a slightly overweight, coffee-addicted, T-shirt-wearing member of a news team at the magazine *Millennium*. The city of Stockholm is a run-down, miserable, gothic city full of danger and malevolence, whereas the rural outskirts and the place of the first murder, Hedeby, mirrors most Swedes' nature-loving preferences. In David Fincher's American adaptation with the same English title, *The Girl with the Dragon Tattoo* (2011), Blomkvist—played by Daniel Craig—is portrayed as an idealized, designer-tailored, socially and sexually desirable, individualistic, and heroic journalist. Contrary to the Swedish-language film, in Fincher's version the Swedish capital is depicted as the civilized and orderly backdrop, while the small village of Hederstadt in the north of Sweden is a wild, uncivilized environment of horror representing the inhumanity of the Vanger family that Blomkvist is investigating.

Already, in the first of a series of ten Swedish crime novels with a clear societal approach, featuring Inspector Martin Beck (*Roman om ett brott* [The Story of a Crime], 1965–75), Maj Sjöwall and Per Wahlöö painted the so-called Swedish model in a quite gloomy light. It would be fair to say that Swedish crime has been one of the more prominent critical channels among popular culture, and it has been so for a long time. But how should we interpret and understand the divergent images of Sweden that have arisen during the decades after the "Record Years" (1950–70), the years of constant economic growth and societal and political development? Is the gloomy picture from Stieg Larsson's books a reasonable depiction of contemporary Swedish society?

POLITICS AND DEMOCRACY SINCE WORLD WAR II

If Sweden was a relatively homogeneous society during the 1950s, 1960s, and 1970s, since then a liberal view has made way for a more tolerant, open, and fragmented community where lifestyles and social roles can differ. In the 1950s, the Swedish model was the concept that described a special blend of general social welfare, income-related social insurance benefits, and highly skilled workers; the Swedish term *folkhem* (people's home) has been used to refer to a mainly national political vision of social democracy. The terms *Swedish model* and *folkhem* have been guiding most of what has been written and discussed concerning Swedish politics internationally. The Swedish model has sometimes been compared to a bumblebee—just as it would seem aerodynamically impossible for such a rotund and heavy insect to fly, so it would seem economically impossible for a society such as Sweden, with its high taxes, to prosper. But Sweden has flown on, regardless. During the 1960s, Swedish society was more expansive than ever, but in the 1970s the structural economic cycles also touched the Swedish economy. Unemployment rose and heavy industry, such as shipbuilding and steel making, faced serious problems. Small-scale farms also vanished during a great urbanization process; in any case, it had become more or less impossible to make farming profitable without huge investments into large-scale agriculture. During that time, the Social Democratic Party lost power in Sweden for the first time since it had formed the government in 1932. In 1976, 44 years of Social Democratic politics came to an end. However, after two terms, the Social Democrats were back in office after having won the 1982 election.

Despite their ideological program, the center-right coalition governments between 1976 and 1982 did not break very much with former policy. Instead, they had to manage an economic crisis, and they did so by spending a lot of tax money, which held off a collapse in the national economy by supporting an industrial structural transformation that had begun in the aftermath of the first oil crisis in 1973. By far the most polarizing political issue during this time was nuclear energy. In a referendum in 1980, the government decided to continue to operate power plants, but they were only to remain in operation until 2010. This issue led to a government crisis because the biggest governing party (Centre Party) had promised not to run any nuclear power plants, while the other coalition parties—the Liberals and the Moderate Party—were in favor of the nuclear alternative. Taxation was also a sensitive issue in the center-right government, because the Moderates wanted much greater tax cuts than the Centre Party and the Liberals were prepared to allow.

In 1982, when Olof Palme returned as prime minister heading a majority Social Democratic government, the most problematic issues were related to economic democracy. During the 1970s, several new laws regulating unions and employees' rights and opportunities in the labor market had been implemented. But for a while, the larger labor unions had been pushing to have some kind of economic sharing model for employees, and the Social Democrats understood that this proposal would mean a huge conflict with the employers' organizations, and they were not keen on bringing that about. Finally, there was a government proposal that was voted on and adopted in the Swedish Riksdag (the Swedish parliament), but that proposal fell far short of what the unions had wanted. Even so, opposition to the idea was massive, not only among center-right voters and the employers' organizations, but also among many prominent Social Democrats.

Sweden's economy flourished anew in the 1980s, and new lifestyles and ideas began to emerge. Swedish political discourse became more and more individualistic and increasingly in favor of liberalizing social public welfare. The so-called neoliberal discourse gained political terrain, and Swedish opinion also became less positive toward public spending and welfare delivered by public authorities alone. During this decade, both Social Democrats and Liberals began to favor a more deregulated economy and were interested in new forms of private initiatives in areas that were once considered to be strictly public sector.

The most remarkable political occurrence, however, was the murder of Prime Minister Olof Palme on February 28, 1986. Palme was shot dead while walking home after attending the cinema with his family. Fortuitously, his wife, Lisbet, was mostly unharmed by the bullet meant for her. The Social Democratic government had won the parliamentary election once again in 1985, and Vice Prime Minister Ingvar Carlsson had to succeed Palme as prime minister. Because the murder was never solved, it still casts a shadow over Swedish politics. Olof Palme became a political icon, comparable with John F. Kennedy in the United States. As recently as 2013, Swedish public service television broadcast two series about his political career and the murder, and two movies (one documentary and one biographical) were made in which his political heritage is discussed. Books on Palme's political life sell in huge numbers, and even to a younger generation his legacy is of political interest.

However, in 1991, opinion had changed so much that a center-right government coalition came into power, with Carl Bildt as prime minister. The conservative Moderate Party was now the biggest political party, the Centre Party was significantly diminished, and the Christian Democrats had entered the parliament and were participating in the government. At the same time, a populist party—New Democracy—also arrived in the parliament, and the new government came to rely on this group every now and then. Under the center-right government of 1991–94, many liberalizations were introduced, although some of these had been implemented already by the Social Democratic government during the late 1980s. During this government term, Sweden underwent an acute currency crisis (1991–92), and all the parties supported a strict plan to make the Swedish economy work again. When the Social Democrats won back power in 1994, they had to manage huge economic problems during most of the 1990s due to the

1991–92 crisis. In that effort, they had support from the Centre Party during the first term and thereafter from the Green Party and the Left Party to make budget restrictions work. A broad settlement targeting the evolving costs of pensions (supported by all parties but the Left) also helped lay the groundwork for economic improvement. Focusing on keeping the economy strong, the Social Democratic prime minister Göran Persson managed to get Sweden back on its feet.

Today, the image of Sweden abroad is in flux. In 2006, a new center-right government came into power, with Fredrik Reinfeldt as prime minister. With a tough command on the national economy, he and Anders Borg as finance minister have been fortunate in success-fully promoting tax cuts and still keeping the general welfare institu-tions more or less intact. The generous immigration policy regarding refugees has been supplemented by a new policy on labor market migrants. In addition, the new coalition government has managed to stay together, although the two minor parties (Christian Democrats and the Centre Party) were at risk of dropping out from the parlia-ment in the 2014 election. The Moderate Party has grown to become by far the biggest in the coalition and is now challenging the Social Democrats as the leading party in the Swedish party system. Nothing regarding general welfare, equality, or relations between the individual and the state has been seriously confronted by the current center-right government. However, government spending has decreased due to higher thresholds and more restrictions on getting public support. Still, many citizens think the social cleavages in Sweden are too large and that vital infrastructure is being sold on the market at too low a price and with meager results. Some of this discontent has paved the way for the emergence of a new populist right-wing party: the Sweden Democrats. They have used the immigration issue as a lever to enter the parliament in the 2010 election and to gain popularity, due to distrust in the government and discontent with the loss of the idea of the Swedish *folkhem*. Many of the party's supporters are male manual laborers, often living in smaller villages in the southern part of Sweden. They dislike immigrants and distrust both politicians and the media. For them, the Sweden Democrats are a feasible political alter-native that is trying to curtail the rapid development from a national, homogeneous, and foreseeable future into a transnational, heteroge-neous, and "flexible" future.

The particular Social Democratic "Swedish model" of progress, consensus, social equality, and centralism has—as has been mentioned—been less fortunate in meeting the challenges of a multicultural society and has lost much of its attractiveness internationally. At the same time, in the current economic crisis in the European Union, Sweden is still considered to be a model of a sound economy and a strong state, but now in a more neoliberal way. Through a very high-profile policy of privatization and outsourcing of welfare, care, and education, Sweden has been a role model for countries such as the United Kingdom, for example. But this policy has met strong opposition, not only from organized members of Social Democracy in Sweden, but also from broad layers of citizens, including employees in the welfare sector and young middle-class families in the country's urban centers.

Policies and attitudes toward immigrants, refugees, and people from other parts of the world in general have also changed. Sweden was a relatively homogeneous society during the 1960s and 1970s; since then, a liberal view has made way for a more tolerant, open, and fragmented community where lifestyles and social roles can differ. Paradoxically, state power has gone from a resource used for ensuring public welfare and economic safety to a means for rallying the public around common values and infusing the population with beliefs about tolerance and ecological protection, as well as more traditional values such as working hard, doing one's share, and not living on public benefits. This development has made it more remarkable to differ with respect to the views one holds than to differ in terms of welfare. The idea of well-being as coupled with specific values has come into the mainstream discourse, and at the same time the idea of well-being as a matter of social and economic circumstances has waned.

Following the introduction of stricter integration policies and the rejection of multiculturalist ideals by leading politicians in most Western European countries, Sweden has become an outlier in the field of integration politics. The basic premises for Swedish immigration politics remain as they have been since the 1970s: cultural assimilation is voluntary for immigrants, citizenship is easy to obtain, and, although the debate on integration issues has intensified over the last decade, it is still characterized by a high degree of consensus between all parties to the left and right, leaving out a minor anti-immigration party disturbing the picture. These developments have strengthened the already well-established Swedish self-image of being an exceptionally open and tolerant country. In the political sphere, national symbols are seldom used; rather, nationalist rhetoric is often rejected as "un-Swedish behavior."

In one area, however, the limits of Swedish tolerance are increasingly being tested, and that is the area of gender equality—in particular when it comes to sexual liberation. As recently as the early 2000s, even recognizing the existence of "honor" murders—let alone specific honor cultures—was highly controversial in the Swedish debate. Millennium trilogy author Stieg Larsson was one of the leading advocates of the relativist perspective, arguing that the notion of specific honor cultures was basically racist. Today, not only honor cultures but also headscarves, religious schools, and religious rituals are often criticized. While originally part of the same narrative, the conflict between sexual freedom and multiculturalism—between the "Swedish sin" and "tolerant Sweden"—has ended, the former having defeated the latter. In order to uphold the notion of Sweden as a tolerant and open-minded nation, the presence of large minority groups (both immigrant and native) challenging the majority norms on sexual and gender issues, as well as religious practices, is often neglected or even rejected. Swedish nationalism is hesitant and has no long history. The National Day of Sweden is observed on June 6 every year, but it was not instituted as a national day until 1983 (until then, it was celebrated as the Swedish flag day), and it became a public holiday only in 2005. But the National Day remains an ambiguous institution, mainly because of lack of public support, and, if celebrated at all, it is conceived as an occasion for official multicultural picnics.

WELFARE AND PROTESTANT VALUES

Ever since the Reformation, religion in Sweden has been understood as Lutheran Christianity, at least officially. Martin Luther's ideas of ecclesial reform reached Scandinavia quite early. It was one of Luther's students, Olavus Petri (1493–1552), who met the Swedish king Gustavus Vasa in 1523, bringing with him new theological ideas that gave the king an incentive to break with Rome (and also with the Danish king) to establish his own nation-state. The religious development in all of Scandinavia was, and perhaps still is, rather uniform, with the Reformation reaching Finland around the same time as Sweden and

Denmark—and then Norway a little later. The result of the Reformation was the establishment of independent Lutheran state churches. Even though this meant a sure break with the pope in Rome, in other respects it should not be seen as a radical break with Catholic Christianity. In the Church of Sweden, there was, first, a liturgical continuity with the Catholic Church, which meant that the people celebrating Mass or attending a service would recognize the way to celebrate from before. Second, there was also a continuity of the apostolic succession, with a (supposedly) uninterrupted line of bishops going back to the original 12 apostles. The Church of Sweden was the established religion by law in Sweden from 1526 to 2000—almost 500 years.

Interesting to us is the relative homogeneity this introduced in Sweden, not only in matters religious, but in cultural and political matters as well. The Reformation meant more than just a religious shift, as religion during that period was considered not only a matter of the individual's private belief but also a matter of culture and politics. In other words, the Reformation meant a consolidation of the nation-state as a religiously and politically independent state. The king took the place of the pope as the head of the church, and political and religious authority thereby merged in a way that had been unheard of before. Moreover, as religious unity was seen as vital for the stability of the young nation-state, this also meant pressure to conform to the state religion. This is a significant difference from the medieval Catholic Church, which—although it surely claimed that all authority, political as well as religious, came from God—still upheld a dialectic between worldly and spiritual authority. The rise of the nation-state also meant, in establishing a definite border that could be surveyed, that an earlier unheard-of disciplining in religious matters was possible. Further, the translation of the Bible into the vernacular helped establish the native Swedish not only as the official language but also as one more or less uniform language, thus opening up a linguistic space for a common literature. As the Lutheran Church emphasized the written as well as the spoken word, it became imperative that the people should learn to read and write. Even though primary-level education did not become compulsory until the nineteenth century (in 1842), literacy reached high levels early on. Participation in the liturgical rites of baptism, confirmation, and burial was mandatory, and children learned Luther's small catechism by heart. The parish pastor was a civil servant, often with duties extending far beyond what would usually be considered "religious" duties: for example, keeping track of the population and introducing new methods in agriculture.

The consolidation of the nation-state as Lutheran confession took place in 1593 at the "Uppsala möte," laying the foundation for the remarkable, but still relative, homogeneity of Sweden: a homogeneity that still had appeal in the twentieth century. The ruling ideas of the Swedish model—progress, consensus, social equality, and centralism—did not spontaneously or inevitably grow out of Swedish history; rather, these are ideas that had been cultivated since the Reformation. If, as the French sociologist Émile Durkheim suggests, "the idea of society is the soul of religion," then religion, as the way society represents and maintains itself symbolically, plays an important role in configuring the nation-state, and Sweden is an excellent example of this.

Religious homogeneity was, of course, only relative. One may presume that, despite the mandatory membership in the state church, dissenting religious movements existed more or less independent of—and maybe sometimes even unnoticed by—the official religion. In the eighteenth century, Pietism from Halle was introduced in Sweden, which emphasized the religious experiences and responsibilities of the individual and argued against doctrinal conformism. In the nineteenth century, a more massive religious awakening came to Sweden in the form of the Moravian Brethren, Methodism, and Baptists. All these were suspect in the eyes of the establishment, however, despite support among members of the Swedish economic and cultural elite. A special law against private convocations was in effect from 1726 to 1858. Compared to other Scandinavian nation-states, in Sweden the percentage of free-church membership was and still is higher, as the other Scandinavian state churches were more successful in their efforts to keep religious awakening within the churches themselves. But dissident religion was not the only threat to religious conformity in Sweden; in the nineteenth century, movements such as liberalism, socialism, rationalism, and positivism influenced popular movements in Sweden, often involving direct polemics against the established church. Despite criticism of the religious monopoly held by the state church, it was not until 1951 that Sweden made it legal for citizens to opt out of organized religion altogether.

Even though freedom of religion was not established in Swedish law until 1951, and the Church of Sweden remained a state church until 1999, the state religion had in fact been retreating from its official position all through the twentieth century. At the beginning of the twenty-first century, Sweden could increasingly be described as a religious pluralist nation. Even though around 70 percent of the population still belongs to the Church of Sweden after its disestablishment, studies have shown that the beliefs of its members are quite varied and do not conform in any significant way to traditional Christian doctrine. Inside and outside the church, then, there exists a significant religious pluralism, including Islam (due to increased numbers of Muslim immigrants), as well as nonreligious alternatives such as various "humanist" movements. The increasing visibility of alternatives to the established church may cast doubt on how religiously homogeneous Sweden was in the first place, and it may raise questions as to whether this homogeneity was just a matter of official policy. Be that as it may, for now, it is a fact that religious homogeneity was a political ideal for a long time that took shape institutionally, not only in churches, but also in the school system and in legislation. Such an ideal has, of course, been active in shaping the Swedish ideals of modernity and their emphasis on consensus. For sure, this ideal of homogeneity has been broken through the prisms of nineteenth-century popular movements such as the free-church movements, the union movement, the labor movement, and the temperance movement; however, the ideal has withstood all these changes and continues to exist, even if in different forms than the original state church conformity. It may be that religion in modern-day Sweden is viewed as a purely private matter; nevertheless, religion has informed many of the ideals that have shaped Sweden into what it is today.

SWEDEN UNPARADISED?

As the former welfare state model dissolves, popular fiction and cinema have become significant forums for articulating critical points of view and struggling over their figurative significance. However, the internationally recognized crime genre is but one of several major discursive sites for the critique of societal development. For example, women's literature—such as today's Swedish chick lit—differs from the Anglophone genre when it comes to ethical questions, gender ideology, and medical issues. Just like the novels in Stieg Larsson's Millennium trilogy, the modern romance stories that compose Swedish chick lit illustrate the sinister aspects of the modern welfare state and its focus on materialistic values and Swedish women's juggling of conflicting obligations and life projects, such as family lives and professional careers. Hence Swedish chick lit is, much more distinctly than the Anglo-American genre, composed of handbooks on how to have a better personal life based on self-improvement and spiritual values. The changing situation in contemporary Sweden means the time is ripe for making a self-critical appraisal of the state of the nation today. In *Culture, Health, and Religion at the Millennium: Sweden Unparadised*, we present a view of contemporary Sweden in significant transformation, as reflected in film, literature, politics, and religion. The authors are six Swedish scholars working at the University of Gothenburg in such diverse fields as film studies, literary studies, political science, religious studies, and theology. Working together since 2010 on a research project titled "Religion, Culture, and Health," we have collaborated in this joint effort to interpret and reinterpret Sweden and Swedish welfare today. We intend that this book shall serve as an analysis of and a comment on the depiction of the Swedish society and the flux of values concerning social welfare, personal freedom, and well-being that is so widely reflected and communicated in media and popular fiction. It is our hope that these six chapters, written by us individually, will give the English-speaking reader of Swedish literature or the cinephile with a particular interest in Swedish movies a broad insight into the state of Swedish society today as well as its historical sources.

The first two chapters give a general introduction and background to two central aspects of Swedish society: the construction of the Swedish ideal of modernity and the transforming conceptualization of the welfare model in political terms, as reflected in governmental policy declarations made in recent decades. In the first chapter, "Hygiene as Metaphor: On Metaphorization, Racial Hygiene, and the Swedish Ideals of Modernity," Ola Sigurdson gives a background of the modernization of Sweden by stressing the importance of the metaphor of hygiene and its connection to welfare and progress. Drawing on Susan Sontag's well-known essay "Illness as Metaphor," he challenges her use of metaphor in his investigation of how the social and cultural phenomenon of metaphors associated with cleanliness, health, and hygiene have been used to establish Swedish modernity and the so-called Swedish model. By exploring two works published in the 1930s, Ludvig Nordström's *Lort-Sverige* (Dirt-Sweden) and Alva and Gunnar Myrdal's *Kris i befolkningsfrågan* (Crisis in the Population Question), Sigurdson demonstrates how certain metaphors and strategies were intimately connected to Swedish politics in order to improve social hygiene and thereby also practice racial hygiene as part of the social ideal of rationality and enlightenment.

In the next chapter, "From Shared Resources to Shared Values," Marie Demker examines politics in Sweden and the transforming political conceptualization of the Swedish welfare state. She gives a survey of how state power (or the authoritative allocation of resources) in Sweden in recent decades has been less focused on ensuring its citizens' material welfare than on protecting their rights to free choice in order to safeguard common and authoritative values such as human rights, secularism, and tolerance. By analyzing Swedish governmental policy declarations from 1975 to 2010, Demker demonstrates that these documents are increasingly used by the government to focus attention on values and ideology and to draw up the grand vision of the state. In this chapter, Demker argues that the welfare state of Sweden has tried to secure welfare (rights to safety and health) by promoting an image of a "cozy," flexible, and inclusive community; by placing a stronger emphasis on cultural aspects in politics; and by opening up a discussion on religion, traditions, and nationhood. The decreasing interest in promoting certain traditional values has, however, resulted in an individualistic country where individual autonomy, independent opinions, and individual rights are highly valued by the population. If there is a certain shared "Swedishness" in contemporary Sweden, it is the ideal of becoming a capable individual like Lisbeth Salander, who does not accept being dominated by anyone or anything.

The following four chapters present four case studies on how the flux in values is expressed and negotiated in public and religious discourse, as well as in fiction, film, and popular literature. Challenging the idea of Swedish tolerance, Henrik Bogdan examines the problematic discourse against certain religious movements, religious sects, and cults, using the example of the Church of Scientology. In his chapter, "'It's Not about Religion, but about Manipulation': Polemical Discourse against Sects and Cults in Sweden," he sets out the limits of

Swedish tolerance toward groups that challenge the notion of "normal" religious practices, especially when it comes to issues connected to the construction of health and illness. By investigating two reputable examples—the so-called E-meter case and the Gillberg affair—he illustrates how brainwashing has been the most recurrent charge against the Church of Scientology and how it has been interpreted as a mental illness or disorder caused by manipulations of cults. Thus in his chapter Bogdan demonstrates the connection between religion and health and religious practices and medical discourse.

In the next chapter, "Something Happened, but What? On Roy Andersson's Cinematic Critique of the Development of the Welfare State," the concept of the Swedish welfare project is tested as Daniel Brodén analyzes and contextualizes the renowned Swedish filmmaker Roy Andersson's provocative narratives of the Swedish welfare state. By investigating his four feature films, including *You, the Living*, and his major polemical commercials from the 1970s to the present day, Brodén asserts the importance of fictional stories in the political debate, as well as their importance in prompting reflection and discussion about societal development and real-world practices—in this case, the contemporary state of the Swedish welfare system. Although Andersson's films are considered to be icons of 1960s Swedish art cinema and the values of the Swedish *folkhem*, Brodén claims that Andersson blames all political parties for the recent corruption of the original welfare project and for thereby promoting nihilism, shortsightedness, and an increasingly inhumane society. He argues that Andersson's films therefore serve as illustrative examples of the "unparadised" theme and the depiction of a societal collapse—that is, the source of today's social and existential ills.

In "Sex and Sin in a Multicultural Sweden," Andreas Johansson Heinö scrutinizes Swedish culture from another angle. Referring to the worldwide myth of the "Swedish sin" as it has been reproduced in movies, literature, art, politics, and science since the 1950s, he investigates how public discourse on sexuality has changed from the 1960s to the present day in Sweden. In his study of public debates on multiculturalism and sexual freedom, Heinö challenges the established Swedish self-image as a country that is open and tolerant when it comes to sexual norms and family life—an image that is especially challenged in relation to immigration and cultural minorities. He pays special attention to the contradiction between what he calls the "sin discourse" and the "tolerance discourse" in public debates on honor culture and female genital mutilation, pornography and sexual education, gender roles, and homosexuality.

In the last chapter, "Chick Lit as Healing and Self-Help Manual?," Yvonne Leffler's approach is to examine Swedish chick lit and contemporary urban romantic fiction in a historical, Swedish context. She highlights some prominent thematic differences between today's Swedish and Anglo-American chick lit novels from a comparative perspective in a way that also points to some current issues in Swedish society. In her analysis of novels by Swedish writers such as Kajsa Ingemarsson and Denise Rudberg, she confirms that popular fiction can be investigated as a source of sociocultural commentary on ethical questions and ideas of happiness and well-being. She rejects the stereotypes of the chick lit genre and redefines it as an instructional genre connected to today's self-help industry and "makeover" formula, as well as a genre that expresses culturally constructed values—for instance, the importance of employment and personal autonomy in contemporary Sweden.

Discourses on health, politics, religion, tolerance, welfare, sin, and romance—such is the stuff from which an image of a particular nation-state is woven. The following six chapters will provide the reader of Swedish literature, and the viewer of Swedish films, some background and insight into what has happened to the image of Sweden in popular media. Perhaps any given nation-state is in a state of tension at any given time, but *Culture, Health, and Religion at the Millennium: Sweden Unparadised* will highlight some of the particular cultural, political, religious, and societal tensions that characterize Sweden at this particular moment in time—at the millennium—informing its self-image as well as the image of Sweden among the international audience of its contemporary fiction.

CHAPTER 1

HYGIENE AS METAPHOR

ON METAPHORIZATION, RACIAL HYGIENE, AND THE SWEDISH IDEALS OF MODERNITY

OLA SIGURDSON

IN HIS AUTOBIOGRAPHICAL ACCOUNT OF GROWING UP in the working-class neighborhoods of Gothenburg on the Swedish west coast, Ronny Ambjörnsson, a professor of the history of ideas, makes the following observation: "Mother fulfilled the commands of hygiene through frantic cleaning. Everything was polished and rubbed to surfaces so shiny that the germs slipped and swirled out through windows that were almost always open for airing. Light, air, and cleanliness became during the 1930s metaphors for enlightenment and rationality. Mother's cleaning and father's studies could be said to belong to the same sphere, two versions of the credo of modernism."[1] This observation is telling in more ways than one. First, Ambjörnsson establishes a connection between seemingly disparate but very mundane activities (such as cleaning and studying) and a certain cultural condition characterized by versions of enlightenment and rationality. Second, this juxtaposition is not incidental or provisional, but actually illustrates "the credo of modernism"—or in other words, a distinguishing belief of a certain period of Swedish modern history. This interrelationship between a domestic duty and a formative belief characterizing an age poses a question that is simultaneously philosophical and historical: how does hygiene work as a metaphor for the version of Swedish modernity that characterized the 1930s and beyond? If Ambjörnsson is correct in his characterization of the Swedish "credo of modernism"—and indeed,

I think there is reason to believe he is—this would provide an important background to the image of Sweden presented and presumed in popular fiction (both then and now), promoted and implied in public policy, and disseminated as a norm in Swedish culture at large. Even when expressions of art, popular culture, policies, or religion wish to question this norm, its hegemonic status will more or less force any interrogations of its status to define themselves in terms of its scope. In relation to the aim of this book, then, this chapter will present an idea about the relation between hygiene and rationality that has been formative for the (self-)image of Sweden in recent history, in policies as well as public perceptions, and in modernist film as well as bestselling novels.

In what follows, I will take a critical look at Swedish self-understanding during the particular historical period of the 1930s and beyond through the lens of its use of hygiene as metaphor. This means that I will not only describe an influential historical idea but also critically discuss the ethical and political shortcomings of that idea. In other words, I will investigate a general question of how our terminology for health and disease takes on a more-than-literal meaning with a Swedish example. Swedish modernity, I think, amply shows some of the hazards involved in such a praxis. But first, let me turn to how Susan Sontag framed a similar question.

HYGIENE AS METAPHOR: THE SONTAG QUESTION

The distinction between illness and disease, even if it is sometimes helpful, is not absolute. Between the subjective experience of being ill and the biomedical symptoms of disease, there is almost always traffic—at least on the existential level. This is especially true if we consider the cultural representations of illness/disease as a third node in this spectrum of ill health. There are always (and almost always conflicting) cultural understandings of what good or ill health consists of, what kind of ill health deserves to be diagnosed, and also the relative cultural "value" of certain forms of ill health—not all diseases are considered equal. These cultural understandings of good and ill health are mediated to the public through advertisements, literature, movies, music, television series, and so on. Although not the topic of this chapter or this book, it would be interesting to ask what impact a medical drama, such as the American television series *ER* or *House* (both televised in Sweden), might have on the public perception of what to expect when treated for a medical condition at a hospital. The inquiry into how fictional narratives represent ill health is growing, and it is of great interest to medical students looking for case studies as well as anyone curious about where our perceptions of particular diseases come from.[2] Just to mention one example from literature, consider how the German author Thomas Mann's *Magic Mountain* is an epic of tuberculosis: TB is placed as perhaps *the* romantic disease of the nineteenth century as well as a kind of diagnosis of modern society as a whole. TB in *Magic Mountain* becomes "metaphorized": it is not just a diagnosis of a particular disease but an existential and societal condition. Today, this inevitably contextualizes Mann's 1924 novel as a historical novel: after World War II, effective antibacterial treatments emerged, although people in many parts of the world still suffer from TB. Sanatorial treatments for TB, such as those described in Mann's novel, are a thing of the past.

That there is traffic between different dimensions of the meaning of a particular disease also becomes a prominent phenomenon if one considers its social dimensions. The British anthropologist Mary Douglas, in her classic work *Purity and Danger*, has shown how the human body has historically functioned (and still does today) as a kind of symbolic system for the body politic and how threats against the social body are often described through metaphors coming from the medical vocabulary.[3] In antiquity as well as in modern times, there exist plenty of conceptions of how personal health, cleanliness, and ill health influence society and vice versa. Not only the physical body of an individual but also the social body can be ill and demand resolute surgical interventions. The connection between individual and social health has to do, among other things, with the fact that the individual body is not as demarcated from the social body as we usually think it is, at least for those of us who have grown up in Western, individualistic societies with a strong emphasis on the autonomy of the person as well as the body. Consequently, it is not very surprising that there is a metaphorical interchange between personal and social levels of existence. For example, we could associate a flu that has struck us with a foreign army "invading" our body, or we can speak about how almost all of the city of Gothenburg, Sweden, was affected by "soccer fever" before the final game when IFK Göteborg won the

Swedish football league on October 28, 2007. Such metaphors could be more or less morally or politically troubling—more so, for example, when a certain ethnic group is considered to be responsible for civic unrest and therefore is described as a "disease" spreading in the body politic. However, that there is a necessary and urgent critique of such metaphorizations should not blind us to the fact that such metaphorical traffic most likely always occurs on some level (sometimes in a more benign way, as I hope my soccer example shows), as it is not always possible to determine which sphere contains the legitimate literal meaning and which the more problematic transferred meaning.

Then again, that the traffic between literal and figurative meanings of disease might be inevitable, as I have already suggested, does not suggest that it is impossible to distinguish between their meanings. The American novelist and writer Susan Sontag, in her influential 1978 essay "Illness as Metaphor," has emphatically criticized confusing metaphorical levels with each other, since it entails a metaphorization of ill health, as in the examples I just have mentioned—disease or illness as an expression of not only a biological but also a cultural or a spiritual condition—which can lead to the idea that we personally bear the responsibility for our ill health and therefore deserve our destiny.[4] It would be better to limit the use of ill-health terminology to the biological and physical, thus avoiding placing the blame on sick people and causing them to feel guilty about their condition. Sontag's prime examples are TB from the nineteenth century and cancer from the twentieth century, both diseases that have to a large extent been associated with personal traits of character (as Mann shows, self-consciously, in *The Magic Mountain*), thus creating a correspondence between the biological and the personal. "The most striking similarity between the myths of TB and cancer," Sontag writes, "is that both are, or were, understood as diseases of passion."[5] She gives numerous examples from literature of how this correspondence has been expressed in writing, but despite the prominence of literature, it is not only in fiction that this attitude is common but also among people in general: "Sickness was a way of making people 'interesting'—which is how 'romantic' was originally defined."[6] Cancer might not be as romantic as TB, but the disease is still associated with certain traits of character, mainly loneliness and discontent. It is, in this new mythology, negative feelings on the part of the sick that are associated with cancer. Cancer is also described in a terminology that suggests a "war" against the disease. What Sontag calls for, then, is a "demythologization" of disease. The reason for such a move is that, according to Sontag, "nothing is more punitive than to give a disease a meaning—that meaning being invariably a moralistic one."[7] The metaphorization of disease or ill health—especially TB and cancer—leads, according to Sontag, to silence as well as shame on the part of patients, making them more reluctant to seek health care. If diseases, especially metaphorically highly charged diseases such as those mentioned, were allowed to be "just" diseases, then much would be won—the temptation of fatalism or fanaticism would be removed, along with the blame and guilt distributed to persons suffering from the diseases in question. Or as she put it on a later occasion, "metaphors and myths . . . kill."[8]

As I have already implied, I think the reform suggested by Sontag is in practice impossible, and I must confess that I am a bit surprised that such a sensitive writer as Sontag does not have a more extended discussion on how metaphors work and how difficult it is, from a philosophical or a literary perspective, to draw a clear distinction between literal and figural uses of a term.[9] It has been suggested that the historical evidence belies Sontag's thesis: experiences of cancer were neither silenced nor particularly shameful compared to other lethal diseases.[10] My objection is of another kind, as I want to suggest that it is hardly possible or desirable to get rid of metaphors as such, even in the medical field, as these are how we symbolically make sense of our illnesses. Nevertheless, the overall aim of Sontag's book is of continuing importance—namely, to avoid blaming sick people for their diseases. Diseases are seldom self-induced, and it is a fact that we *suffer* diseases beyond our control. Thus there is a need to avoid any stigmatization of disease. Further, that the traffic between the literal and figurative sense can be hard to police in any absolute or final sense does not mean that distinctions cannot be drawn. For instance, the World Health Organization, in its definition of health, implicitly distinguishes between at least two dimensions—health as the absence of disease and health as well-being—and although these two dimensions belong together (not least in our personal experience), this does not mean that they are the same thing or cannot be separated, however provisionally. To achieve Sontag's legitimate aim, then, we need a critical vigilance of the use of metaphors associated with ill health, but perhaps we also need to be a little more nuanced in our perception of the inevitable need for metaphors.

In this chapter, I will tweak the use of Sontag's legitimate aim for slightly different purposes: I wish to take a closer look at different dimensions of the term *hygiene* as it figures in some seminal works of Swedish modernity. The term *hygiene* comes from the Greek *hygies*, which has rich connotations, one of these being "healthy." In Greek mythology, Hygieia was the daughter of Asclepius, the god of medicine and healing, and she herself was the personification of health, cleanliness, and sanitation. There is, then, a clear relation between the metaphors of illness and disease and hygiene as a metaphor. The reason for choosing to focus on hygiene in this chapter is that this term has been central for the self-understanding of Swedish modernity, which I alluded to in the introduction and which I hope to demonstrate further. In a way, then, my investigation turns Sontag's on its head: it is the social and cultural phenomenon of metaphorization that is at the center of this chapter, not the physical, even though my interest lies in the traffic between these different dimensions of human existence. Before I deal with two important Swedish works from the 1930s, one reportage and one more scientific text, I shall give a short background of the modernization of Sweden so as to put these two works into their historical context. Finally, I will conclude with a more general reflection on hygiene as a metaphor.

THE SWEDISH MODEL: PROGRESS, CONSENSUS, AND CENTRALISM

"The Swedish model" is a term used in secondary literature about Sweden, most often to describe a certain kind of compromise between an employer's interest in profits and an employee's interest in good wages as well as general welfare. Such a compromise was crucial for Sweden's economic and social policy from the 1930s to the 1970s. This is symbolized by the agreement between the trade union *Landsorganisationen i Sverige* (LO) and the employers' organization *Svenska arbetsgivareföreningen* (SAF) at Saltsjöbaden in 1938, supervised by the government, where it was agreed that market stability would be achieved by recognizing both the manufacturing sector's need for profit and the workers' need for stability. This "spirit of Saltsjöbaden" came to characterize the specific Swedish economic, political, and social stability that lasted from the 1930s until the 1970s. Significant for this period, besides the agreement, was that the Social Democrats held government continuously from 1932 to 1976, although there was a coalition government during World War II. Even if the Swedish model did not begin in a specific decade nor end in another, this period represents the heyday of this particular configuration, and it became internationally renowned quite early on, not least through Marquis Childs's 1936 book *Sweden: The Middle Way*.[11] According to historians Per Thullberg and Kjell Östberg, there were three main ingredients in the Swedish model: a modern welfare state, institutionalized cooperation between the parts of the labor market ("the spirit of Saltsjöbaden"), and political governance that strove for consensus and compromise between parties.[12] Another way to describe it is to suggest that the Swedish model rested on three ideational pillars: progress, consensus, and centralism. Without entering into the entire discussion about the impact on history of material institutions versus concepts, let me suggest here a middle way: I see the social processes as the institutional embodiment of these concepts whose meaning, at the same time, grows out of the very same institutions. As the Swedish model is both a social process and an idea, as I will show later, both aspects are important in this context. As a way of introducing the Swedish model as a background to my discussion of hygiene as metaphor, let me comment briefly on each of the concepts of progress, consensus, and centralism.[13] Without doubt, equality would also qualify as a central concept for understanding the Swedish model, but as it has been thematized already in the introduction (and in several of the other chapters), it should be regarded as included in, and even implied by, this discussion of progress, consensus, and centralism.

To begin with, progress is, of course, central to the understanding and self-understanding of Sweden in the early twentieth century. It is a fact that Sweden, like many other Western countries, experienced a rapid change in economic as well as technological, social, and political terms during that period. At the beginning of the twentieth century, Sweden was a relatively poor nation with an essentially agrarian economy. The industrialization and urbanization of the nation took place, quite rapidly compared to other countries, in the 1930s. From 1870 to 1940, the number of people dependent on agrarian employment fell by 30 percent, and from 1940 to 1975, it fell by another

75 percent.[14] Industry in Sweden began to thrive at the end of the nineteenth century as export levels rose. Among the goods exported were commodities such as grain, ore, and wood and refined goods produced by local industries. A number of companies that continue to play an important role in the Swedish economy today were established during the late nineteenth century, including ASEA, L. M. Ericsson, SKF, and Alfa-Laval. The profits were reinvested into building a national railway during the 1870s. This expansion of industry also led to growing urbanization, which in turn led to an increase in housing. During the 1890s, industry's share of the gross domestic product exceeded agriculture's share. In the 1920s, Sweden was hit by a major recession. Prices fell and so did employment levels. But from 1925 through the rest of the 1920s, a boom replaced the recession. Between the wars, as well as during World War II, the economy was fluctuating, but Sweden's relative neutrality and the fact that its infrastructure was intact led to major growth in the economy after the war; the gross national product increased by 5 percent annually between 1946 and 1950. The uniqueness of Sweden's economic growth might be its stability, not its magnitude.

The constant and stable growth of the economy in the period under discussion made room for a considerable expansion of the public sector. Full employment became a goal for the labor market policy, and the high number of employed persons further enhanced domestic consumption. Public spending expanded during this period, and private consumption also expanded as a result. The real wage increase as well as industrial mass production made it possible for a majority of people to buy a refrigerator and freezer, and eventually also a television, stereo, and car. To summarize, from the 1870s to the 1970s, Sweden went from being one the poorest countries in Europe to one of the richest in the world. Its strong economic growth, together with technological advances that had been made available to large parts of the population, meant that the idea of progress took a central place in the Swedish model. Economic growth created, not unexpectedly, the notion that history was moving toward an increasingly bright future. The fact that such economic and technological progress took place in such a relatively short time gave birth to the idea that the method applied there could also be applied to other areas and with similar success. According to mathematician and futurologist Lars

Ingelstam, "the doctrine of the invariably continuous *progress*" is one of the dominant and most problematic public myths of contemporary Sweden. This myth has been, by and large, unarticulated and therefore mostly tacit, but nevertheless its core has been "technological progress, scientifically founded and rationally administered in (as it goes) 'socially acceptable forms.'"[15] To the myth of progress belongs the thought that all obstacles, in principle, can be overcome and all problems can be solved through political technology, given that progress is not hindered by irrelevant factors (obsolete traditions, irrational viewpoints, etc.). A life as effective and useful as possible became a self-evident ideal for those who prevailed over this interpretation of the development of Sweden. The engineers could see themselves as the avant-garde of the new society.[16]

I have already mentioned the agreement between the trade union LO and the employers' organization SAF at Saltsjöbaden in 1938 as characteristic of Swedish economic, political, and social stability. It also exemplifies the second pillar of the Swedish model—namely, the virtue of consensus. One could take a longer historical perspective on the politics of consensus by remembering that Sweden, in the centuries before the modern breakthrough, was, relatively speaking, an ethnically and religiously homogeneous country (as described in the introduction to this book), with an interplay between a strong, centralized state and an autonomous peasant population. But the immediate predecessor to the politics of consensus is rather, as political scientist Bo Rothstein suggests, the corporative solutions of the Swedish state in the early twentieth century: "Instead of the parliamentary channel the Swedish state opened the corporative way of representation to the workers' influence on politics."[17] This means that elected delegates of an association—for example, a labor union—were appointed as that association's legitimate representatives. Accordingly, those associations were given representatives in central state organizations and could influence policies that were relevant to them. One example of this given by Rothstein is how, in 1903, local employment agencies were instituted whose boards consisted of equal shares of representatives of workers and employers and a neutral chairman. This corporative model was then an example and a predecessor of later corporative models of representation.

There is no straight line from these local employment agencies to the spirit of Saltsjöbaden, however. The dawn of the 1900s was characterized not only by corporative political solutions but also by open conflicts between employers and workers. But eventually these conflicts were recognized by organizations from both sides as being, in the long run, detrimental to the national economy and therefore also to the profit or income of the respective parties. Bargaining between the Centre Party (agrarian party) and the Social Democrats in 1933 helped the move toward a politics of consensus. The consensus achieved in parliamentary politics and in the labor market was not, however, between all possible parties but between some; for instance, the syndicalist labor union SAC (Sveriges Arbetares Centralorganisation) was marginalized by the agreement between LO and SAF.

As is the case with progress, consensus is not only a matter of actual politics but also an idea, important for the self-understanding of Sweden during this time. Consensus was sought both as a working model for the labor market, for instance, and as an ideal in itself, and this ideal was firmly established in the 1930s. In 1935, at the 500-year anniversary of the Swedish parliament, King Gustaf V held up the spirit of consensus as a typically Swedish characteristic: "In troubled times, not least during the Engelbrekt feud [a 1434–36 rebellion led by Swedish nobleman Engelbrekt Engelbrektsson against the king of the Kalmar Union, Eric of Pomerania], the Swedish people saw as their most precious possession Swedish legislation as an expression of both the country's independence outward and the people's care for social peace inward."[18] Earlier, in February 1914, the Swedish king had caused the liberal government's resignation through an extraparliamentary speech, but little more than twenty years later, he saw social peace or consensus as an expression of the typical Swedish way of handling conflict. And in a way, he was right. The Swedish parliament during the twentieth century (at least until the 1970s) was characterized by an extensive consensus between parliamentary parties on the basis of a technocratic-political view of reality.[19] However, consensus is a virtue not only in politics but also in the wider culture, as suggested, for instance, by Danish sociologist Gösta Esping-Andersen: "Swedish solidarity has always rested upon a society characterized by homogeneity, likeness, localism, and, actually, provincialism. It was never a society that tolerated a significant differentiation."[20] Of course, for those residing in Sweden but outside of Swedish solidarity—such as the Sami people living within the borders of Sweden as well as in Norway and Finland, or other ethnic or religious minorities—the politics of consensus have not always seemed as attractive.[21]

This leads us to the last of the three pillars: centralism. Progress in technology and economics in Sweden gave rise to the idea, as I have previously noted, that social progress could also be achieved with the same scientific and rational means. This would require an ability to oversee the society as a whole, and here the state found its task: administrating and distributing progress. Swedish sociologist Gunnar Olofsson has pointed out how positive state metaphors have been used in both political and scholarly debate about the role of the state in the Swedish context, correlating this with the prime minister in chief: "The political phraseology launched concepts such as '*folkhemmet*' [the people's home] (Per Albin Hansson in the 1920s and 30s), the 'strong society' (Tage Erlander in the 1950s and 60s), and the 'common sector' (Olof Palme in the 1970s)."[22] The state is seen as the agent of a positive development of society—an agent that, like the engineer, was able to monitor the changes that were necessary: "Optimism in regard to planning and the state looked upon political power from the horizon of the engineer of society. In the same way as science, through domination of nature, has been able to produce better conditions, an intentional power over society's development could lead to better social conditions."[23] Public policy is oriented toward economic growth, and the state serves as the agent that distributes this growth and also as the agent that monitors to ensure that such growth is actually achieved. State planning is seen according to a top-down model.

Again, such central planning is not necessarily something that begins with the Swedish model of the 1930s. Centralism had a long history in Sweden before the modern breakthrough. Another Swedish sociologist, Göran Therborn, writes the following about Swedish state history: "Sweden was probably the first country in Europe to obtain a uniform state apparatus, with courts and central administration with demarcated areas of competence, a uniform, centrally controlled provincial administration, and a tax-collection system wholly controlled by the state—instead of leasing the collection to individual entrepreneurs—and a state budget."[24] In matters of law and administration, Sweden was unified during the seventeenth century. The central state became powerful since there were no significant counterbalances to the state apparatus, such as a powerful aristocracy, strong cities, or the Roman Catholic Church.

Through Gustavus Adolphus's successful campaigns (at least from the perspective of Swedish foreign policy at that time) during the Thirty Years' War, the power of the king was strengthened. The government drew stability from the compromises and collaboration between the aristocracy and the crown, and the aristocracy won the positions of public officials: positions that, in the nineteenth century, were reserved for them. The Lutheran Church after the Reformation was a state church, with the king as its official head and the priests as public officials with duties against the state; force was used against other faiths, and Sweden was, in 1951, one of the last nations of Western Europe to adopt legislation on freedom of religion. Even the democratic breakthrough came relatively late to Sweden compared to most of Europe, but it was quite swift when it finally arrived; the shift from a traditional, hierarchical political system to a parliamentary democracy governed by the Social Democrats (labor party) took only a couple of decades. The sum of it all is that, even after the democratization and modernization of Sweden, centralism survived through changing political systems.

That central power was awarded a leading role in the Swedish political system before and after the democratic breakthrough did not mean, however, that the state was seen as oppressive. A part of the Swedish version of centralism was the belief that the state was good and fair. As the historian of ideas Roger Qvarsell puts it, "The Swedish government is sometimes said to be paternalistic, not patriarchal, a father figure more benign than strict. Whether this is a proper description or not is not easy to tell, but that the image of the good state has played a large role in social development is undeniable."[25] This is, most likely, also the reason the popular movements at the end of the nineteenth and the beginning of the twentieth centuries were not overly critical of the Swedish state, despite their criticism of the traditional state as such. Even popular movements in Sweden were characterized by a rather extensive homogeneity, and they were also characterized by an emphasis on popular education—an emphasis that eventually made social education a central issue in Swedish politics. When the royal prerogative in politics gave way to a more democratic organization, the belief in centralism as well as the good state, combined with the importance of social education, merged into a trust in the possibility of transforming society with the state as the instrument of change. The state was both willing and able to change life for most of the population for the better, and thus it was prepared to take on responsibility for the individual's well-being through an interventionist policy.

Swedish policy during the breakthrough of Swedish modernity in the 1930s might fairly be characterized as pragmatic. Nevertheless, I would contend that this was a pragmatism underpinned by certain ideas, or tacit assumptions, of what counts as reasonable politics. Those ideas eventually became articulated in official speeches and on other occasions involving discussions of what counted as typically Swedish. One way of conceptualizing these ideas, in retrospect, is to call them ideas about progress, consensus, and centralism, as I have done in this brief introduction to the Swedish model. That such ideas actually underpinned a pragmatic policy means that pragmatism (at least in this case) is not neutral but in itself carries a particular political vision, perhaps unacknowledged, that is played out in many different ways and that is far from self-evident, at least seen from the outside or from the margins. I will now turn to the main focus of this chapter—namely, how hygiene is used as a metaphor for social development in two different expressions of Swedish modernity. First, I turn to a commentary on the social state of the Swedish countryside and then to a more scholarly account; both examples are from the years around the breakthrough of Swedish modernity.

DIRT-SWEDEN

On the morning of Monday, April 25, 1938, Swedish journalist and writer Ludvig "Lubbe" Nordström, together with sound technician Axel Hedin, started out from his home on Söder in Stockholm on a field trip by car. His aim was to visit 43 district doctors and 27 priests from the state church, both to inquire about the living conditions in the Swedish countryside and to see whether those conditions correlated with the spiritual conditions of the citizens. This was going to be the topic of the radio broadcast that would later be issued as a book, *Lort-Sverige* (Dirt-Sweden), published the same year.[26] Although Nordström was a prolific writer of poetry, as well as fiction and journalistic prose, with this book he became well known as an advocate for the modernization of Sweden. *Lort-Sverige* has been seen as emblematic of a particular era in Sweden, and it is also central, as one of its prime examples, to my interest in the metaphorization of hygiene in Swedish modernity. Nordström himself has been described as "the prophet of the Swedish model."[27]

Nordström decided to make the trip after he read a census report from the official institute *Statistiska Centralbyrån* (Statistics Sweden)—the collection of demographic data began in Sweden in the eighteenth century—where he was alarmed to learn that the living conditions in many places were atrocious. According to Nordström's account of the 1935–36 census, 15.1 percent of the homes were "completely *ruined*," 18.6 percent "*thoroughly wretched*," 40.7 percent "*miserable*," 51.4 percent in need of improvement, and only 7.9 percent "*satisfactory*."[28] Although one might wonder what exactly the difference is between living in a home that is completely ruined, thoroughly wretched, or just miserable, the point of Nordström's list is not to present an exact description of the situation but to convey a sense of urgency, especially since, according to him, the Swedish population is "the world's most advanced culture" (*världens ledande kulturfolk*).[29] The poor living conditions were simply not becoming to such a great people, but they could also be detrimental to the country's business reputation. So Nordström set out on a field trip to see with his own eyes if this was true and what it looked like, and he came to see what he had not expected to see (at least that is what he says): "dirt-Sweden." The dirt that he came to see was not only "physical" but also "spiritual"—"and in *all* classes."[30]

Let me make some observations regarding Nordström's use of the term *dirt*. Central to my interest in Nordström's *Lort-Sverige* is his correlation between "physical" and "spiritual" dirt. Physical dirt is easy to imagine, and Nordström gives several vivid examples of it throughout his book: "A smell of herring brine and fuggy air, composed of odors from woodwork rot, mold, chamber pots, old sweat-soaked clothes, sour-smelling shoes, dirty socks, filled the cottage";[31] or, in a description of a stairway, "The steps half rotten, black with dirt, walls gray-black with dirt. A stale smell of basement."[32] Nordström repeatedly dwells on the sights but perhaps most of all on the smells of the places he visits, and his nose seems to be as sensitive in distinguishing bad smells as any perfumer's would be.[33] But it is a contrast not only between clean and dirty buildings but also between clean and dirty persons.[34] Persons living in a dirty house seem to develop the same characteristics themselves, as in the following description, given after an account of a dreadfully dirty home: "By the window table a tiny, tiny, shrunken, toothless old woman in a dirty kerchief, a face like an old wasted, wrinkled brown bag, two small boils instead of eyes. Brown-black fingers like roots gnawed by rats."[35] Then he finishes off his description with an account of what he smells in her home.

What amounts to spiritual dirt, however, is not as obvious. To begin with, "spirituality," for Nordström, is not necessarily associated with institutional religion. He has both good and bad things to say about the priests that he meets on his trip, but in general, he believes that religion as practiced by the Church of Sweden has been made obsolete, a thing of the past, and thus is not concerned with "real life."[36] Quite early on in his journey and in his book, Nordström decides to cancel visits to the priests, a decision that he does not hold to throughout the book. Spirituality, then—which is a word Nordström uses only occasionally—is a way of talking more generally about a "view of life." He is very clear that, to get at the problem he describes in his book, a revolution is needed—a revolution more radical than any social or economic revolution thus far, but still dependent on the progress, not least the technological progress, achieved in a hundred years in the "civilized" part of the world.[37] Spiritual dirt, for Nordström, is a question of bad traits of character. He believes that part of the problem with dirt-Sweden is moral; there is what he calls a "mentality of taking subsidies" (*understödstagarmentalitet*), where people trust in the government to take care of them rather than care for themselves by using their own abilities and strengths. *Understödstagarmentaliteten* was a public issue at the time, and hotly debated, not only by Nordström. This mentality is essentially passive and is contrasted with more active, and positive, traits of character such as "self-discipline, self-reliance, and self-respect" or "strong independence and entrepreneurship."[38] The Swedish people were in need of a spiritual awakening to meet the demands of modernization—and such an awakening is not just "a tranquil, sleepy process that takes place. It is a war of souls."[39] In other words, Nordström's rhetoric is not only graphic but sometimes positively apocalyptic, and throughout the book he revels in contrastive comparisons between the old and the new, the dirty and the hygienic. The spiritual dirt that needs to be cleaned away is passivity, egoism, and dependence on others, whereas spiritual "cleanliness" involves a sense of responsibility and solidarity.

In the preface to *Lort-Sverige*, Nordström refers to the radio broadcast he had recently conducted, in which he stated that Sweden might not *be* dirt, but it "*has* dirt within its borders, too *much* dirt to be tolerated calmly."[40] This dirt had to be removed as swiftly as possible, not only as a matter of "national prestige" but most of all as a matter of "national efficiency": "We cannot afford to have so much dirt in the national machinery."[41] The preface sets the tone for the whole book: a nation-state is likened not to an organism but to a machine. Organic metaphors in this context would probably lead thoughts in the wrong direction, as an organic state would be both the preferred metaphor of a philosophical idealism and the guardian of the national tradition that Nordström believes is obsolete. Instead, Nordström chooses the mechanistic terminology of the nation-state as a machine that can run efficiently; this is, the book implies, the metaphor of progress and of the future. In this, he is in line with a general emphasis on the virtues of the coolheaded engineer who is able to fix whatever problems he encounters. But Nordström's suggestions are not uncontested; we learn in the very same preface that two camps have formed in relation to his account: one that denies it or thinks it is exaggerated and another that agrees with it and "hopes that the fortunate citizens will have their eyes opened through this depiction of the lack that exists and that no one has expressly denied."[42] To Nordström himself, this is a question of the future destiny of the nation, and anyone who fails to see that is "afraid of reality" or is simply a coward. In other words, a highly moralizing language characterizes the tone of the preface. Let me exemplify this through a longer quote that also highlights some of the apocalyptic implications of disregarding Nordström's warning: "You must be blind in both eyes if you don't see that the fear of facing reality and its various problems, that precisely in this growing moral cowardice, that precisely in this spiritually lazy and egotistic attempt to turn away from reality, that precisely in this mentality is found the critical threat to what one confesses with the lips is highest of all: *the national freedom*, the national democracy. If this mentality is victorious, then the ground for this democracy has crumbled and then we stand, as certain other nations have done ahead of us, before chaos."[43] The district doctors Nordström meets on his field trip are often described as hardheaded and matter-of-fact and are generally presumed to have economic, statistical, and technological competence.

They have been assigned a mission—it is not clear by whom or what, but nevertheless—to educate the people out of their ignorance. It is interesting to note that whatever the doctors or Nordström have to say is rendered in correct spelling and syntax, whereas the speech of non-medical persons that Nordström meets on his trip is often rendered in (a written version of) their local dialect.

Lort-Sverige extends the idea of hygiene from the personal sphere to the ethnic. It would most likely be unfair to characterize Nordström as a national socialist, as ideas of "racial hygiene" abounded in 1938, when the book was written. There is no sign in this book that Nordström was an anti-Semite, and neither do traditional classes or conditions impress him in any way. On the contrary, there is a strong tone of social reformism of a certain kind in his book, toward the betterment of the poorest in society. But this social reformism is of an authoritarian kind, typical for his time, and he has strong opinions about how the "human material"—that is, the population of Sweden—could be furthered through active cultivation. The force that will be able to demolish obsolete structures in Swedish society is "*cleanliness, absolute cleanliness.*"[44] It is not entirely clear from the passage what kind of cleanliness is meant here, but in the context of the book, this becomes a passage that illustrates how cleanliness becomes a metaphor for the new, successful Sweden that not only has done away with atrocious housing conditions but has also taken on a more active role in racial hygiene—one centered not on caring for or supporting the "worst racial elements" but rather on leading the best toward a bright new future.[45] Although Nordström attributes some of the more problematic views to others (there are many interviews throughout the book), it becomes clear through his use of italics in the text that he regards it as a problem that "*the weak are allowed to reproduce.*"[46] The threatening passivity of the people may, if it continues, result in a need to bring foreign labor to Sweden—and what would become of Sweden then, he asks rhetorically, when it eventually becomes "populated by a foreign people?"[47]

The remedy for Sweden's malaise, in both its physical and spiritual forms, was to make a clean break with the past. Sweden needed to modernize, and just as there is no point in trying to mend a pair of broken shoes by resoling them, there was no point in trying to rebuild old, substandard buildings.[48] What is old should just be discarded, and only in this way could Sweden proceed with modernization. This meant the abolition of "dirt-Sweden" and the promotion of "villa-Sweden." The "villa," in Nordström's book, refers to a house that is built according to functional standards rather than traditional or sentimental ideas of what a home should look like (and that most likely has central heating and a proper bathroom and kitchen). The villa was a symbol of the growing middle class that had broken free from the past. But Nordström's suggestion entailed more than just a reform of housing. In the final chapter of *Lort-Sverige*, he discusses the need for a spiritual reorientation, away from laziness and toward responsibility, as well as the need for a thorough reorganization of agriculture through rationalization, modernization, and centralization.[49] Far from being a national socialist or a Marxist, Nordström is clearly oriented toward the social engineering that was prevalent in Sweden at the time: a mix of pragmatism and absolute belief in progress. Repeatedly, there is a call for a "plan" that will lead Sweden into the future. Nordström is, in *Lort-Sverige*, alternately a sensitive writer, a prophet, a scientist, an aesthetic and moral judge, and someone who is always sure of the soundness of his own description of the situation.

I hope my exposé of Nordström's *Lort-Sverige* has succeeded in expressing some of the main ideas of his suggestions for reform, but what I have especially tried to highlight is how he regards the correspondence between different dimensions of human existence—dirty housing conditions correspond, in his account, to physiognomic appearances and spiritual conditions. One final quote may illustrate this correspondence: "The rooms were and stayed dark and dreary. The people were and remained dark and dirty."[50] I have no quarrel with his suggestion that a lot of the population in Sweden in the 1930s lived in poor and substandard conditions, except that perhaps some of his most colorful descriptions seem too detailed to be true. But the very intimate traffic between different senses of a concept such as hygiene was (and still is) problematic is, of course. Hygiene, in Nordström's book, is a question not only of personal but also of mental, social, and even ethnic hygiene. Indeed, the level at which we find the literal use of "hygiene" in *Lort-Sverige* is not self-evident. Further, the call for cleanliness is aligned with a vision of how to achieve it, very much in line with the three pillars of the Swedish model: progress (necessary for the sake of "national efficiency" and possible through rational planning), consensus (the conviction that all rational people would agree with Nordström's own perspective), and centralism (the belief that change can be engineered from the state's central perspective).

CRISIS IN THE POPULATION QUESTION

Nordström's *Lort-Sverige* was in no way unique. It had an even more famous predecessor in Alva and Gunnar Myrdal's 1934 book *Kris i befolkningsfrågan* (Crisis in the Population Question). Alva and Gunnar Myrdal were the very symbols of engaged intellectuals in Sweden at the time. Well-read, well-travelled, and active in the political debate in Sweden from the 1930s onward, they were both members of the Social Democratic Party and had a great deal of international experience. Alva was trained as a teacher, but her main occupation involved political and diplomatic work in Sweden and elsewhere; Gunnar was a professor of political economy and, later, international economy, but like his wife, he also did diplomatic work for the United Nations. Alva Myrdal was awarded the Nobel Peace Prize in 1982 and Gunnar Myrdal the Nobel Prize in Economic Sciences in 1974 (together with Friedrich von Hayek). When it comes to academic publications, the most well-known works for an international audience are most likely Gunnar Myrdal's 1944 book *An American Dilemma: The Negro Problem and Modern Democracy*, a study of the situation of African Americans in the United States, and also *Asian Drama*, published in 1968. *Kris i befolkningsfrågan* is very interesting with regard to my question about hygiene as metaphor, but to explain that, first I need to say something about the background of the book as well as its contents.

To a reader acquainted with *An American Dilemma*, with its emphasis on "the American Creed" as a liberal ethos that can be used to criticize the actual—often illiberal—actions of American people and institutions, such as racial segregation, *Kris i befolkningsfrågan* may come as something of a surprise. This ethos of the American Creed, in Myrdal's understanding of it, speaks of "the essential dignity of the human being, of the fundamental equality of all men, and of certain inalienable rights to freedom, justice, and a fair opportunity."[51] Myrdal—who philosophically ascribed to a version of emotivism where, in short, moral statements were seen as referring to emotional attitudes rather than propositions with truth value—argued that, in the case of the American Creed, there was no confusion between value and fact, since this creed was based on explicit value judgments that were empirically observable. The function of the American Creed was as a "conscience of a nation," and since most people in the United States wanted to live according to this creed, there was no contradiction involved in criticizing actual acts or policies on its behalf, as long as one ascribed to the notion that values and acts should be consistent with each other. In other words, in *An American Dilemma*, Myrdal opened up for normative reasoning within political economy in a way that puts it slightly at odds with the general drift of *Kris i befolknings-frågan*. The latter book was rather an expression of the three pillars of the Swedish model.

The 1934 book was perhaps the most publicly debated book in Sweden in its time. It is above all a discussion of the implications of what its authors regarded as a modern and socially oriented family policy. But the family policy is considered in its social context, which is why the book also has broader implications for a future Swedish welfare policy. The Myrdals write that "the population question must primarily be studied as a problem of social psychology and sociology of culture."[52] It is their own scholarly disciplines that deliver the perspective from which the "population question" is approached, and this is a novelty in the debate about the population in Sweden. Even if *Kris i befolkningsfrågan* was initially received rather indifferently, quite soon its sales picked up, and it was printed in several revised editions. It could also be argued that it had a real influence on the actual policy in the government of Prime Minister Per Albin Hansson and the Social Democrats. In 1981, Gunnar Myrdal, writing about the book he had cowritten with Alva, stated that the "welfare program that we had strongly recommended was so profoundly in line with Per Albin's dream about the good welfare state [*folkhem*]."[53]

The rhetoric used in *Kris i befolkningsfrågan* is robustly modernistic and rigorously "objective." The Myrdals refer to the latest statistical results, quoting them extensively. They present the modernization of society as both highly desirable and inevitable. Further, they declare that the views they put forward belong to those who are "awake," in contrast to those who exist in society's "cultural backwaters," and the very choice of words here indicates a moral judgment.[54] Tradition is defined as "the irrational binding of our notions and views."[55] It is imperative to liberate oneself from irrationality in order to reach a rational view, even in the population question. They write that rational progress in all areas of society is already rapid and is increasing in speed. Here, it is technological development that is the motor of progress and that also demands reforms within the economic and social areas: "Technological development requires continually renewed organization of the forms of human coexistence."[56] Progress is often portrayed as an inevitable destiny that is neglected only to the detriment of society. The rationalization of society increasingly has an impact on all spheres of life, which, according to the Myrdals, is noticeable in the rationalization of procreation and birth control. Procreation—among certain classes—is increasingly a question of will rather than instinct. This means that prospective parents can control procreation and rationalize and moralize it by placing it under the control of the moral will rather than the amoral instinctual life.

Despite the seeming inevitability of the modernization of society, it still seems to need some help from progressive social politics to develop in what the Myrdals call a desirable course. To make sure that society keeps pace with progress, they advocate what they call a "prophylactic social politics" that will "enhance the quality of the 'people material' [folkmaterialet]" and make the "supply of children" a concern for society as a whole.[57] We may note here that all through the book people are objectified, referred to as "people material" or "human material." This could be ascribed to a rhetorical strategy that is supposed to indicate a matter-of-fact and technical attitude toward the problem in question. In an article from 1932, "Socialpolitikens dilemma" (The Dilemma of Social Politics), Gunnar Myrdal refers to what he calls the "romanticism of engineering," which, in essence, leads to a notion of a logical and objective engineer who, after unbiased deliberation, is able to solve all problems, technical as well as social.[58] This rhetorical strategy means, however, that in Kris i befolkningsfrågan, the "people" are not recognized (at least not rhetorically) as being able to maintain any agency, which can raise serious opposition to the suggested policy; the "people material" is essentially an object for whose sake the social politics are proposed by those granted subjectivity—the experts.

According to the Myrdals, what is needed is a more centralized social planning as well as education and socializing of people, especially the young. Bad habits, irrational views, and irresponsible actions need to be corrected. The aim of the proposed social politics, however, is even wider: "The immediate task of the prophylactic social politics is to produce a better human material."[59] The conscious or unconscious direction of "the future" or "everybody" is to "rationalize, elaborate production and the whole of human life and thereby raise the quality of ourselves and our fellow human beings"; this is a development that is "sincerely affirmed by all sound human beings."[60] Such a reform has consequences for many areas of society—for instance, the school system, whose aim must be more social: "The social adaptation of individuals must be the primary objective of the school."[61] The authors argue that human beings need to be brought up to value cooperation and mutual accommodation. But social planning is not only a question of schooling, and here we finally see why *Kris i befolknings-frågan* is of interest to the question of hygiene as metaphor in Swedish modernity. Hopefully this exposition has given some indication of it already, but when the Myrdals come to the question of eugenics, where they explicitly state that there are individuals "whose procreation is not desirable from a racial hygienic perspective," it becomes all but obvious.[62]

As previously mentioned, apropos Nordström, racial hygiene was a phenomenon not limited to national socialism. Eugenics and sterilization were seen as ways of refining the "human material." Even though the Myrdals recognized that scientific eugenics had shaky foundations and could be used for dubious purposes, they still saw some future potential in eugenics together with sterilization precisely in refining the available "material" and avoiding maladjusted procreation. In *Kris i befolkningsfrågan*, the Myrdals comment on the legislation about sterilization that was passed in the Swedish parliament in 1934 and that was to take effect on January 1, 1935, as something positive that should be extended to include even people of age, against their will, and as something that should be as strong as possible right from the start.[63] If the arguments for eugenics were not yet strong enough, the reasons of social pedagogy were more than convincing. A positive view of eugenics was, in other words, connected to the need for racial hygiene with the purpose of forming the "human material" for the good of society. Those competent to supervise this massive task were the "experts": the civilized and enlightened representatives of the true interests of the people.

"Racial" hygiene was not the only hygiene discussed by the Myrdals. Other uses of the term include "mental hygiene," "social hygiene," and "habitation hygiene"—and more physiological and nutritional aspects are also included: for example, "'health food' prepared by our nutrition experts" is highlighted as important for growing children.[64] There are also "moral health" and "spiritual health," the latter of which, incidentally, is explicitly connected to the housing policy, just as Nordström stated in his book four years later. Interesting for my purposes here is the Myrdals' passing remark about the concept of health: because health is reduced to a "physiological-materialistic notion" atrocious living conditions are not recognized as a health hazard, and thus no actions are taken to address them (e.g., by prohibiting overcrowding).[65] Like Nordström, the Myrdals see "a connection between overcrowding, on the one hand, and psychic ill health, general inferiority, and asocial tendencies on the other."[66] Better housing conditions are as important to a more progressive social politics as better, but also free, health care. Even if making a connection between housing conditions and general health in itself does not necessarily suggest any illegitimate traffic between distinct dimensions of health, we may note how many times *hygiene* is used in the body of the text. This might be interpreted as an indication of a less controlled traffic between different dimensions, especially if one also takes note of how the question of hygiene in *Kris i befolkningsfrågan* is intimately related to the question of improving the quality of the "human material." The verbs describing how the suggested improvement is to occur are as interesting as they are telling: "leading," "monitoring," "enlightening," "waking," and "rearing."[67] All these verbs suggest a central viewpoint from which social and personal change is managed.

Even though the terminology of *hygiene* is not nearly as frequent in *Kris i befolkningsfrågan* as in its successor, *Lort-Sverige*, and the tone of its rhetorical style is less alarmist, it is easy to see how Nordström was influenced by a way of thinking similar to that of the Myrdals. Common to both books is a belief in the unprejudiced and rational power of an enlightened elite and the feasibility of central planning. By presenting the problem as a matter of hygiene (whether it concerns housing or ethnicity or anything else), both books try to give the impression of an argument that is self-evident, because who wants to take sides with "dirt"? And self-evident is how the solution is represented, as the outcome of actions taken by those with the power of unprejudiced reasoning and a "clear" vision of the problem, untroubled by the distorted residues of tradition and history. As the sociologist Zygmunt Bauman puts it, the kind of authority the authors claimed for themselves could be described as legislative: "The authority involved the right to command the rules the social world was to obey, and it was legitimized in terms of better judgment and superior knowledge guaranteed by the proper method of its production (i.e., shapeable yet heretofore shaped in the wrong way); the new legislative authority of men of knowledge established its own necessity and entitlements."[68] One could even suggest that both Nordström and the Myrdals exemplify a certain kind of teleological apocalypticism in their insistence both on knowing where history is actually going—given a little help—and on their ability to clearly distinguish between the past and the future. It needs to be said, finally, that at least the Myrdals came to change their rhetorical strategy later and that they also came to recognize how tradition might actually have influenced their reasoning, as when Gunnar Myrdal, in a speech to the Lutheran Council of America on March 11, 1976, insisted that the normative agenda of political economy was his way of "expressing my Lutheran inheritance."[69] But this was, of course, forty years later, and it remains a fact that hygiene was very much a root metaphor for talking about societal change in the 1930s in Sweden. That we find all three pillars of the Swedish model in the Myrdals' *Kris i befolkningsfrågan* is not at all surprising, as it was a central text for the interpretation of this model in the 1930s. Together with Nordström's *Lort-Sverige*, it clearly shows how hygiene was very much part of the image of how Sweden was to modernize itself as a country. This has been observed earlier in much of the literature on the era, so let me now turn to some more general observations on this period.

RACIAL HYGIENE AS A POLITICAL PROJECT

Hygiene—from personal to racial hygiene—was a central theme in Sweden between the two world wars. Racial hygiene, such as Nordström and the Myrdals talk about, should not be seen as a part of national socialistic racial biology and metaphysics but rather as an integrated part of a general idea of progress. In comparison to other nations at this time, Sweden saw itself as progressive in matters of racial biology and also, at a later time, suggested extensive reforms motivated by racial hygiene. In Sweden, an official institute for racial biology was inaugurated at Uppsala University in 1922, supported by several well-known biologists and members of parliament. The purpose of the institute was to propagate knowledge about the value of racial hygienic reforms in managing social problems. As two Swedish ethnologists, Jonas Frykman and Orvar Löfgren, write, "Hygiene, regardless of the context in which it occurs, is the central keyword of the time between the wars. Through hygiene, it should be possible to do away with what is unclean or disturbing and finish up with the good and the normal as the end product. Through the 'human material' that the nation holds, a happy, healthy, and harmonious race shall finally be cultivated."[70] Racial hygiene was a part of the bigger framework of the effort to achieve better living conditions through social hygiene. If the "human material" could be improved, the land of the future could be conquered. At the beginning of this chapter, I quoted Ronny Ambjörnsson's autobiographical account of how hygiene and rationality became two sides of the same coin as the "credo of modernism" in his childhood. Ambjörnsson's colleague in the history of ideas, Karin Johannisson, suggests that, "in the 1930s, social hygiene was merged with a new type of social engineering that not only wanted to create a healthy human being, but a *new* human being: sound, strong, rational, willing to subordinate its irrational body to the rational social body."[71] In the next sentence, she quotes Alva and Gunnar Myrdal from *Kris i befolkningsfrågan.*

Racial hygiene in the 1930s, then, was not necessarily motivated by biological, Darwinian arguments (which of course were prominent then, too, but more so in the 1920s) but rather by an idea of social engineering that presumed that social planning was possible and hoped that it would become a reality.[72] As mentioned, the parliament passed legislation for sterilization in 1934; it came into effect on January 1, 1935, and was extended in 1941. Through this legislation, the parliament wanted to inhibit reproduction among people with mental disabilities and mental illnesses and consequently to "refine" the people. The 1934 legislation allowed for the forced sterilization (for racial or social reasons)of individuals deemed incompetent in the eyes of the law. There were even discussions about sterilizing individuals deemed to be "asocial," such as alcoholics, prostitutes, vagabonds, and criminals. This legislation of sterilization was proposed by the government and was adopted with strong support across the political spectrum in the parliament. In 1941, however, there was widespread agreement that this legislation was not enough, so the possibility of forced sterilization was extended to individuals carrying a "severe disease or severe deformity of another kind." Other medical reasons for sterilization were also referred to, and even social reasons were extended, as the legislation claimed that individuals living in an "asocial way" could be sterilized.[73] The justification remained the presumed utility for the state. In 1960, the legislation and the motive of racial hygiene behind it began to be questioned in an inquiry about impediments to marriage. In 1975, the 1941 legislation was abolished, and all forced sterilization was banned. During the period 1935–75, about 63,000 individuals were sterilized in Sweden. According to historian Maija Runcis, about 95 percent of these were women.[74] One explanation for the wide scope of the period when forced sterilization was practiced is given by Gunnar Broberg and Matthias Tydén, two Swedish historians: "That the politics of sterilization could last so long has to do with its scientific legitimization; perhaps the reason was less a confidence in racial hygiene as such and more a trust in science in general."[75] The politics of sterilization was a way of pushing the Swedish society forward, with the state taking responsibility in the sphere of "hygiene," and it rested firmly on the three pillars of the Swedish model: progress, consensus, and centralism.

THE INEVITABILITY OF METAPHOR

Let me conclude by returning to my initial discussion of hygiene as metaphor with the help of Sontag. As Sontag suggests, in a sentence I quoted earlier, "metaphors and myths . . . kill," and it would seem that racial hygiene could be seen as an example of this. By talking of sterilization as a kind of "hygiene," its practice can be made to sound more legitimate, since few would quarrel with the importance of personal hygiene for the health of the person; consequently, social hygiene could trade on the value of personal hygiene. The traffic between the personal and the social senses of hygiene could make a deplorable practice seem more acceptable. Hygiene, in Nordström's and the Myrdals' books, was used as a central metaphor intimately connected to the growth of the welfare society, both as its presupposition and as a moral imperative for it to occur. It is interesting to note, even if this is only a matter of degree, that the associations in Nordström's account are of a more domestic kind than the Myrdals' more scientifically minded use of the term *hygiene*. However, in both accounts, a chain of associations is established—from the personal (in both physical and moral respects), to the material (in terms of housing), and finally, to the more abstractly social. No dimension of hygiene could be ignored, because doing so would threaten the entire edifice of the coming welfare state. Thus also the apocalyptic tone of Nordström's writing in particular.

In one way, hygiene could perhaps be seen as a root metaphor in an entire worldview, as is hinted at in the earlier quote from Ronny Ambjörnsson; if hygiene was part of the Swedish "credo of modernism," it entailed, as seen in the writing of Nordström and the Myrdals, beliefs as well as rituals and perhaps also faith in the sense of trust in progress. Hygiene was—understandably—a part of the effort to achieve better living conditions not just for the few but for the many, but at the same time it must be understood—regrettably—as a technique for disciplining the "people material" into conformity with the ideals of a certain kind of Swedish modernity and, moreover, for the people's own supposed good. We need not suppose any vicious motives behind the suggestions for the modernization of Swedish society to understand how this became a legitimization for an expansive politics of sterilization that violated the autonomy of persons for the common good. The metaphor of hygiene became a central tool in this process. Despite the criticisms previously made of Sontag, the critical vigilance she called for regarding the uses of metaphors associated with health would have been very beneficial.

Although the political uses of hygiene metaphors have decreased drastically since the 1930s in Sweden, one may suppose that this is not due to an increased insight into the hazards of metaphorization. Indeed, the politics of sterilization has fallen out of favor and has also been the subject of public debate. Increasingly, the ideals of Swedish modernity have been critically scrutinized at the same time as the homogeneity of Swedish society has crumbled. Sincere belief in the inevitability and goodness of continuous progress has waned. But one may well ask whether the thing itself has disappeared because the metaphor has fallen out of favor. As Henrik Bogdan shows in Chapter 3, about how minority religions are treated and what this tells us about official tolerance in contemporary Sweden, a similar pattern can be seen even if it does not involve the metaphor of hygiene. Also, having sex could be seen as a matter of hygiene, as Andreas Johansson Heinö shows in Chapter 5 about Swedish sin. Finally, Wilhelm Kardemark has shown in his 2012 dissertation (not in this book), *När livet tar rätt form: Om människosyn i svenska hälsotidskrifter 1910–13 och 2009* (When Life Takes the Right Shape: On Anthropology in Swedish Health Magazines 1910–13 and 2009), how "good health" has been put forward as a central ideal for contemporary Swedish (and perhaps also Western) citizens in a way that should make us wonder whether the hygiene metaphor really is no longer being used politically.[76] This chapter does not try to answer these questions, but some of the following chapters will add something of their own to this quite complex picture.

If there is something to Mary Douglas's thesis that the human body functions as a symbolic system for the body politic, including medically charged metaphors describing the threats against the social body, we should hardly be surprised to encounter additional health metaphors in contemporary politics. Rather than suggesting, as Sontag did (albeit in a distinctively different context), that we might get rid of the traffic between different senses of health-related vocabulary and the metaphorical charging of certain diseases, we should instead devote our critical efforts to distinguishing and examining that vocabulary—hopefully preventing its metaphors from turning vicious. As far as we can see, from the vantage point of today, Nordström and (especially) the Myrdals were using metaphorization in order to build society from as "de-metaphorized" a political vision as possible. To suggest today that the "de-metaphorization" needs to go even farther than they were able to take it runs the risk of only prolonging a strategy that might be flawed from the outset. One may even suggest that the "de-metaphorization" aspiration is part of the same quest for hygiene (now in the sphere of language) that produced the problem to begin with. Modernity, as Bauman has demonstrated, is characterized by precisely this anxiety about ambivalence, and the aim of modern politics is to "exterminate" or "suppress" ambivalence: "The horror of mixing reflects the obsession with separating."[77] What Nordström and the Myrdals can help us with, as historical examples rather than examples of a viable practice, is instead the self-critical insight of the inevitability of metaphor. This leaves us ample room to examine what kinds of metaphors we live by and the extent to which they are valid or should be criticized—or even what metaphors might be good for, and when. And it saves us from the possibly fatal mistake of thinking that we can look at the world and at ourselves from a position beyond metaphor. Only in this way, I suppose, could Sontag's legitimate aim of critical vigilance in regard to the traffic of metaphors be upheld. Hence there is also a need to scrutinize the self-images of a society such as Sweden, whether in its official policies or in its cultural expressions—as will be done in the following chapters.

NOTES

1. Ronny Ambjörnsson, *Mitt förnamn är Ronny* (Stockholm: Bonniers, 1998), 28.
2. Cf. the Norwegian book *Sykdom som litteratur: 13 utvalgte diagnoser* [Sickness as Literature: 13 Selected Diagnoses] by Hilde Bondevik and Knut Stene-Johansen (Oslo: Unipub, 2011).
3. Mary Douglas, *Purity and Danger. An Analysis of the Conception of Pollution and Taboo* (London: Routledge, 2002).
4. Susan Sontag, *Illness as Metaphor and AIDS and Its Metaphors* (New York: Picador, 1990), 3–87.
5. Ibid., 20.
6. Ibid., 30.
7. Ibid., 58.
8. Ibid., 102.
9. For a helpful philosophical account of metaphors, see Paul Ricoeur, *The Rule of Metaphor*, trans. Robert Czerny (London: Routledge, Kegan & Paul, 1978).
10. See, for instance, Barbara Clow, "Who's Afraid of Susan Sontag? Or, the Myths and Metaphors of Cancer Reconsidered," *Social History of Medicine*, 14:2 (2001), 293–312.
11. Marquis Childs, *Sweden: The Middle Way* (New Haven: Yale University Press, 1936).
12. Per Thullberg and Kjell Östberg (eds.), *Den svenska modellen* (Lund: Studentlitteratur, 1994), 5.
13. This account draws upon my book *Den lyckliga filosofin: Etik och politik hos Hägerström, Tingsten, makarna Myrdal och Hedenius* (Stockholm: Brutus Östlings bokförlag Symposion, 2000), especially chapter 7.
14. See Lennart Jörberg, "Svensk ekonomi under 100 år," in *Svensk ekonomi*, 3rd ed., ed. Bo Södersten (Stockholm: Rabén & Sjögren, 1984), 24–25.
15. Lars Ingelstam, *Framtidstron och den svenska modellen*, Tema T Rapport 15 (Linköping: Universitetet i Linköping, 1988), 15.

16. Mats Lindqvist, "Ingenjör Fredriksson i framtidslandet," in *Modärna tider: Vision och vardag i folkhemmet*, ed. Jonas Frykman and Orvar Löfgren (Lund: Liber förlag, 1985), 141, 183.

17. Bo Rothstein, *Den korporativa staten: Intresseorganisationer och statsförvaltning i svensk politik* (Stockholm: Norstedts, 1992), 98.

18. Quoted from Stig Hadenius, *Svensk politik under 1900-talet: Konflikt och samförstånd*, 4th ed. (Stockholm: Tiden Athena, 1996), 70–71.

19. Emil Uddhammar, *Partierna och den stora staten: En analys av statsteorier och svensk politik under 1900-talet* (Stockholm: City University Press, 1993); Leif Lewin, *"Bråka inte!" Om vår tids demokratisyn* (Stockholm: SNS Förlag, 1998).

20. Gösta Esping-Andersen, "Jämlikhet, effektivitet och makt," *Den svenska modellen*, 105.

21. For an account of this in the form of a novel, see Mikael Niemi's *Popular Music*, trans. Laurie Thompson (London: Flamingo, 2003), 67–71.

22. Gunnar Olofsson, "'Den stränge fadern och den goda modern': Sociologiska perspektiv på den moderna staten," in *Sverige—vardag och struktur: Sociologer beskriver det svenska samhället*, ed. Ulf Himmelstrand and Göran Svensson, 2nd ed. (Stockholm: Norstedts, 1993), 588.

23. Ibid., 589.

24. Göran Therborn, "Hur det hela började: När och varför det moderna Sverige blev vad det blev," in *Sverige—vardag och struktur: Sociologer beskriver det svenska samhället*, ed. Ulf Himmelstrand and Göran Svensson, 2nd ed. (Stockholm: Norstedts, 1993), 32.

25. Roger Qvarsell, "Mellan familj, arbetsgivare och stat: En idéhistorisk essä om det sociala ansvarets organisering under två århundraden," in *Medmänsklighet att hyra? Åtta forskare om ideell verksamhet*, ed. Erik Amnå (Örebro: Libris, 1995), 20.

26. "Lort" has wider connotations: besides "dirt," it may also refer to "filth" or "muck."

27. Sverker Sörlin, "Utopin i verkligheten: Ludvig Nordström och det moderna Sverige," in *I framtidens tjänst: Ur folkhemmets idéhistoria*, ed. Ronny Ambjörnsson (Stockholm: Gidlunds, 1986), 181. See further pp. 166–95 for an introduction to and an analysis of Nordström's work.

28. Ludvig Nordström, *Lort-Sverige*, 3rd ed. (Stockholm: Kooperativa förbundets bokförlag, 1938), 16.

29. Ibid., 16. This fact is confirmed by a mailman in Jamestown, a chauffeur in Detroit, and a singing teacher in Chicago—see ibid., 15.

30. Ibid., 18.

31. Ibid., 31.

32. Ibid., 104.

33. Cf. especially 118–19, where Nordström seems to be able to distinguish between smells from at least 25 different sources, among them "several different kinds of weapons" and "earth that is urine steeped since decades, maybe centuries."

34. Ibid., 68, 83, 118.

35. Ibid., 120.

36. Ibid., 43. Cf. 80, 85–86, 91–92.

37. Ibid., 250.

38. Ibid., 138, 230.

39. Ibid., 72.

40. Ibid., 11.

41. Ibid.

42. Ibid.

43. Ibid., 12.

44. Ibid., 173.

45. Ibid., 236.

46. Ibid., 432.

47. Ibid., 375.

48. Ibid., 298.

49. Ibid., 429–34.

50. Ibid., 135.

51. Gunnar Myrdal, *An American Dilemma: The Negro Problem and Modern Democracy*, vol. 1 (New York/London: Harper & Brothers, 1944), 4.

52. Alva and Gunnar Myrdal, *Kris i befolkningsfrågan* (Stockholm: Albert Bonniers förlag, 1934), 79.

53. Gunnar Myrdal, *Hur styrs landet?* (Stockholm: Rabén & Sjögren, 1982), 188.

54. Myrdal, *Kris*, 10.

55. Ibid., 15.

56. Ibid., 295.

57. Ibid., 11.

58. Gunnar Myrdal, "Socialpolitikens dilemma II," *Spektrum*, 2:4 (1932), 25.

59. Myrdal, *Kris*, 205.

60. Ibid., 206, 256–57.

61. Ibid., 265.

62. Ibid., 75.

63. Ibid., 217, 220.

64. Ibid., 227.

65. Ibid., 231.

66. Ibid., 233.

67. Ibid., 250.

68. Zygmunt Bauman, *Intimations of Postmodernity* (London: Routledge, 1992), 11.

69. Gunnar Myrdal, "A Worried America," *Current*, 202 (April 1978), 47–48.

70. Jonas Frykman and Orvar Löfgren, "På väg—bilder av kultur och klass," in *Modärna tider: Vision och vardag i folkhemmet*, ed. Jonas Frykman and Orvar Löfgren (Lund: Liber förlag, 1985), 74.

71. Karin Johannisson, "Politisk anatomi," in *Kroppens tunna skal: Sex essäer om kropp, historia och kultur* (Stockholm: Bokförlaget Pan, 1998), 227.

72. Cf. Gunnar Broberg and Matthias Tydén, *Oönskade i folkhemmet: Rashygien och sterilisering i Sverige* (Stockholm: Gidlunds, 1991), as well as Maija Runcis, *Steriliseringar i folkhemmet* (Stockholm: Ordfront, 1998).

73. Broberg and Tydén, *Oönskade*, 94, 180ff.

74. Runcis, *Steriliseringar*, 277.

75. Broberg and Tydén, *Oönskade*, 186.

76. Wilhelm Kardemark, *När livet tar rätt form: Om människosyn i svenska hälsotidskrifter 1910–13 och 2009* (Göteborg: Institutionen för litteratur, idéhistoria och religion, 2013).

77. Zygmunt Bauman, *Modernity and Ambivalence* (London: Polity Press, 1991), 7–8.

CHAPTER 2

FROM SHARED RESOURCES TO SHARED VALUES

MARIE DEMKER

"COZY" LITTLE *FOLKHEM*?[1]

DURING THE LAST THIRTY YEARS OR SO, we have seen a change in the conceptualization of the Nordic welfare state. The popular image, both abroad and at home, of a neutral and fair state apparatus that mediated conflicting interests and distributed resources has been replaced by a new image of a flexible and inclusive community that promotes common values and safeguards our rights concerning personal safety and health. However, that shift could also be formulated as a move away from an image of a high-tax socialist state known for suicides, drugs, and its open-minded views on sex, into a liberal, individualistic welfare state with reduced taxes and a high degree of individual choice—including in traditionally government-directed areas such as health and education, where people can access both free services and those they pay for themselves.[2]

A development toward a more liberal view of society and individuals has taken place in the Western hemisphere as a whole, but the Nordic welfare states have been especially touched by this development. The explanation for this is that in most of the Nordic countries—unlike in other Northern European states such as the United Kingdom, Germany, and the Netherlands, for example—the political agenda for solving problems regarding allocation of material resources has been focused almost solely on removing unfair class inequalities through redistributive mechanisms. In doing so, most of the solutions have been tied to governmental processes either by the state itself or by regional or local tax communities. This is also the case in Norway, Denmark, Iceland, and Finland, but it has been particularly evident in Swedish society because of its highly developed welfare state, and I argue that the discourse has moved away from ensuring that (mostly) material welfare is equally distributed and has taken a more elusive turn. A stronger and broader emphasis on what are called the cultural aspects in politics, instead of a narrow materialistic focus, has opened up the political space for discussions on religion, traditions, and nationhood. And, of course, this development has also opened up the political discourse to forces that strongly promote the value of a homogeneous and traditional nationalistic society.

As mentioned in the introduction to this book, it is now widely acknowledged that Stieg Larsson's Millennium trilogy portrays a chilly and cynical Swedish society where the protagonist, Lisbeth Salander, is left to seek vengeance herself for the mistreatment she endured as a result of past public negligence. With the ambivalent help of an independent journalist, she reveals how the welfare state not only manipulates its own citizens but is also manipulated by forces stronger than the soft state can withstand. This development described in the book can be understood only if viewed within a wider Swedish political frame. Since the late 1960s, Western society has undergone enormous changes due to the communication revolution, with an increase in individualization and destabilization as the most prominent features.[3] During the 1980s, liberal values had an important breakthrough.[4] By putting the individual at the forefront and calling for free choice regarding both schools and lifestyle, the liberal winds got quite strong in Swedish society.[5] In the late 1980s, most citizens said they wanted more public welfare services to be delivered by private alternatives—a change that was remarkable considering the earlier Swedish development described briefly in the introduction to this book.[6] In my view, there was, at the same time, both a strong call from citizens for a society that permitted a rich variation of lifestyles and a call from the same citizens that precluded these variations from diminishing their chances for self-realization. Most Swedes wanted it both ways, so to speak. They wanted individual freedom and choice but also the safety of the highly developed welfare state. One way for the government to address this dilemma was to politically upgrade the national common value frame focusing on human rights and individual liberties while at the same time offering citizens a multiplicity of choices (both private and public) framed by these ideas and values. In political practice, the solution is deregulation, privatization, and an assortment of offers on the welfare market, which are guaranteed by state power by means of special conditions and the establishment of controlling bodies to ensure that the values and safety of the public are protected.

In the older materialistic outline focusing on spreading welfare and redistributing public goods, the national collective value frame was not questioned at all, and therefore citizens were guaranteed a certain amount of freedom concerning values such as those associated with religion, traditions, and ecological awareness. In the new outline, instead of focusing on individualization and letting cultural themes and values be the foundation, freedom regarding religious tradition or family values has to be restricted but in a "cozy" and "inclusive" way.[7] Today, state power is conceptualized to socialize, educate, and control citizens in order to protect certain values rather than to ensure that citizens have the resources and material opportunities that they require for development, progress, and a future in which they have the authority to make their own choices. Those choices have been outsourced to the market although under the supervision of governmental bodies.

As one piece in a broader jigsaw, I will analyze whether there is any empirical evidence to support the assumed development, portrayed in Stieg Larsson's books, from a society characterized by collectivism and equally distributed welfare to one of individualism and bureaucratic and restricted welfare distribution. Is there a reason to believe that the gloomy, Millennium-based picture of Sweden that was sketched in the introduction to this book has any resemblance to real politics? I would suggest that the answer is partly yes. Based on a time-comparative analysis of the annual policy declarations of Swedish governments and also the expressed views of Swedish citizens, I will develop an argument on how and why the authoritative resource allocation in Sweden has moved from providing its citizens with material welfare and enough income to support them in making new choices, over to safeguarding common and compelling values such as human rights, secularism, tolerance, and ecological awareness.

MORE CONCERNED ABOUT VALUE ORIENTATION
THAN ABOUT MATERIAL RESOURCES?

Executing state power is the most basic role of an open society, and the Swedish view of how that power should express itself in society has shifted over time. Framing a community or society through values is a condition for shaping its future. As we mentioned in the introduction, and as Ola Sigurdson developed further in Chapter 1, Sweden was a relatively homogeneous society during the 1960s and 1970s. Since then, however, a liberal view has paved the way for a more tolerant, open, and fragmented community where lifestyles and social roles can differ. At the same time, Swedish living standards have risen and the material circumstances have improved substantially for all social groups. It seems contradictory, then, that the expression of state power has gone from securing welfare and economic safety to gathering around common values and infusing the population with beliefs about tolerance, ecological views, and national identity. This development has made room for a discussion about the risks that can arise when different views clash rather than about the material vulnerability of groups that are struggling to get by or have been left behind.

In 2012, an animated discussion took place in the leading Swedish newspapers on how black stereotypes are used in art and culture. One of the most respected and beloved Swedish children's writers and filmmakers ended her work on a character called *Lilla Hjärtat* (Little Heart) after she was accused of racism.[8] At the same time, "Tintin in the Congo" was discussed because a librarian wanted to move all the Tintin books from the children's library and into a section for adults, where "Tintin in the Congo" was already situated. Another artist—who created a cake reflecting a racist stereotype—prompted a scandal when the Swedish minister for culture was invited to eat some of it and did so without noticing the stereotype. A huge discussion on racism followed: the minister had been caught in a trap, as she really had no choice other than to be a part of the artist's performance.[9] These are examples of how ideas and norms have been more important topics in the public debate about racism and discrimination rather than they have been in discussions about the labor market, education, and social integration. An idea of well-being coupled with specific values has come into the mainstream discourse at the same time as the idea of well-being as a matter of social and economic circumstances has decreased.

In order to find out more systematically whether, how, and when this change took place, I have studied the annual declarations of the Swedish government every five years from 1975 until 2010. A policy declaration is read by the prime minister on the opening of the parliament each year. The declaration is an assessment of the state of affairs in Sweden, and it used to be an account of reforms and propositions expected to occur during the coming parliamentary term. It could be compared to the American State of the Union speech, but in a parliamentary system the speech does not have the same heavy influence as in a presidential one. On the other hand, the policy declarations made by the prime minister used to be more down to earth, introducing the plans that the government was prepared to undertake. I have also taken into consideration in the analysis all the declarations from 1991 to 1994, and also from 2004 to 2006. In all, I have analyzed eight declarations thoroughly with an in-depth qualitative textual analysis and seven declarations through a systematic and analytical contextual reading, searching for indicators of policy change.

POLICY DECLARATIONS 1975–90

The policy declarations of 1975, 1980, 1985, and 1990 are more or less entirely dedicated to economy, income taxes, material resources, and the labor market. In 1975, 1985, and 1990, Sweden had a Social Democratic, one-party government, but in 1980 it had a coalition government consisting of three center-right parties, where the Centre Party (agrarians) had the prime minister post.[10] On some rare occasions value-related statements were made, and the declarations also made a special effort to promote a climate of "mutual understanding"(*samförstånd*) during the economic crisis, and to defend the value of full employment.

In 1980, Prime Minister Thorbjörn Fälldin (Centre Party) mentioned mutual understanding in a time of crisis, and he argued forcefully that the main goal for the government was to stabilize the economy. In 1985, Prime Minister Olof Palme (Social Democrat) discussed a common responsibility[11] for the economy and for the future of the country. He stressed that the main goal for the government was to address employment issues.[12] Palme also put forward the tradition of political cooperation[13] in Swedish politics. In 1990, Prime Minister Ingvar Carlsson (Social Democrat) talked about how "we Swedes"[14]

ought to show that people can live together in "freedom and safety."[15]
He also mentioned that "we" feel "proud" of our democracy, our well-
educated citizens, our well-equipped industry, and our preservation of
nature. These are the only examples of policy declarations from these
years that advocate fostering a common value ground. The 1990 declaration also touches on the subject, using terms related to common
values and national heritage.

POLICY DECLARATIONS 1990–2000

Between 1990 and 1995, something happened: there was a value turn
in the declarations from the early 1990s. In the 1995 declaration of
government policy, Prime Minister Ingvar Carlsson specifically and
explicitly spoke about the political struggle against racism, discrimination, and xenophobia. This marks, presumably, a step toward policy
declarations that are more of a documentation of common values than
an enumeration of political goals that have been promised or achieved.

In 1995, Ingvar Carlsson spoke about improving the integration
of immigrants and counteracting discrimination. He emphasized that
this is a task for everyone who believes in the very heart of democracy—
the equality and inviolable human rights of all people. Again, as in
1990, the words "we all want to feel proud of our country" were used,
but now contextualized in a discussion of human rights as being the
heart of democracy. Further, Carlsson stressed the broad cooperation
that is a tradition in Swedish politics, just as Olof Palme did in 1985.

During 1991–94, Sweden had a center-right coalition government
led by Prime Minister Carl Bildt (Moderate Party/Conservative). At
the same time, a populist party called New Democracy, entered parliament demanding fewer immigrants, lower taxes, and less bureaucracy.
This party did not manage to get into the parliament for a second
term. In 1994, the Social Democrats won the election and (again)
formed a one-party government. But during this period, the Social
Democrats began to receive the explicit support and cooperation of
the Centre Party (1994–98) and thereafter with the Green Party/Ecol-
ogists and the Left Party/Left Socialists (1998–2006). It was due to
the support of the Centre Party/Agrarians that Prime Minister Göran
Persson was able to so strongly direct and succeed in surely the most
rigorous reconstruction of the Swedish economy ever, including Swedish defense policy. Without the support of at least one party at the

center-right position, it would have been a remarkable political risk to take. The Centre Party left the cooperative arrangement after the 1998 election. During the 1998–2006 period, the Social Democratic minority governments instead leaned on parties in the center-left spectrum, and this cooperation included setting up political working groups on several key topics as well as having personnel from the supporting parties in the departments.

If we take one step backward and investigate the development between 1990 and 1995, we immediately notice that the change in declaration style is *not* tied to party politics or ideological current. In the first year of the center-right government, Prime Minister Carl Bildt did not discuss values or ethics in politics at all. The new government did put forward four main tasks: membership in the European Union, stabilizing the economy, introducing freedom of choice in the welfare sector, and preserving the environment. None of these goals were underpinned with discussions of values, morals, or ethics. Quite the contrary, the government had a solid program consisting of precise political strategies that were meant to lead to the articulated goals. The whole declaration was made in quite "materialistic" language, but Bildt mentioned that "we" were grateful to all people from other countries that had contributed to the progress of the Swedish society, and he underlined that everyone, regardless of faith and/or culture, should have an opportunity to live together in Sweden. Regarding Swedish foreign policy, Bildt pointed out that human rights, freedom, and democracy were guiding values. Ingvar Carlsson's and Carl Bildt's declarations of 1990 and 1991, respectively, were consequently quite similar in terms of the amount of effort they put into mentioning issues concerning values, morals, and/or ethics.

But in 1992, Prime Minister Carl Bildt discussed ethics apropos education, the environment, and primary schooling and also emphasized that Sweden should be an "open" and "tolerant" country, and that it was essential to oppose "xenophobia" and "racism."[16] But in a paragraph in the 1992 declaration, he explicitly articulated a moral standard for Sweden as a society:

> A dynamic society is faced with new ethical issues. Not least, the recent economic developments show the significance of morals for social climate. Where morality fails, so does confidence in the rules of society, and institutions erode. It is now more important than ever that policy

be based on a solid ethical foundation. The government's starting point is the view of human equality and human life that is so deeply rooted in our country through the sanctity of the Swedish Christian and humanist traditions. Each person is unique. Every human being has the right to be respected as an individual. The collective must never stifle individual freedom, responsibility, creativity, and the right to choose. The right to security and privacy and the solitary right to participation for the weak is the basis for a policy that upholds human dignity and social cohesion. (Carl Bildt, October 6, 1992, in the Swedish Parliament)[17]

Carl Bildt here shows that ethics, morals, and common values are the cornerstones in politics. It is only through value-based propositions that a government has the legitimacy to hold power and to set political goals. Also, Bildt stresses that it is the individual that comes first, and that only through respecting the individual is it possible to "protect" a society that holds together. In giving individual values and human rights a prominent place in the policy declaration, Carl Bildt both criticizes the former Social Democratic government and brings the focus onto the ideological heart of the issue. Bildt and his Moderate Party have been among the most outspoken critics of Swedish neutrality policy, which they thought was a cowardly political strategy that had sold out moral values and human rights—especially toward the Eastern bloc. Bildt was one of the first politicians who took the initiative to organize and then support the weekly protests in Stockholm against the Soviet Union, demanding freedom for the Baltic States. By stressing the issue of human rights so emphatically, he also showed how the new government had clearly broken with the former political praxis, although the breakdown of the Eastern bloc had made the old praxis obsolete.

In the policy declaration from 1993, Prime Minister Carl Bildt advanced his position slightly and talked about "a national identity" as making an important contribution to a multicultural Europe. Swedish national identity is tied to a "dynamic" cultural climate: "Public support for an independent cultural life is an important contribution to an open and dynamic social climate. Protecting our cultural heritage is the safeguard of a national identity that has an obvious place in a multicultural Europe" (Carl Bildt, October 5, 1993, in the Swedish Parliament).[18] Regarding integration policy, Bildt stressed the importance of countering xenophobia in all forms: "Sweden should be a tolerant society. Immigration and refugee policy must be characterized by humanity and openness. Racist and xenophobic tendencies must be resisted" (Carl Bildt, October 5, 1993, in the Swedish Parliament).[19] In the declaration, Bildt makes a clear connection between national identity and resisting xenophobia. Here, having a national identity is not equated with ethno-nationalism, instead, Bildt wants to promote an inclusive nationalism (civic nationalism). Being a sincere European, Bildt wants to focus on a multicultural Europe as a step forward toward integration. As one who also cares about national identity, he includes a ruthless fight against all forms of xenophobia and distrust between natives and immigrants.

By 1993, the term "moral" had disappeared from the declaration, but "ethics" was still there. School should be built on norms that are grounded in "Christian ethics and Western humanism," said Prime Minister Bildt,[20] adding that "family and school should give children and adolescents a clear insight into right and wrong." The declaration was still focused on policy reforms of an economic and political nature, but ethical considerations and values were much more prominent in this declaration than in the one from 1991.

In the election of 1994, Carl Bildt and the center-right government were voted out of power and a Social Democratic, one-party government took over. The new prime minister, Ingvar Carlsson, delivered his government's first policy declaration in 1994, which accentuated shared values as an overt collective ground for togetherness and solidarity. Carlsson talked about a "global sentiment of citizenship"[21] and a "common responsibility and solidarity" in his declaration. He expressed a desire to invoke a new spirit of common understanding in "the interest of the nation." But it is in the section on immigration and integration where the most pronounced discussion on Sweden as a value community comes up:

> Democracy's core is the idea that all people are of equal value and sanctity. Therefore, discrimination, xenophobia, and racism should be fought wherever they are found. The responsibility lies with each of us who believe in democracy. Sweden will defend the right to asylum. But it is not enough. Sweden is today a multicultural society. We must jointly ensure that our society is not split by tensions between people from different countries and cultures. Our entire society must now be mobilized to increase integration and combat segregation. All areas of importance will be affected. This applies to employment and housing. This applies to schools and cultural life. This applies to municipalities and organizations. The immigration minister has the

overall responsibility for coordinating policies on integration. The goal is clear: There must not be one Sweden for us and another Sweden for them. (Ingvar Carlsson, October 7, 1994, in the Swedish Parliament)[22]

Hidden in this paragraph is an implicit threat—one of a society divided. Carlsson mentioned that both sectors where shared values may be of less importance (housing and the labor market) and sectors that are permeated by values (culture and education) were touched by this threat. But it is very difficult not to read this paragraph as an appeal to the population for increased tolerance and a more welcoming attitude toward immigrants, and therefore as a movement in the direction of a society of shared values. Carlsson was as positive as Bildt was regarding a multicultural future, but he focused more on integration policy than Bildt did. Bildt relied more on identity-based openness, whereas Carlsson put his efforts toward strengthening society's capacity in terms of housing and employment, and also toward civil society.

In the 1995 declaration, Prime Minister Carlsson followed up on his earlier message, underlining the importance of everyone taking up the fight against racism and xenophobia:

> Let it be said so that it can be heard across our country: The Parliament, consisting of the Swedish people's elected representatives, will never allow discrimination, xenophobia, and racism to take root in our country. We are not going to move one inch from that position. The whole of Sweden must be mobilized to reduce conflicts between people from different cultures and countries. The Immigrant Policy Committee will complete its work early next year. Then the work on one of the truly great challenges of the future must be intensified: to increase integration and reduce segregation. (Ingvar Carlsson, October 3, 1995, in the Swedish Parliament)[23]

In this paragraph Carlsson indicates very clearly that the fight against xenophobia and racism is not a fight for political parties or specific ideologies but a fight for everyone, a fight about social responsibility. He underlines that "the whole nation"[24] is to be mobilized in fulfilling the goal of decreasing antagonism between people from different "cultures and countries." Sweden is addressed as if it is(in these matters)a homogeneous value community.

Carlsson was appealing to a common norm of antiracism and tolerance that he wished to expand. He also put some effort into articulating how crucial he and the government considered these matters to be. The expression "We are not going to move one inch"[25] from the fight against racism and discrimination reveals a firm position. Carlsson, like Bildt before him, was concerned about several uprisings against asylum camps in some municipalities and especially about a series of sensational shootings targeting immigrants, and the subsequent trial. One man, John Ausonius, was found guilty of murder in 1995 in one case, and of causing severe injury in 11 cases, and he was condemned to a life sentence. In 1991–92, he had been shooting at persons with darker hair and skin, motivated by his hatred of foreigners. The trial took a long time because of the situation regarding evidence (several shootings took place over a long period, and there were several victims), and also because the accused attacked his own defense lawyers and the court had to find new ones. This experience lingered in the public's consciousness throughout the first half of the 1990s and reflected an increasingly negative attitude toward immigrants. That development ended rather quickly, and since the middle of the 1990s, Swedes have been increasingly generous in their attitudes toward immigrants and refugees.[26]

Introduced by Carl Bildt in 1992, and developed and fulfilled by Ingvar Carlsson in 1995, common and shared values finally became a vital underpinning for governmental policy declarations, as will be discussed in the following sections.

POLICY DECLARATIONS 2000–2010

In the first year of the new millennium, the new Social Democratic prime minister, Göran Persson, took on the tradition and spoke at great length on human rights, the equal rights of all people, and democracy. He also mentioned "racism" and "discrimination" as well as "anti-Semitism." Persson was unreservedly clear on the importance of decreasing antagonism between people from different "cultures and countries." He was even more outspoken on the importance of values than either Carlsson or Bildt had been. The latter were explicit only regarding children, youth, families, and the education system, but Persson spoke in more general terms:

> Equality of value for every human being is the basis of democracy. But democracy can never be taken for granted. It must constantly be won

again, with each new generation. The discussion of democracy's fundamental values must be kept alive. Its practical expression in nonprofit
organizations, NGOs, and local development, as well as in emerging
networks, must be affirmed. Efforts to increase young people's influence should continue. The findings of the Democracy Investigation
[a special committee of researchers evaluating Swedish democracy in
1997–2000] are now being discussed in an extensive consultation process. Special support is being provided to local democracy. Another
special committee on integration and power is now at work. The
struggle for human dignity—against racism, anti-Semitism, and xenophobia—is one of the crucial issues of our time. It is a struggle that
can only be overcome through concerted action and the commitment
of many. A national action plan is to be presented. Broad efforts are
being made to increase the competence of the judiciary. The EXIT
Project [a project for defectors from extremist milieus] will have continued support. The Stockholm International Forum on the Holocaust
receives annual follow-ups. The next conference, Stockholm Forums
for Knowledge and Humanism: The Fight against Intolerance, will be
held on January 29–30, 2001. It will focus on specific prevention for
greater mutual understanding between people in their everyday lives.
The goal is to define international cooperation in these matters and
to increase awareness and preparedness among the professionals who
often have to deal with people in anti-democratic movements. (Göran
Persson, September 19, 2000, in the Swedish Parliament)[27]

Persson's propositions were meant to promote a common and all-
embracing understanding between individuals of all ages and social
groups. He also made appeals for engagement from "the many"
(*många*) and he coupled local democratic development with the fight
for human rights and against racism and xenophobia. Furthermore,
he tried to expand the political sphere so that it would go beyond
improving the premises for antiracist work and appealing to people's
ethical principles by providing economic support for direct and professional actions against racism.

But five years later, in 2005, much less was said about shared values
and Sweden as a value community. In 2005, Prime Minister Göran
Persson talked about solidarity and unity but had less to say about
other kinds of values. A few lines on "folk education" ("*folkbildning*")[28]
and on "culture" were included in a section discussing reforms regarding youth reading books, developing literacy, Swedish filmmaking, and
design. But the policy declaration of 2005 corresponds much more
closely with pre-1990 policy declarations, although, of course, with an

updated rhetorical substance. In 2005, Persson spoke about the labor market and welfare, and he also said a great deal about environmental issues and also discussed international matters at great length.

Five years later, in 2010, Sweden brought in a new government. In 2006, the Social Democratic, one-party government lost the election and Sweden saw the entry of a new, center-right coalition government. Prime Minister Fredrik Reinfeldt represented the conservative Moderate Party (as did Carl Bildt before him), and the three other parties were the Liberals, the Centre Party, and the Christian Democrats. After the 2010 election, Reinfeldt and his government remained in power but in a minority position. The Swedish parliament again saw the entry of the Sweden Democrats: a new, populist nationalist-conservative party with its roots in the old white-power networks. None of the other parties wanted to cooperate with the Social Democrats in order to overthrow the minority government, and therefore Reinfeldt was able to keep the position as prime minister, and he also kept the same parties in government. Not having a voting majority against him was equivalent to having the support of the parliament, a situation that held in Sweden until after the 2010 election. Since then, new rules have been introduced and the prime minister must thereafter have a voting majority *supporting* him or her.

In an unusually all-embracing policy declaration in 2010, Fredrik Reinfeldt talked a lot about the need for unity, about managing together, and about a society that is "cohesive."[29] Reinfeldt also emphasized that Sweden is an "open" and "tolerant" society founded on "indisputable values where we separate right from wrong." Like his former party colleague Carl Bildt, he emphasized that the government is sensitive to the individual and to the needs of the individual. Reinfeldt discussed the ideas of spiritual improvement and enhanced individual freedom for everyone, and he spoke about the inherent ability in everyone to take responsibility and shape their own lives.

In the declaration of 2010, Reinfeldt discussed immigration issues extensively and highlighted that it is the structure that shapes inequality, not any lack of capabilities among immigrants. He began his remarks by declaring Sweden to be an open and tolerant country, and he spoke about how the country has benefited from that; he chose to address the problems that he identified in political terms and not in value terms. Reinfeldt lined up a wide range of reforms and propositions to improve immigrants' welfare and labor status. The fact is that words such as "racism" and "xenophobia"[30] were not mentioned in the 2010 declaration. In some sections, where Reinfeldt talked about civil society and about educating and raising of adolescents, values and ethics were only implied.

If we look briefly at the first policy declaration from the Fredrik Reinfeldt government (in 2006), there is much less promotion of values than in the early 1990s but more than in Göran Persson's policy declaration from 2005. Reinfeldt's most explicit paragraph from 2006 on tolerance and shared values concerns, as is so often the case in the declarations, the immigration issue: "The open society should be safeguarded. Differences and diversity must be affirmed. Ethnic and cultural diversity enriches our society. A free and open exchange of views, and respect for individual integrity are fundamental values of our democracy. The government is concerned about the rise in xenophobic tendencies and extremism. The principle that all individuals have inviolable value must be defended vigorously. By implementing policies that address the social problems underlying these tendencies, we can prevent extremism and xenophobia from taking root" (Fredrik Reinfeldt, October 6, 2006, in the Swedish Parliament).[31] Reinfeldt urged that the "open society" be defended and that heterogeneity and differences be affirmed. But exactly as in the 2010 declaration, the prime minister did not appeal to all citizens or to a national community but instead proposed political means to address the issues. In other parts of the declaration, Reinfeldt gave detailed examples of these means, which involved the labor market, welfare, and education. In his declaration, Reinfeldt assumed that Sweden should be an "inclusive" society with regard to all social groups. However, his statements did not mention immigration or integration but instead regional differences and social variations.

It is somewhat surprising that Reinfeldt, in his first declaration from the *second* term of his government, gave more room than he did in 2006 for a discussion of common values and holding the society together.

There is a great and undeniable difference between the declarations made in 2005 and 2010, but it is not possible to arrive at any immediate conclusions about possible ideological motives that might have prompted such change in the early 1990s. Comparing the declaration from 2005 (Persson) with the declaration from 2006 (Reinfeldt), the most significant difference is the length (Reinfeldt's is about 50 percent longer)—but, of course, also a change of subject. Where Persson talked a lot about environmental issues, Reinfeldt was more occupied with employment and the economy. But regarding the perspective in this chapter—shared values—there are more similarities than differences.

SHARED VALUES IN GOVERNMENTAL POLICY DECLARATIONS 1975–2010

Comparing governmental policy declarations from 1975 to 2010, the most significant development is that these documents have gone from a less poetic record of what should be done to a more poetic version of ideological positions. These documents have also grown considerably longer. The latest policy declarations include a lot of rhetoric and promises, but they don't set out any precise reforms, arguments, or proposals; instead, the policy declarations seem more like appeals, visionary statements, and articulations of political directions. The point of departure is that the values expressed in a policy declaration are already shared, or ought to be shared, throughout the society. The policy declarations are more and more inclusionary and less and less explanations of what is to be done during the coming government term.

What in the 1970s and 1980s was considered to be cooperation at the elite level came to be a matter of common understanding among citizens at the beginning of the 1990s. Further, what was seen as the government's responsibility in 1975 and 1980 came to be seen as a responsibility for us all and for "our" Sweden. It is evident that the introduction of common values and the talk about a value community took place shortly after the end of the Cold War. It is also evident that this development coincided with an increase in the level of opposition toward immigration and also with overt xenophobic societal expressions.

The period 1992–94, when the development toward an emphasis on values, morals, and national identity was most obviously expressed, was marked by a severe economic crisis. The Swedish currency was very close to extinction and was rescued only by abandoning the stable exchange rate. This period was also characterized by a growing xenophobia among the Swedish population, and, at the same time, Sweden was receiving more refugees than ever. In the parliament, the entry of a populist, antiestablishment party that overtly expressed its distrust in politics and its discontent with the refugee policy was a political problem for the minority government.

Concerning ideological differences, there are no evident explanations to be found. In the early 1990s, it was both center-right and social democratic prime ministers who changed the declarations and made the expression of shared values more and more prominent. The differences in how Carl Bildt and Ingvar Carlsson expressed the idea of shared values were minor. They both stood up against racism, explicitly and decisively, in their policy declarations. In the 2000s, we notice that Persson and Reinfeldt both embrace the idea of Sweden as a community of shared values, but in quite different ways. For Persson, it was xenophobia and anti-Semitism that stood out as reasons for mobilizing and taking direct political action, whereas Reinfeldt had focused mainly on societal unity and openness. For Persson (and for Carlsson), the ideological battle against racism was a prominent element in his political discourse, whereas for Reinfeldt it is not an ideological fight but an economic and political battle—a battle his government wants to wage not in the ideological arena but through political reforms. Although shared values are a basis for these reforms, Reinfeldt does not want to promote these values through direct political action or by mobilizing political forces to support them. It is, however, somewhat unexpected that he takes for granted that these shared values must be upheld, and, at the same time, he does not propose any particular political reforms to underpin them.

SHARED VALUES AS THEY ARE INTERPRETED AMONG SWEDISH CITIZENS

Over the course of three decades, Swedish citizens had answered questions about their opinions and attitudes in connection with the national elections. The surveys were administrated by the Swedish National Election Studies, conducted at the University of Gothenburg in the Department of Political Science.[32] Do these surveys show any signs of a Swedish population that is more interested in shared values than in shared resources? The general answer is no.

Through a row of propositions on what kind of society the respondents want to "promote,"[33] it is quite clear that the Swedish population does not want to focus more on shared values than on shared resources!

When respondents were asked to give their thoughts on a proposition such as "reducing the income gap,"[34] it was evident that their desire for this had grown stronger between 1988 and 2010, not weaker. As shown in Figure 2.1, the Swedish population over time has been slightly more supportive of reducing income gaps from 1988 to the present. In 1988, 60 percent of the Swedish population thought it was a very good or a rather good idea to reduce income gaps in Sweden, compared to 69 percent in 2010. There is absolutely no evidence of a population that is *less* interested in sharing material societal resources equally, rather the contrary.

The support for promoting a society with high economic growth remained fairly steady from 1982 until 2002. In 1988, as much as 76 percent supported promoting a society with high economic growth, and in 2002 the share is 79 percent. The support for a society that uses advanced technology (computers and machines) to increase productivity, on the other hand, rose from 29 percent in 1982 to 53 percent in 2002.[35] The Swedish population shows no concerns or anxieties about developing the industrial sector and making use of new technologies. On the contrary, the Swedish population seems to welcome innovation in the workplace, and there are no signs of reduced support for developing the economy and raising production to new levels.

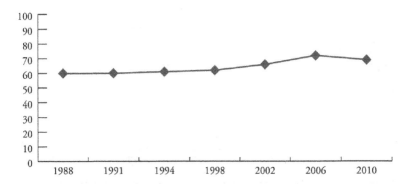

Figure 2.1 Part of the Swedish population that thinks it is a "very good" or "rather good" proposition to reduce the income gap in Sweden.
Commentary: Swedish National Election Studies (SNES). The item was "Reduce the income gap" and the respondents were shown a card with five possible alternatives: Very good, Rather good, Neither good nor bad, Rather bad, and Very bad proposition.

However, even if we see no signs of decreasing support for sharing economic resources and developing new technology, is there any indication of a growing desire for homogeneity in values or for a common value ground in Swedish society? As shown in Figure 2.2, support for a multicultural society increased after the tone of the policy declarations started to change in the early 1990s. Between 1994 and 1998, support for a multicultural society increased from a share of 47 percent up to 56 percent. As was discussed earlier, it was in 1992–94 that the governmental policy declarations began to stress the importance of shared values. Moreover, the increased support for a multicultural society corresponds to a decrease in the disapproval over receiving refugees. In 1992, 65 percent of the Swedish population thought it was a good idea to receive fewer refugees, which is the highest proportion during the whole period from 1990 to 2011. By 1994, the percentage had dropped to 56 percent and reached its lowest level (41 percent) in 2011.[36]

Instead of being focused on shared values, during the 1990s the Swedish population grew more open and tolerant toward immigrants and different lifestyles, religions, values, and cultures. A growing economy, a developing technical industrial sector, and a welcoming of a multicultural society seems to be the Swedish mix.

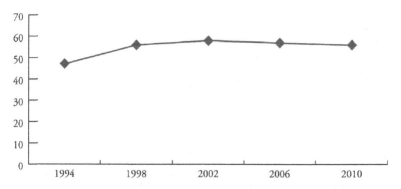

Figure 2.2 Part of the Swedish population that supports a multicultural society with a high tolerance toward diverse lifestyles and religions (1982–2010)
Commentary: SNES. The item was "Promote a multicultural society with a great tolerance toward diverse lifestyles and religions?" and the respondents were shown a card with a scale from 0 to 10, where 0 indicated that it was a very bad proposition and 10 a very good one. The graph shows the share that chose a position from 6 to 10 on that scale.

But if support for multiculturalism is stronger today—and therefore also support for divergent values and lifestyles—how does the population decide that certain traditional values should be promoted in a future society? It is clear from Figure 2.3 that the only value that has held its ground is gender equality: as much as 85 percent of Sweden's population wants to promote a society where men and women are equal, and that proportion has increased since 1991 (72 percent). But the desire for a society that promotes family values, Christian values, traditionally Swedish values, or law and order has decreased during the last two decades. Supporting multiculturalism and feminism in Sweden goes together with supporting high technical skills and a growing economy. Liberal values and a modern view on labor and industry are strong features in Swedish society in the new millennium. The Swedish model has been rejuvenated.

Most remarkable, perhaps, is that the support for "traditional Swedish values" has decreased since 1991. At the same time as a majority of the Swedish population supports the promotion of a multicultural society, it is also less interested in upholding traditional Swedish values. In 1991, more than two-thirds of the population (72 percent)

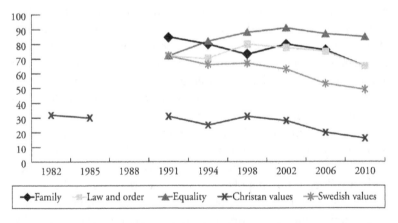

Figure 2.3 Part of the Swedish population that supports a society that strengthens the position of family; strengthens law and order; and promotes gender equality, Christian values, or traditional Swedish values (1982–2010)
Commentary: SNES. The item was "Promote a society where Christian values/family values/law and order/gender equality/Swedish values have greater importance," and the respondents were shown a card with a scale from 0 to 10, where 0 was a very bad proposition and 10 a very good one. The graph shows the share on each item where the respondent chose a position from 6 to 10 on that scale.

thought promoting Swedish values was a good idea and in 2010, less than half of the population (49 percent) expressed the same opinion. These two trends converge in a conclusion that Swedish citizens—during the very same period where the governments' policy declarations were more focused on shared values—have been *less* interested in shared values. On the contrary, the Swedish population still supports economic growth and technological improvement and wants greater equality with respect to both gender and income, but does not at all support the idea of a cozy, little "*folkhem*" where we all share the same values and frames of reference.

NOT A COZY LITTLE *FOLKHEM*, BUT BECOMING AN INDIVIDUAL

How, then, can we interpret the fact that the Swedish government has been more and more convinced that shared values are the most important at the same time as Swedish citizens would prefer to focus on shared (and growing) resources?

I would like to interpret these results as only seemingly contradictory. National politics has become narrower due to globalization and European integration. Swedish politicians know, as do their European counterparts, that they have much less room to maneuver than before. Policy declarations therefore increasingly fulfill the role of documents where the government draws up the grand plans and additional visionary pieces, appealing for support and participation in the projects. Focusing on values and ideology and appealing to a general, public-spirited outlook are therefore effective strategies for showing some kind of political power and vigor. Swedish politicians also know that Sweden, as a small country, is heavily dependent on its industrial production, foreign trade, its innovative capabilities, and its well-educated population—resources that have to be upheld in order to benefit further from economic globalization. Domestic collaboration and stimulating economic growth are therefore indisputable political means, regardless of political ideologies. The values that the policy declaration tries to encourage are therefore not specific ideological party values or traditional values, but instead an appeal to modernity in terms of equality, cooperation, and tolerance. In an individualistic society such as Sweden, this plea is the only possible one. So, intertwined in the policy declaration's proud words of national unity, national identity, and a firm stand against racism, there is a demand for the only possible collective shared value: human rights and individuals' rights to their civil liberties.

For the Swedish population, globalization has led to an open society where it sounds increasingly awkward to talk about "Swedish values" or traditional authorities. Immigration has changed the population, and today about 20 percent of Swedish inhabitants have a foreign family background. Through liberalization of formerly firm regulations concerning welfare, education, and employment, individual preferences can be both articulated and met. From an individual's point of view, the appeal to human rights and civil liberties could be seen as both a precondition for their own self-realization and a necessary condition for Swedish collective progress. Considering the decreasing interest among Swedish citizens in promoting certain traditional values, a strong idea of individualization might instead be the most promising interpretation.

Sweden is often described as a society where individualization has gone further than in other comparable countries. Political scientists Ronald Inglehart and Christian Welzel, in their book *Modernization, Cultural Change, and Democracy*, have examined the authority patterns in 57 countries:[37] Sweden shows up as the most individualistic country of all. Swedes place individual autonomy, independent opinions, and individual rights higher than all other examined populations; while religion, nation, and tradition are not of great importance. In their analysis, Inglehart and Welzel also single out Sweden as the country where this pattern is most significant. Sweden is a country where a rational and secular culture has the second strongest hold, and the country in which self-realization is most important among all the countries studied. The strongest connection is to be found between self-realization and rationalism, respectively, and a postindustrial socioeconomic structure. Sweden is nearly a statistical ideal type and is situated exactly on the regression line, farthest out on both dimensions. In table after table in Inglehart and Welzel's statistical examinations, Sweden proves to be either the most individualized country in the world or, if not, then among the most individualized.

Is the new focus in the policy declarations on shared values a way of coping with the fact that Sweden as a country does not share any traditional or national values? By putting a stronger emphasis on tolerance, ethics, and cultural variance regarding politics—instead of such materialistic matters as economy and employment—a political space is created for discussions on religion, traditions, and nationhood. This was not an intended course. Sometimes, Swedes are said to take pride in not being nationalistic. Swedish nationalism is therefore understood as a kind of antinationalism. At the same time, though, as Swedes are proud of Swedish democracy and Swedish equality, they could also be said to share a collective identity of tolerance and inclusion. But it is only a conditional inclusion—an inclusion of individuals into a group of individuals. Not being as individualistic as a Swede, keeping authoritarian or traditional values high, will be seen as uncooperative or stubborn. And, of course, this also opens up the political discourse to arguments that will master and condemn cultures that do not promote the individual as much as Swedes do (i.e., religious groups, migrants with strong family values, or foreigners who wish to keep their nationalistic cultures alive).[38]

In conclusion, as was the point of departure for this study, since the early 1990s there has been a strong call—both among citizens and from the government—for a society that permits a rich variation of lifestyles. Politically upgrading ethical, moral, and value frames is a political answer to increasing European political integration and individualization, by offering all citizens a multiplicity of choices regarding welfare, lifestyle, and faith. The problem (if there is one) is the somewhat paradoxical fact that interest in shared values such as general moral standards seems to have decreased at the same time as the variety of choices has increased. Swedes are instead willing to promote more equality, both regarding gender and incomes, and to tolerate a wide range of foreign cultures, lifestyles, and religions. Rather than sharing any national values, to exhibit "Swedishness" is to become a capable individual and not be absorbed by the mass or dominated by anyone or anything. In this respect, Lisbeth Salander in the Millennium trilogy is a very good example of the new Swede: a capable, gifted woman with economic resources and an attitude. In response to the lack of material support for her trajectory from any state authority, she takes her fate into her own hands and is not afraid of violating traditional codes of conduct and social behavior. Welcome to individualist Sweden!

NOTES

1. *Folkhem* is a Swedish term commonly used in reference to the welfare state that was constructed during the years after the World War II. Ideologically, the term is connected to the Social Democratic Party, especially during the 1950s and 1960s.
2. For an example of the first picture, see the ultranationalist Kevin D. Williamson describing Sweden in a chapter titled "Why Sweden Stinks" in his book *A Politically Incorrect Guide to Socialism* (Washington, DC: Regnery, 2011).
3. Ulf Bjereld and Marie Demker, *I Vattumannens tid: En bok om 1968 års uppror och dess betydelse idag* (Stockholm: Hjalmarson and Högberg, 2005).
4. Ulf Bjereld and Marie Demker, *Kampen om kunskapen: Informationssamhällets politiska skiljelinjer* (Stockholm: Hjalmarson and Högberg, 2008).
5. Kristina Boréus, *Högervåg: Nyliberalismen och kampen om språket i svensk debatt 1969–1989* (Stockholm: Tiden, 1994).
6. Lennart Nilsson, "Svenska folket, den offentliga sektorn och välfärdsstaten," *Lyckan kommer, Lyckan går*, SOM-report no. 36, ed. Sören Holmberg and Lennart Weibull (Göteborg: University of Gothenburg, 2005).
7. Andreas Johansson Heinö, *Vi gillar olika? Hur den svenska likhetsnormen hindrar integrationen* (Stockholm: Timbro, 2012).
8. Radio Sweden had a short review of this: "Library Removes 'Lilla hjärtat' Books," http://sverigesradio.se/sida/gruppsida.aspx?programid=2054 &grupp=3578&artikel=5387600 (accessed January 3 2013).
9. *The Mirror* had an article: Natalie Evans, "'A Racist Spectacle': Swedish Culture Minister Slammed for 'Black Face' Cake," http://www.mirror.co.uk/news/world-news/swedish-minister-of-culture-slammed-for-racist-797906 (accessed January 3, 2013).
10. Sweden has two bigger parties: a conservative party (the Moderates) and the Social Democratic Party (left reformist). Besides these two, as of 2013 there were six other parties in the parliament, three of which are in a coalition with the conservative party (the Centre Party/Agrarian, the People's Party/Liberal, and the Christian Democrats/Social Conservative) and three opposition parties besides the Social Democrats (the Left Party/Left Socialist, the Green Party/Environmental, and the Sweden Democrats/Nationalist Conservative).
11. "Gemensamt ansvar."
12. "Sysselsättning."
13. "Samverkan."
14. "Vi svenskar."
15. "Frihet och trygghet."
16. The Swedish terms are *öppet, tolerant, främlingsfientlighet*, and *rasism*.

17. "Ett dynamiskt samhälle ställs inför nya etiska frågor. Inte minst de senaste årens ekonomiska utveckling visar moralens betydelse för samhällsklimatet. Där moralen sviktar, urgröps också tilltron till samhällets spelregler och institutioner. Nu skärps kraven i politiken på en fast etisk grundåskådning. Regeringens utgångspunkt är den syn på människors lika värde och människolivets helgd som genom Sveriges kristna och humanistiska tradition är så starkt förankrad i vårt land. Varje människa är unik. Varje människa har rätt att respekteras för sin särart. Kollektivet får aldrig kväva den enskildes frihet, ansvar, skaparförmåga och rätt att välja. Den svages rätt till trygghet och integritet och den ensammes rätt till delaktighet utgör grunden för en politik som slår vakt om människans värdighet och samhällets sammanhållning."

18. "Det offentliga stödet till det fria kulturlivet är ett viktigt bidrag till ett öppet och dynamiskt samhällsklimat. I vården av kulturarvet ligger värnet av en nationell identitet som har en självklar plats i ett mångkulturellt Europa."

19. "Sverige skall vara ett tolerant samhälle. Invandrings- och flyktingpolitiken måste präglas av humanitet och öppenhet. Rasistiska och främlingsfientliga tendenser skall bekämpas."

20. "kristen etik och västerländsk humanism."

21. "global medborgaranda."

22. "Demokratins innersta kärna är idén om alla människors lika värde och okränkbarhet. Därför måste diskriminering, främlingsfientlighet och rasism bekämpas varhelst sådana tendenser förekommer. Det ansvaret åvilar var och en av oss som tror på demokratin. Sverige skall slå vakt om asylrätten. Men det räcker inte med detta. Sverige är i dag ett mångkulturellt samhälle. Vi måste gemensamt förhindra att samhället splittras genom motsättningar mellan människor från olika länder och kulturer. Hela vårt samhälle måste nu mobiliseras för att öka integrationen och motverka segregationen. Alla områden av betydelse kommer att beröras. Det gäller arbetsmarknaden och bostadsmarknaden. Det gäller skolorna och kulturlivet. Det gäller kommunerna och organisationerna. Invandrarministern har ett övergripande ansvar för att samordna politiken för ökad integration. Målet är givet: Det får inte finns ett Sverige för oss och ett annat Sverige för dem."

23. "Låt det sägas så att det hörs över hela vårt land: Denna riksdag, bestående av svenska folkets valda representanter, kommer aldrig någonsin att tolerera att diskriminering, främlingsfientlighet och rasism får fotfäste i vårt land. Vi viker inte en tum från den hållningen. Hela Sverige måste mobiliseras för att minska motsättningar mellan människor från olika kulturer och länder. Invandrarpolitiska kommittén kommer att slutföra sitt arbete i början av nästa år. Då måste arbetet med en av framtidens verkligt stora utmaningar intensifieras: att öka integrationen och minska segregationen."

24. "hela Sverige."
25. "viker inte en tum."
26. Marie Demker, "Racism, Xenophobia and Opposition to Immigration in Sweden," in *Stepping Stones: Research on Political Representation, Voting Behavior and Quality of Government*, ed. Stefan Dahlberg, Henrik Oscarsson, and Lena Wängnerud (Göteborg: Department of Political Science, University of Gothenburg, 2013).
27. "Alla människors lika värde utgör grunden för demokratin. Men demokratin kan aldrig tas för given. Den måste ständigt vinnas på nytt, för varje ny generation. Diskussionen om demokratins grundläggande värden måste hållas levande. Dess praktiska uttryck i ideella organisationer, folkrörelser och lokala utvecklingsgrupper, liksom i nya framväxande nätverk, måste bejakas. Arbetet med att öka ungdomars inflytande fortsätter. Demokratiutredningens slutsatser diskuteras i ett omfattande rådslag. Särskilt stöd lämnas till lokal demokratiutveckling. En integrationspolitisk maktutredning arbetar. Kampen för människovärdet—mot rasism, antisemitism och främlingsfientlighet—är en av vår tids ödesfrågor. Det är en kamp som bara kan vinnas med aktiv handling och mångas engagemang. En nationell handlingsplan presenteras. Breda insatser görs för att höja kompetensen inom rättsväsendet. Projektet EXIT ges fortsatt stöd. Stockholms internationella forum om förintelsen får årliga uppföljningar. Nästa konferens, Stockholms forum om insikt och humanism—i kamp mot intolerans, hålls den 29-30 januari 2001. Den kommer att handla om konkret förebyggande arbete för en större ömsesidig förståelse mellan människor i vardagen. Målet är att precisera det internationella samarbetet och att öka kunskapen och handlingsberedskapen bland de yrkesgrupper som ofta har att hantera personer i antidemokratiska rörelser."
28. The Swedish word *folkbildning* means adult education, combining civil education and developing democratic skills.
29. "håller samman."
30. "främlingsfientlighet."
31. "Det öppna samhället skall värnas. Olikheter och mångfald skall bejakas. Den etniska och kulturella mångfalden berikar vårt samhälle. Ett fritt och öppet meningsutbyte, och respekt för den enskildes integritet är grundläggande värden i vår demokrati. Regeringen ser allvarligt på ökade främlingsfientliga tendenser och extremism. Principen om alla människors okränkbara värde måste försvaras med kraft. Utvecklingen kan motverkas genom en politik som möter de samhällsproblem som gör att extremism och främlingsfientlighet lättare kan slå rot."
32. Swedish National Election Studies (SNES) homepage, http://www.valforskning.pol.gu.se/english/ (accessed January 3, 2013). SNES has been governed and performed by the Department of Political Science at

Gothenburg University since 1954. The latest report is Henrik Oscarsson and Sören Holmberg, *Nya svenska väljare* (Stockholm: Norstedts Juridik, 2013).

33. In a Swedish context, this issue is part of a battery of so-called *satsa på-frågorna.*

34. "Minska inkomstskillnaderna."

35. The items were as follows, "Promote a society with high economic growth and high productivity" and "Promote a society where advanced technology such as industrial robots and computers are used to make production efficient." The respondents were shown a card with a scale from 0 to 10, where 0 was a very bad proposition and 10 a very good one. The percentage given in the text shows the share of respondents that chose a position from 6 to 10 on that scale (SNES).

36. Demker, "Racism, Xenophobia."

37. Ronald Inglehart and Christian Welzel, "The WVS Cultural Map of the World," *World Values Survey,* http://www.worldvaluessurvey.org/wvs/articles/folder_published/article_base_54 (accessed April 11, 2014), and Inglehar and Welzel, *Modernization, Cultural Change, and Democracy: The Human Development Sequence* (Cambridge: Cambridge University Press, 2005).

38. Mette Pedersen, *Not One of Us: National Identity Versus Islam; A Comparative Discourse Analysis of the Danish People's Party, the Party for Freedom, and the Sweden Democrats* (Master's thesis, Aalborg: Aalborg University, 2011).

CHAPTER 3

"IT'S NOT ABOUT RELIGION, BUT ABOUT MANIPULATION"

POLEMICAL DISCOURSE AGAINST SECTS AND CULTS IN SWEDEN

HENRIK BOGDAN

ONE OF THE KEY DISCOURSES OF THE Swedish welfare state was, and
to a certain extent still is, the tolerance of religious, cultural, and ethnic minorities, and the post–World War II public debate was indeed
characterized by open-mindedness toward and acceptance of non-
mainstream forms of religion. Although the welfare state was, on the
surface, a secular and social-democratic construct, it was firmly built
upon the Protestant ethics of the Swedish state church, as discussed
in the Introduction to this volume. However, as the homogeneity of
Swedish society began to crack and eventually fell apart, the limits
of Swedish tolerance toward groups that challenged the image of a
"normal" or accepted religion became apparent. Central questions
related to the place of religion in "unparadised Sweden" thus came to
the fore at an increasing speed: What is the role of religion in Sweden
today? Are there forms of religion that are not acceptable? Can religion
be dangerous? Questions like these are often raised when the issue of
"cults" and "sects" is being discussed.

This chapter argues that the self-image of Sweden as a tolerant and
inclusive society—as discussed in the Introduction—is highly problematic, since the tolerance only applies to those groups that are seen as
"normal" and "accepted." The limits of this tolerance become apparent

when religion in Sweden is being analyzed. Although Sweden is often used as an example of a thoroughly secularized state—understood in the sense that religion is increasingly seen as belonging to the private sphere of the society—and national polls show that Swedish citizens often perceive themselves as open-minded and tolerant toward minority religions; membership in new religious movements often challenges the notions of accepted religion in Sweden.[1] Compared to more traditional forms of religion, any mention of alternative forms of religion in Swedish newspapers is often conspicuously polemical and condemning. The criticism leveled against new religious movements (often termed "sects" by the media[2]) is often centered on the belief that membership in these groups leads to mental and physical harm. One thus frequently encounters claims that groups such as the Church of Scientology, the International Society for Krishna Consciousness, and the Raëlian movement "brainwash" or "manipulate" the minds of their members; or that the effects of their therapeutic, meditational, and ritual practices are harmful from a psychological perspective. Other forms of criticism include allegations of sexual abuse and various forms of economic exploitation, and also that the organizational structures of these groups are essentially incompatible with Swedish democracy on account of their apparent hierarchical structures and the secret or nontransparent nature of many aspects of their activities. Significantly enough, this polemical discourse is an (apparently) secularized construct devoid of religious arguments: it is rare to come across criticism that focuses on the religious teachings and tenets of these movements, but when such criticisms are made, they take the form of ridicule and irony rather than approaching the groups as perceived religious or moral threats.

The secularized nature of the polemical discourse reflects, of course, wider trends in Swedish society—due to the processes of modernity, secularization, and globalization, traditional religious discourses are being marginalized at an increasing rate, and arguments based on explicit religious grounds have consequently lost much of their earlier claims to authority and legitimacy. The criticisms leveled against new religious movements can be used as revealing examples of the changes in attitude toward religion as such in Swedish culture and society. Although these movements are extremely small in terms of members, counting only a few hundred members each (see note 13), and have had only a very small or nonexistent impact on Swedish society as a whole; the popular image of these movements, the critique against them, and the self-images of the groups themselves illustrate central theoretical issues in the study of religion in Sweden. By analyzing *the way that we talk about* minority religious groups and, more specifically, the way that we talk about new religious movements, questions such as "What is an accepted religion?," "Who defines religion?," and "What are the limits of religious freedom?" come to the forefront.

The polemical discourse against new religious movements in Sweden can, in part, be explained by the fact that journalists and politicians tend to rely on the expertise of members of the Swedish anticult movement. The "anticult movement" is a term used by scholars and others to refer to people and groups who oppose "cults" or new religious movements.[3] Sociologists David G. Bromley and Anson Shupe defined the anticult movement in their work *Strange Gods: The Great American Cult Scare* (1981) as a collection of groups that advocated the brainwashing theory, but as this theory gradually became discredited during the late 1980s and 1990s, there occurred a significant shift in ideology toward a "medicalization" of membership in "cults" and "sects"—that is, the claim that it is psychologically harmful to be a member of this type of religious group.[4] The leading anticult group in Sweden, *Föreningen Rädda Individen* (FRI, the Save the Individual Association, founded in 1984) has, since April 2001, been a member of the *Fédération Européenne des Centres de Recherche et d'Information sur le Sectarisme* (FECRIS, or the European Federation of Centers of Research and Information on Sectarianism), and the Swedish anticult movement is thus part of the larger European movement, which has considerable political influence in countries such as France, Belgium, and Germany.

The primary target of both the Swedish and the international anticult groups is, for all intents and purposes, the Church of Scientology. Founded by the American science fiction author L. Ron Hubbard (1911–86) in the early 1950s, the Church of Scientology is one of the world's most successful new religious movements, claiming to have more than 700 centers in 65 countries, but it is also one of the most notorious religious groups to have emerged in the twentieth century. Indeed, it was labeled the "Cult of Greed" by *Time* magazine in 1991, and the historian of religions Hugh B. Urban has described Scientology as the "world's most controversial new religion." In his recent study *The Church of Scientology: A History of a New Religion* (2011), Urban argues that the history of Scientology reflects major changes in the American religious landscape (viz., anti-Communism, interest in Asian religions, fascination with the occult, etc.) and that Scientology can be used as a test case for the study of religion as a whole:

> Scientology, I will suggest, is a critically important test case for think-ing about much larger legal and theoretical issues in the study of reli-gion as a whole. Not only does it raise basic questions such as what gets to count as religion and who gets to decide; more important, it also raises profound issues of privacy and freedom of religious expression in a post-9/11 context of religious violence and rapidly expanding gov-ernment surveillance. Finally, it also forces us to rethink the role of the academic study of religion in the interpretation of controversial groups such as Scientology. How do we balance a truly serious, critical analysis of problematic groups like these while at the same time countering sensationalistic media attacks and respecting basic rights to privacy and freedom of religious expression?[5]

Adopting a similar approach to Scientology, but within a specifically Swedish context, this chapter sets out to discuss the limits of Swed-ish tolerance toward groups that challenge the notions of "normal" religion and to analyze the polemical discourse against new religious movements expressed by the anticult movement and (by extension) the media.[6] Using the Church of Scientology—perhaps the most contro-versial new religious movement, not only in Sweden, but throughout the world—as a case study, this chapter will address issues connected to the constructs of health and disease, the ongoing conflict with the National Board of Health and Welfare, the so-called Gillberg affair, and the limits of religious freedom. The Church of Scientology will thus be used as an example to show the changing attitude toward reli-gious discourse in contemporary Sweden.

NEW RELIGIOUS MOVEMENTS ON THE SWEDISH RELIGIOUS LANDSCAPE[7]

In September 1998, the Swedish Ministry of Health and Social Affairs published a report on new religious movements (NRMs) in Sweden, titled *I God Tro—Samhället och nyandligheten* (In Good Faith—Society and the New Spirituality).[8] The report was 378 pages long, and its primary object was to ascertain the extent to which former members of NRMs needed help from the government when leaving their groups. Although the premises for the report were implicitly negative regarding the effects of membership in NRMs, the authors showed an awareness that general information about NRMs in Sweden was polarized between criticism from the anticult movement and an apologetic approach from the members themselves. Furthermore, it was stated that research into NRMs in Sweden was largely nonexistent, and that the few scholars dealing with NRMs agreed that more research needed to be done in this particular field. One of the main conclusions of the report was the suggestion that a government-funded association for information about and research into NRMs should be created, to be called *Kunskapscentrum för Livsåskådnings- och Trosfrågor* (Center for the Study of Questions of Belief). Although this laudable enterprise never materialized, the report itself was nevertheless an important step toward an official recognition that NRMs were an established and integrated part of the Swedish religious landscape—a landscape that had changed drastically over the past decades, with new actors competing against traditional institutions such as the Swedish state church (on January 1, 2000, the Church of Sweden was separated from the state). One of the better-known new actors is the Church of Scientology, which has been active in Sweden since 1968.

Until the 1960s, Sweden was—in comparison with most other European countries—a relatively homogeneous country, from both an ethnic and a religious perspective. The official evangelical-Lutheran religion, as formulated and propagated by the Swedish state church, was characterized by nationalism, unity, and homogeneity, whereas other forms of religion were often met with hostility and suspicion. In effect, being Swedish actually meant being a member of the state church, and the only other forms of religion practiced from the time of the Reformation until the nineteenth century were those of immigrant Jews and Catholics. It was not until 1860 that Swedish citizens were allowed to leave the state church, but only on the condition that they become members of congregations approved by the state—which in practice meant joining the Catholic Church or the Methodists.[9] From the mid-nineteenth century, various new Christian denominations were established throughout Sweden, such as the Church of Jesus

Christ of Latter-Day Saints (1850), the Plymouth Brethren movement (1876), Seventh-Day Adventists (1880), Jehovah's Witnesses
(1899), and Christian Science (1905), along with a number of alternative forms of religion including various spiritualist organizations
and esoteric movements such as the Theosophical Society (1888), the
Martinist Order (1890s), and the Hermetic Brotherhood of Luxor
(1890s). However, these new organizations posed no real threat to the
hegemony of the state church, and membership in the new organizations was very limited compared to that of the state church.

It was not until 1951 that freedom of religion was formally established in Sweden, with the passing of the law of religious freedom that
granted Swedish citizens the right to leave the state church and to
choose their own religious beliefs and practices. From the 1960s on,
the religious landscape in Sweden changed dramatically, with regard
to the number of new Christian denominations and churches as well as
the increased presence of non-Christian religious institutions. The primary reason for the changes was the increasing number of immigrants
coming into Sweden who brought new forms of religion with them.
The increased presence of new denominations and non-Christian
religious traditions occurred while the whole of Swedish society was
undergoing profound changes due to the impact of secularization, globalization, and the processes of modernity/late modernity. The notion
that the established religious institutions were the only legitimate and
accepted forms of religion was questioned, and religious seekers began
to look for alternative answers and solutions—as people were already
doing in other parts of Europe and in the United States.

The 1960s and 1970s saw the establishment of a number of international NRMs in Sweden that reflected the broader trends of contemporary religious changes in the United States and Western Europe.
The first Transcendental Meditation group in Sweden was established
as early as 1961, only four years after Maharishi Mahesh Yogi founded
the Spiritual Regeneration Movement in Madras. The formation
of the Transcendental Meditation group was probably prompted by
the fact that Maharishi had visited Sweden in 1960 while traveling
around the world. The Unification Church was established in 1969—
that is, around the same time as the Church of Scientology—and two
years later the Family/Children of God appeared in Sweden. Other
international NRMs that established themselves in Sweden at this

time were the International Society of Krishna Consciousness (ISK-CON) in 1973, with Bhaktivedanta Swami Prabhupada visiting Sweden the same year, and the Osho movement in 1978.[10]

The Church of Scientology in Sweden

When the Church of Scientology came to Sweden in 1968, it was during a period of social and political turmoil characterized, on the one hand, by university students protesting against the Vietnam War and agitating for socialist and communist changes (often in the form of revolution), and, on the other hand, by an increased interest in alternative forms of religion among members of the counterculture movement in Sweden. The commotion was particularly intense at the universities, and many students joined or formed radical political groups; whereas others turned their attention to alternative forms of religion, joining existing NRMs or coming into contact with religious groups in other countries. Thus it is not surprising that the first forms of Scientology activity were organized by a small group of students in the university town of Lund.[11] In Stockholm, the first Scientology group met at the home of a young art student, Tomas Tillberg, who had visited the Church of Scientology headquarters at Saint Hill in East Grinstead, Sussex, during the spring of 1968. After another visit to Saint Hill a few months later, during which he completed a course in communication, Tillberg set up a Scientology group at his home on Birkagatan 33, in the Vasastan area of Stockholm. In April 1969, the group was elevated to the status of a formal church by the headquarters at Saint Hill. In Göteborg, the Church of Scientology established itself in a similar manner, with people interested in Scientology traveling to Saint Hill in 1967 and then setting up a group in May 1968. As was the case with the Stockholm group, the group in Göteborg initially had the authority only to teach the course in communication.

The Church of Scientology spread quickly across Sweden, with a number of centers established in various cities such as Eskilstuna and Örebro, but it was in the three largest cities—Stockholm, Göteborg, and Malmö—that the Church of Scientology would be most successful. The Church of Scientology apparently attracted a large number of members during the first couple of years, and, according to one source, the number of sympathizers had reached around seven thousand in 1970, although it must be stated that this figure appears to be unduly high.[12] The organizational structure of the Church of Scientology in Sweden followed the same pattern as in other countries, and when the Citizens Commission on Human Rights was established in 1969 with the aim of fighting against "human rights crimes" committed by mental health professionals, it only took a year before a Swedish branch, *Kommittén för Mänskliga Rättigheter* (Citizens Commission on Human Rights), was set up. In 1970, the publication of *Freedom* was launched in Sweden: this being the official newsletter of the Church of Scientology. Other organizations linked to Scientology in Sweden include Criminon, dedicated to the rehabilitation of criminals, and Applied Scholastics Sweden, which promulgates study techniques based on the teachings of L. Ron Hubbard. However, it is Narconon—its drug rehabilitation program established in Sweden in 1972—that is the perhaps the best-known Scientology organization in Sweden.

From 1970 onward, the church has been very active in translating and publishing books by L. Ron Hubbard, including *Dianetics: Utvecklandet av en vetenskap* (Dianetics: The Evolution of a Science [1970]); *När du tvivlar, kommunicera* (When in Doubt, Communicate: Quotations from L. Ron Hubbard [1971]); *Scientologi: Tankens grunder* (Scientology: The Fundamentals of Thought [1972]); *Dianetik: Den moderna vetenskapen on mental hälsa* (Dianetics: The Modern Science of Mental Health [1973]); and *Scientology: Tjugonde århundradets religion* (Scientology: Twentieth-Century Religion [1974]).

It would take thirty years for the Church of Scientology in Sweden to be legally recognized as a so-called voluntary organization with a religious purpose, and, on November 23, 1999, the tax authorities decided to grant the Church of Scientology tax exemption. The following year, on March 13, 2000, the Church of Scientology was registered as a religious community by the National Judicial Board for Public Lands and Funds following a new law—titled the Act on Religious Communities (Swedish Code of Statutes 1998:1593)—which took effect on January 1, 2000, and separated the Church of Sweden from the state. On June 10, 2000, the first legal Scientology wedding in Europe was celebrated in Stockholm.

Today, the Church of Scientology has churches in Stockholm, Göteborg, and Malmö, and Narconon has one center, in Eslöv; according to their website, the number of active Scientology members in Sweden is around 3,500.[13] In addition, there is an independent school, Stude-maskolan, in Bandhagen, Stockholm, that uses the study techniques of Applied Scholastics. The school was founded in 1991 and is open to students from the first to ninth grades and has about one hundred students. Ever since its start, the Church of Scientology has maintained an active profile in Swedish society, with activities ranging from demonstrations against the National Board of Health and Welfare and, in the past few years, the erection of large yellow tents in central locations in major cities where volunteer ministers offer help.[14] In comparison with other NRMs active in Sweden, the Church of Scientology maintains an open attitude toward academics and students, illustrated by the fact that on their website the Church of Scientology offers information to students at compulsory high school and university levels.

RELIGION, CONFLICT, AND MENTAL HEALTH

Its active role in society has made the Church of Scientology one of the best-known NRMs in Sweden, but it has also attracted a lot of negative attention. Many of the misconceptions and prejudices found among the public often stem from the yellow press, which has accused the Church of Scientology of being manipulative and dishonest. Chief among the allegations is the notion that the Church of Scientology practices brainwashing, and that members are being forced to spend huge amounts of money on the courses offered by the church. The latest trend in the gossip press is to focus on celebrities such as Tom Cruise and to emphasize what is often seen as "weird" or "strange" in the Church of Scientology. There are, however, two particular events that stand out in the history of Swedish Scientology and that have attracted a lot of attention—even from the more respectable media—namely, the "E-Meter case" in the 1970s and the controversy over the "Bible of Scientology" during the late 1990s.

The "E-Meter case" was brought about by criticism leveled against the content of a number of advertisements placed in the Swedish Scientology magazine *Start* in 1973.[15] According to the advertisements, the E-Meter could measure the mental state of human beings, a claim that attracted the opposition of psychiatrists and certain members of the health department. The advertisements were reported to the consumer ombudsman, and, in 1976, the Swedish Market Court banned the Church of Scientology from formulating their advertisements in such a manner. The decision was appealed by the Church of Scientology on the grounds of religious freedom. The case eventually reached both the Supreme Court and the European Commission of Human Rights but without any results. The case received widespread media attention, and it became clear that Scientology and Dianetics stood in sharp contrast to the more traditional forms of psychiatric health care. Criticism from psychiatrists was fierce, and it was argued that information provided by the Church of Scientology was misleading and false. The criticism was reflected in the rhetoric of the Church of Scientology, which argued not only that traditional forms of psychiatry violated human rights but also that psychiatry's use of diagnoses is not based on scientific or medical premises and that the treatments used in psychiatry (particularly the use of drugs) have a negative effect on patients. The debate was highly polarized, and the general public, through the media, tended to side with the psychiatrists and representatives of health-care institutions and to view the use of the E-Meter as something suspect or fraudulent. But as Swedish sociologist of religion Jonas Alwall has argued, the critics did not take into account the fact that the use of the E-Meter was an integral part of the religious belief system of Scientology, and that the claims of effectiveness of the E-Meter should be placed in the wider religious discourse of Scientology.[16] The controversy surrounding the use of the E-Meter was not, however, something new in the history of Scientology. In fact, as early as the 1950s, the United States Food and Drug Administration had investigated whether unwarranted medical claims were being attached to the E-Meter by the Church of Scientology. The investigation led to a raid on January 4, 1963, at the Founding Church of Scientology in Washington, DC, and all the E-Meters present in the building were confiscated, only to be returned eight years later after the issue had been resolved in court. The E-Meter had been declared a legitimate religious artifact.[17]

Alwall argues that a similar lack of contextualization of Scientology within the broader context of religious discourse underlies some of the criticism leveled against Scientology in connection with the much-publicized "Bible of Scientology" case of the late 1990s. On June 1, 1996, Swedish citizen Zenon Panoussis posted a number of secret—and copyrighted—OT (Operating Thetan)-level documents on the Internet, which the media erroneously labeled the Bible of Scientology.

The OT-level documents are reserved for the more advanced members of the Church of Scientology and reveal Scientology's inner teachings, such as the Xenu myth, which is basically Scientology's founding myth.[18] However, the posting of the material on the Internet was not something new in itself, but reflected what had been going on for a while in other countries as well.[19] According to the Church of Scientology in Sweden, the material that Panoussis posted was in violation of copyright law, and, furthermore, it claimed that the material had been stolen from the church. The website was closed down following a court decision, but this did not deter Panoussis from trying to spread Scientology materials. Through an appeal to the Swedish constitution and the principles of public domain, Panoussis deposited copies of the documents in question at public institutions such as the Ministry of Justice, the Chancellor of Justice, and the Riksdag (the Swedish parliament), thereby making them accessible to the public. This stratagem worked for a while, but, in October 1997, the government decided to place the documents under secrecy, thereby restricting them from the public. The official reason for this decision was that the documents were protected by foreign secrecy: "That is, the rule that states that information pertaining to citizens or legal persons in another country shall be protected by secrecy if its publication threatens to interfere with Swedish foreign relations."[20] It became known that the Swedish government had come under pressure from the United States in this particular case, a fact that prompted critics of Scientology to also criticize the Swedish government. The case of the "Bible of Scientology" did not, however, end here; sometime later the decision of the government was overruled by the Supreme Administrative Court, only to be challenged by the proposition of a new law by the government. The legal implications notwithstanding, it was the contents of the OT-level documents that received the most attention from the public. The documents were often described as "bad" science fiction, and it was questioned on what grounds normal persons could believe them to be true. As in other countries, Scientologists were often ridiculed for believing in the religious worldview formulated by Hubbard, but, as with the "E-Meter case," the critics tended to overlook the fact that the documents should be interpreted in the light of religious discourse. Religious texts are, more often than not, interpreted in symbolic and allegorical ways, and they are often characterized by self-contradiction and nonempirical arguments.

In recent years, the Church of Scientology has been involved in one of the most controversial academic affairs in Sweden, the so-called Gillberg affair. On May 9, 2004, three researchers at the Department of Child and Adolescent Psychiatry at the University of Gothenburg informed the university's vice-chancellor that they had destroyed tens of thousands of documents related to a 15-year longitudinal study of children with severe attention deficit disorders. It was an act that went against a decision of the Supreme Administrative Court, which stated that the data had to be made available to other researchers. The background story to this event is long and complicated, fused with conflict, polemics, and bitter professional disagreement. In March 1997, Professor Christopher Gillberg of the Department of Child and Adolescent Psychiatry at the University of Gothenburg published an article in which he stated that 120,000 Swedish children suffer from some kind of neuropsychiatric problem, such as attention deficit disorders, Asperger's, or Tourette's syndrome.[21] Gillberg is described as "a world expert in autism and attention deficit disorder and a leading proponent of deficits in attention, motor control, and perception (DAMP), a Nordic concept developed in the 1970s to describe a combination of hyperactivity, lack of concentration, and clumsiness and later regarded as a subcategory of attention deficit hyperactivity disorder."[22] He was questioned by Dr. Leif Elinder in an article published in the *Swedish Medical Journal*, particularly on account of Gillberg's claim that 10 percent (120,000) of all Swedish children suffer from neuropsychiatric problems.[23] Elinder was soon joined in the criticism of Gillberg's work by an associate professor of sociology from Lund University, Eva Kärfve, who in 2000 had published a highly critical book—but one that was unfair and poorly researched, according to Gillberg's supporters, titled *Hjärnspöken—DAMP och hotet mot folkhälsan* (Brain Ghosts—DAMP and the Threat to Public Health).[24] Gillberg and his colleagues protested against the book to Lund University and accused Kärfve not only of "lies and misrepresentation" but also of having received classified documents from the journalist Janne Larsson, who writes for the Swedish branch of the Church of Scientology's Commission on Human Rights.[25] In 2002, the debate escalated when Kärfve and Elinder accused Gillberg and his colleagues of research fraud—a very serious charge in academia—and they proceeded to file several applications to gain access to the raw data on which Gillberg and his colleagues had based their findings. Gillberg refused to make his data available, arguing that the material was confidential and that releasing it would be unethical toward the participants of the study (60 children from the 15-year study). Kärfve then proceeded to take the case to the Administrative Court of Appeal, and the Gillberg affair received even wider attention—not least in the media—and the debate became polarized between those who agreed with Kärfve and Elinder's basic stand that research needs to be transparent and verifiable by other scientists, and those on Gillberg's side, who argued that research ethics need to be respected, and that it would have been unethical to reveal data that had been collected on the basis of confidentiality.

The affair continued to unfold, with each party accusing the other of fraud and misconduct, but I will limit my account to the role of the Church of Scientology in the Gillberg affair. Gillberg's group not only claimed that confidential material used by Kärfve in her book *Hjärnspöken* (2000) came from Janne Larsson, associated with the Church of Scientology and its Commission on Human Rights, but also claimed that in the autumn of 2002, "at the height of the battle to gain access to their data, Professor Kärfve attended an antipsychiatry Scientology conference in Germany. She admits attending the meeting, but has maintained that she did so only as an observer and in her role as a sociologist. Scientology, she said, was a 'scary' movement about which she had written critically."[26] The claimed association with Scientology was raised as an argument against Kärfve's scientific objectivity. In fact, in 2003, when two of Gillberg's colleagues lodged a formal complaint to Lund University accusing Kärfve of scientific dishonesty in her book, they also "suggested that she might be linked to the Church of Scientology."[27] Although the two experts appointed by the Swedish Research Council to investigate the claims did not concern themselves with the allegation that she was allied to Scientology, it is nevertheless telling that the charge of being connected with Scientology was seen as such a significant issue that it merited inclusion in the complaint against her by Gillberg's colleagues.[28] The Church of Scientology has a long international history of conflict with the established forms of psychiatry; the church is particularly critical of the use of drugs to "cure" mental disorders (they claim that drugs cannot cure deficit disorders, and instead they argue that their own form of therapy, auditing, is successful in curing such disorders).[29] The journalist Janne Larsson, mentioned previously, not only has been covering the Gillberg affair in a very polemical and critical way but is also seen by some Swedish psychiatrists and journalists as working with a hidden agenda. For instance, in an article published in 2007 in *Läkartidningen* (the Medical Journal, published by the Swedish Medical Association), Larsson is described as a member of the Church of Scientology and a representative of the Swedish branch of the *Citizens Commission on Human Rights* (CCHR), whose stated aim is to investigate and expose "psychiatric violations of human rights."[30] Larsson is criticized for "working in the dark" and for requesting large amounts of material on issues related to attention deficit hyperactivity disorder from governmental departments, which he then selectively interprets according to the "conspiracy theory" promoted by the CCHR.

As might be expected, the Church of Scientology interprets things differently, as is evident in many of the articles published in the official journal of the Swedish branch of the Citizens Commission on Human Rights, called *Mänskliga rättigheter tidningen* (Human Rights Journal), or by reading the articles posted on their website.[31] There are a number of reasons why the Church of Scientology is widely regarded as not falling into the domain of religious discourse, one of which is to be found in the language of Scientology itself and the way the church presents itself to the public, which is often interpreted as a form of pseudoscience falling into a liminal position somewhere between science and religion. This state of liminality is illustrated by the fact that Scientology in Sweden is often perceived by its critics as not being a true or proper form of religion, and at the same time failing to meet the criteria to be recognized as a science. However, it is not only in the public mind that Scientology is often separated from religious discourse. This can also be seen as central to the criticisms leveled against Scientology by the Swedish anticult movement. The anticult group FRI, arguably the fiercest opponent of the Church of Scientology in Sweden, has as its motto on its website: "It's not about religion, but about manipulation," while stating at the same time that the activities of groups such as the Church of Scientology are indeed based on religion.

SCIENTOLOGY AND THE SWEDISH ANTICULT MOVEMENT

Criticism against the Church of Scientology has been expressed in the Swedish media right from the very outset in the late 1960s, but it is the anticult movement and the individuals connected to it that have been the strongest opponents. The leading anticult group in Sweden, FRI, was founded in 1984 by a group of friends and relatives of members of various "destructive sects" (as mentioned earlier, the term "sect" has negative connotations in Sweden, similar to the term "cult" in the United States). Since 2002, FRI has had a suborganization called Sesam that consists of former members of "destructive" and "totalitarian" groups. Since April 2001, FRI has been a member of FECRIS. According to Liselotte Frisk, the primary arguments expressed by FRI against movements such as the Church of Scientology are that they exploit the insecurity and idealism of young people, they are dishonest about their real objectives, they systematically break down their members through techniques that aim to change members' behavior, they confiscate the assets of their members, the religious status they seek to acquire is often a cover for receiving tax-exempt status, their true goals are power and money, they use psychological and sometimes physical violence against their members, they represent a fascist ideology and ethos, they have authoritarian leaders, and they practice mind control or brainwashing.[32]

According to the organization's website, FRI has been in contact with more than 500 defectors, 200 of whom have been subjected to deprogramming, and, according to Frisk, FRI claimed that between 20 and 30 of these deprogrammed individuals had belonged to the Church of Scientology. In discussing the Church of Scientology on their website, FRI enumerates four aspects that Scientology allegedly shares with other "totalitarian" groups. First, they manipulate their members by withholding important information and by using suggestion during the auditing process and in their courses. Second, they control their members through confessions and surveillance and by encouraging members to inform on one another. Third, they restrain members through the notion that the words of L. Ron Hubbard are a law that must not be questioned or discussed. Fourth, Scientology bullies its members if they fail to make progress, and questions their judgment if they do anything "wrong." FRI is frequently used by the Swedish media as an expert body when the subject of NRMs is being discussed.

Another example of an anticult spokesperson is Karl-Erik Nylund, who frequently appears in the press as an "expert on sects." Nylund (born in 1942) is a retired priest in the Swedish Church and the author of a well-known book titled *Att leka med elden: Sekternas värld* (Playing with Fire: The World of Sects, rev. ed. 2004), in which he identifies the Church of Scientology as the most dangerous sect in the world.[33] In discussing the Church of Scientology, Nylund addresses in particular the ways in which the church tries to silence its critics, and he states quite bluntly that Scientology—which he identifies as "psychotherapy characterized by occult science fiction"—is about money. In common with other critics, he dismisses the religious dimension of Scientology, stating that after reading some of the OT-level documents, he came to the conclusion that it was nothing but rubbish.[34]

What is significant about the criticism directed against the Church of Scientology by FRI and authors like Nylund is that they are not criticizing the religious beliefs and practices as such, but rather the claims of what Dianetics can accomplish, the cost of the courses and auditing sessions, and what they see as deceptive behavior. This type of criticism is part of an international anticult movement that is secular in character, as opposed to religious countercult groups that largely base their criticism on theological grounds. FRI shares many similarities with other anticult groups in Europe, such as the British organization FAIR (Family Action Information Resource), which in 2007 evolved into the Family Survival Trust, and it is perhaps not surprising that both organizations belong to FECRIS.[35]

The Problem of "Cults" in a Welfare Society

Although Christianity is still the dominant religion in Sweden—about 75 percent of the Swedish population are members of the Swedish Church—the religious landscape has changed dramatically since the 1960s, with a wide range of new religious traditions on the scene. The Church of Scientology and other international NRMs established themselves in Sweden at a time when the whole of Swedish society was undergoing profound changes and when Swedes were increasingly looking for alternative religious answers. Although most of the NRMs active in Sweden have a comparatively small number of members, they have nevertheless received a lot of attention from the public through the media, from the academic world, and from the anticult movement. Government recognition of the importance of NRMs in Swedish society was made evident by the report commissioned by the Swedish Ministry of Health and Social Affairs in 1998. As one of the largest and most active NRMs in Sweden, the Church of Scientology stands out as perhaps the best-known NRM but also as one of the most controversial groups in Sweden. As discussed previously, the controversy surrounding the Church of Scientology stems to a large extent from the "E-Meter case" in the 1970s and the controversy over the "Bible of Scientology" during the late 1990s. These two events were not only hotly debated and the focus of extensive media attention but also illustrative of the conflict and tension that can arise when secular and religious worldviews meet. The E-Meter was questioned on scientific grounds, and the controversy over the OT-level documents posted on the Internet and later deposited in public institutions focused on questions of copyright and freedom of speech. But from the perspective of the Church of Scientology, both controversies were ultimately seen as an infringement on the freedom of religion or the right to exercise and to protect religious beliefs and practices.

Moreover, the criticism from the anticult movement has added to the controversy that sometimes surrounds the Church of Scientology, in that spokespersons from the anticult movement are frequently used as "experts" by the media. When comparing the development of the Church of Scientology in Sweden with that of its development in other countries, one is immediately struck by the apparent lack of idiosyncratic tendencies. The establishment and later development of the Church in Sweden parallels that in many other countries, and the organizational structure is identical for the Church of Scientology in all countries. Both the "E-Meter case" and the posting of OT-level documents echo conflicts that the Church of Scientology has experienced in other countries, as is the tendency to answer criticism from outsiders in an often polemical fashion and to use the legal system to protect the church. The criticism from the anticult movement, and also the anticult movement as such, resembles what we see in many other countries.

But when all is said and done, the question remains, What is it about religious organizations such as the Church of Scientology that obviously provokes such mistrust, fear, and ridicule in Swedish media (and apparently among Swedish people in general)? What are the reasons for the openly polemical discourses leveled against "cults" by the

media in a society that is otherwise characterized by "political correct-
ness" and an almost paranoid fear of offending religious minorities? I
would argue that there is an inherent tension between the self-image of
Sweden as a welfare state—although, as discussed in the other chapters
of this book, the welfare system is being dismantled and the self-image
is beginning to crumble—and the polemical discourses on "cults." If
we analyze the criticism leveled against cults by the anticult movement and the media at large, we see that the charge of brainwashing is
the most recurrent charge since at least the 1970s, and brainwashing
is almost exclusively interpreted as an anomaly or a mental disorder
caused by the manipulations of cults. The notion of a healthy society
with healthy citizens is thus in conflict with the popular view of cults:
the cults threaten the health of the welfare state. Moreover, the notion
of brainwashing stands in sharp contrast to the ideals of the integrity,
inviolability, and sanctity of the individual, which are fundamental
for a democratic society, since the individual is believed to have been
deprived of his or her own free will and ability to make rational and
critical choices. The fact that scholars have dismissed brainwashing as
an ideological construct rather than a psychological or clinical "state"
is irrelevant: the polemical understanding of the "cult" implies a threat
against the mental health of the citizens of Swedish welfare society.

It is my contention that the polemics against NRMs in general, and
against the Church of Scientology in particular, clearly show a para-
digmatic shift in the understanding of what constitutes the founda-
tional values of Swedish culture—that is, a shift from moral, religious,
nationalistic, and political values (which are constitutive of the "grand
narratives of modernity") to those of economy and health (which I
believe are the grand narratives of late modern Swedish society). The
medicalization and economization of moral and religious issues are
obvious in how Scientology is portrayed in Swedish media; not as
a theologically questionable or "evil" movement, but as a money-
making, swindling business and a brainwashing, manipulative form
of pseudotherapy.

As stated at the outset of this chapter, national polls show that
Swedish citizens often perceive themselves as open-minded and tolerant toward minority religions, but when we look more closely at what
sort of minority religions Swedes tolerate, they are the "traditional"
forms of religion, such as Islam, Judaism, Hinduism, Buddhism, and

ethnic Christian churches and denominations. The fact that Swedish national polls do not even mention new religious movements is indicative of their perceived lack of relevance for Swedish society at large, but more important, it also indicates that these types of movements are not even considered to be part of the Swedish religious landscape. As such, controversial groups like Scientology actualize the very question of religion itself as a category, or in the words of Hugh Urban, "Scientology is thus an ideal case for thinking about religion—that is, for thinking about how religion is defined, who gets to define it, and what the stakes are in laying claim to or being denied such status."[36]

NOTES

1. Although national polls on general attitudes toward religion are regularly conducted in Sweden, so far no nationwide survey has been done specifically on the attitudes toward new religious movements in Sweden.

2. The use of the term "sect" in Europe is similar to the use of the term "cult" in the United States—that is, it is used in a normative and implicitly and/or explicitly negative way to label new or deviant religious groups. Most scholars studying these groups have adopted the term "new religious movement" (NRM) as a neutral alternative to the polemical and derogatory terms "cult" and "sect." The NRMs discussed in this chapter can be described as "new" in the sense that they were founded fairly recently (especially during the second half of the twentieth century, with most members being first- or second-generation members) and that the teachings differ to such an extent from the dominant religious traditions of the West that it is valid to speak of "new" forms of religion.

3. It should be stressed that the "anticult movement" in singular form is somewhat misleading since we are dealing not with a single, unified movement but rather with a wide range of groups and individuals that share the common belief that "sects" and "cults" are harmful and should be combated. Some of these groups and individuals have cooperated and formed national and international organizations such as FECRIS, mentioned earlier.

4. David G. Bromley and Anson Shupe, *Anti-Cult Movements in Cross-Cultural Perspectives* (New York: Garland, 1994), 9–14.

5. Hugh B. Urban, *The Church of Scientology: A History of a New Religion* (Princeton, NJ: Princeton University Press, 2011), 5.

6. The use of "polemical discourse" in this chapter follows Hanegraaff's use of the term and is thus subject to five basic conditions: it requires (1) a sense of unrest or threat; (2) that the source of threat be not entirely clear and readily accessible; (3) a target; (4) an audience; and (5) simplicity—that is,

the discourse must be based on simple oppositions (Wouter J. Hanegraaff, "Forbidden Knowledge: Anti-Esoteric Polemics and Academic Research," *Aries* 5:2 (2005), 226–27).

7. Parts of this chapter are based on my article "The Church of Scientology in Sweden," in *Scientology*, ed. James R. Lewis (Oxford: Oxford University Press, 2009), 335–44.

8. Statens offentliga utredningar (Statens offentliga utredningar 1998:113), *I God Tro: Samhället och nyandligheten*. (Socialdepartementet, Betänkande av Krisstödsutredningen, no. 113, Statens offentliga utredningar, September 1998).

9. Daniel Anderson and Åke Sander (eds.), *Det mångreligiösa Sverige–ett landskap i förändring* (Lund: Studentlitteratur, 2009), 27–34.

10. Liselotte Frisk, *Nyreligiositet I Sverige: Ett religionsvetenskapligt perspektiv* (Nora: Nya Doxa, 1998); Bo R. Ståhl and Bertil Persson, *Kulter, Sekter, Samfund: En studie av religiösa minoriteter i Sverige* (Stockholm: Proprius förlag, 1971).

11. Ståhl and Persson, *Kulter*, 104.

12. Ibid.

13. According to the report published by the Swedish Ministry of Health and Social Affairs, in 1998, the Church of Scientology was estimated to have about 1,000 active members and about 10,000 passive members. This can be compared with other NRMs such as Summit Lighthouse, with about 200 members; ISKCON, with about 150–80 "full-time" members and 1,000–2,000 affiliated members; and the Raëlian movement, with only about 10 members. According to Swedish scholar Peter Åkerbäck ("Scientologi-kyrkan," in *Religion i Sverige*, ed. Ingvar Svanberg and David Westerlund [Stockholm: Dialogos förlag, 2008], 328), the estimated number of active Church of Scientology members is about 500, which is a considerably lower figure than the Church of Scientology's own estimate.

14. Åkerbäck, "Scientologi-kyrkan," 329.

15. An E-Meter, short for electropsychometer, is a device used by Scientologists to measure electrical resistance and skin conductance. Often referred to as a sort of "lie detector," it is used during auditing (Scientology's form of therapy) to discover engrams (traumatic experiences).

16. Jonas Alwall, "Scientologerna och samhället: Dialog eller konflikt?," in *Gudars och gudinnors återkomst: Studier i nyreligiositet*, ed. Carl-Gustav Carlsson and Liselotte Frisk (Institutionen för religionsvetenskap, Umeå universitet, 2000).

17. J. Gordon Melton, *The Church of Scientology* (N.p.: Signature Books, 2000), 13, 14.

18. Mikael Rothstein, "'His name was Xenu. He used renegades . . .': Aspects of Scientology's Founding Myth," in *Scientology*, ed. James R. Lewis (Oxford: Oxford University Press, 2009), 365–87.

19. Melton, *Scientology*, 36–38; Urban, *Scientology*, 178–200.

20. Alwall, "Scientologerna," 112.

21. Christopher Gillberg and Sophie Ekman, "Skolan knäcker 120 000 barn," *Dagens Nyheter*, March 20, 1997.

22. Jonathan Gornall, "Hyperactivity in Children: The Gillberg Affair," *British Medical Journal*, 335 (2007).

23. Leif Elinder, "Dyslexi, DAMP och Aspergers syndrome—Friska sjuk-förklaras i diagnostiskt samhälle," *Läkartidningen*, 94:39 (1997), 3391–93.

24. Eva Kärfve, *Hjärnspöken—DAMP och hotet mot folkhälsan* (Stockholm: Brutus Östlings bokförlag Symposion, 2000).

25. Gornall, "Hyperactivity."

26. Ibid.

27. Ibid.

28. Ibid.

29. Katharine Mieszkowski, "Scientology's War on Psychiatry" (2005), http://www.salon.com/2005/07/01sci_psy (accessed January 8, 2013).

30. Vanna Beckman, "Offentlighetsprincipen exploateras," *Läkartidningen*, 104:39 (2007).

31. Kommitén för mänskliga rättigheter homepage, http://www.kmr.nu (accessed January 3, 2013).

32. Frisk, *Nyreligiositet*, 216.

33. According to Nylund, *Att leka med elden: Sekternas värld*, 2nd ed. (Stockholm: Sellin & Partner Bok och Idé AB, 2004), 58–60, the five most dangerous sects in the world are (1) the Church of Scientology, (2) the Raëlian movement, (3) the Unification Church, (4) the Family/Children of God, and (5) ISKCON. In Sweden the top five dangerous sects are a bit different, but it is still the Church of Scientology that is identified as number 1. The other groups in the top five include (2) the Raëlian movement, (3) the Unification Church, (4) Kristi Församling, and (5) Linbufonden (Nylund, Att leka, 301). According to Nylund, manipulative sects are characterized by four criteria—namely, (1) *aggression* toward members who think differently, (2) *aversion* toward outsiders, (3) *alienation* from society, and (4) claims to *absolute truth*.

34. Nylund, *Att leka*, 218.

35. Elisabeth Arweck, *Researching New Religious Movements: Responses and Redefinitions* (London: Routledge, 2006), 111–201.

36. Urban, *Scientology*, 17.

Chapter 4

Something Happened, but What?

On Roy Andersson's Cinematic Critique of the Development of the Welfare State

Daniel Brodén

THE NARRATIVE ABOUT THE SWEDISH WELFARE STATE developed by internationally renowned filmmaker Roy Andersson is one of the most iconic and pessimistic variations on the "Sweden Unparadised" theme. As the introduction of this book clarifies, the critical investigation of the welfare state in Sweden has, for a long time, been a major theme in Swedish film and literature. But few, if any, filmmakers have scrutinized the development with the same depth, consistency, and zeal as Andersson. Although not as internationally well known as Ingmar Bergman, Andersson is a strong contender for the title of not only the most original auteur of Swedish cinema but also the famed critic of the state of the welfare state. In fact, a closer look at his oeuvre reveals a critical perspective that is as relentless as it is broad in scope.

Roy Andersson burst onto the international art-house scene in 2000 with the Jury Prize winner at the Cannes Film Festival, *Songs from the Second Floor* (*Sånger från andra våningen*), a film described by veteran critic J. Hoberman as "slapstick Ingmar Bergman," and about which Robert Ebert wrote, "You have never seen a film like this before. You may not enjoy it but you will not forget it."[1] In a series of loosely strung together, absurdist vignettes, Andersson presented a stunning dystopian panorama of a modern society in a state of disintegration, plagued by rampant materialism, human indifference, lost ideals, and apocalyptic phenomena. In the film, a perpetual traffic jam lurches through a city populated by pale, lifeless citizens bereft of hope. Unscrupulous capitalists flee the country in hordes after having plundered the economy, while hidebound politicians try to solve the crisis by, literally, sacrificing the young generation. The protagonist, a small-minded salesman, flogs cheaply made crucifixes for "Jesus's two-thousandth birthday," while his son, who is confined in a mental institution, is unable to stop crying, having realized the utter lack of compassion in society.

Songs from the Second Floor established Roy Andersson, then in his late fifties, as an international auteur with a cinematic vision that is idiosyncratic even by the standards of art cinema. Andersson not only makes exceptionally bleak films, but he also exclusively shoots his scenes in static, wide-angle long shots, rendering his offbeat, some-times laugh-out-loud funny, depictions of the human condition all the more striking. Drawing on a range of European high-modernist influ-ences, including Otto Dix's *Neue Sachlichkeit* paintings, Samuel Beck-ett's tragicomic play *Waiting for Godot* (1953), Luis Buñuel's surrealistic satire *The Discreet Charm of the Bourgeoisie* (1972), and Federico Fellini's allegorical fresco *And the Ship Sails On* (1983), Andersson has culti-vated a personal critical realist style, which he refers to as "the complex image."[2] He meticulously crafts every single image, shooting his films in his privately owned Studio 24 and, when needed, utilizing *trompe l'œil* technique to create the impression of vast sceneries. It can take months for Andersson to perfect a single shot, and the results can be likened to heavily stylized *tableaux vivant*, mirroring the Russian formalist Vik-tor Shklovsky's notion of defamiliarization—that is, the capacity of art to make the everyday world unfamiliar and to provoke reflection through the uses of unconventional artistic forms.[3] Andersson's visual traits include strangely abstracted sceneries and odd-looking amateur actors, wearing white, powdered makeup and delivering seemingly banal lines with blank faces.

However, Roy Andersson occupies a contradictory place in Swed-ish culture. On the one hand, he is an old-school modernist—after the follow-up film to *Songs from the Second Floor, You, the Living* (*Du levande;* 2007), his oeuvre was exhibited at the Museum of Modern Art in New York—and many cinephiles around the world hold him in higher esteem than his fellow auteur, compatriot Lukas Moodysson, the director of international hit films such as *Together* (*Tillsammans*; 2000) and *Lilya 4-Ever* (*Lilja-4-Ever*; 2002). Just prior to the publication of this book he won the prestigious Golden Lion award at the Venice Film Festival for his latest film *A Pigeon Sat on a Branch Reflecting on Existence* (*En duva satt på en gren och funderade på tillvaron*; 2014). On the other hand, Andersson is a broadly popular survivor from the heyday of 1960s art cinema, with his debut feature, *A Swedish Love Story* (*En kärlekshistoria*; 1970), usually ranking among the top ten domestic films of all time.[4] In fact, many Swedes are more familiar with his films than with Ingmar Bergman's. Andersson is widely known for his work in advertising, and a special kind of deadpan, ironic, single-shot commercials—similar to the FedEx "Fast-Talking Man" and Wendy's "Where's the Beef?" television spots by Joe Sedelmaier—have been his trademarks in the last decades. As a director of commercials, he has managed to combine the humorous with the serious to an exceptional extent and, as a critical statement about the state of Swedish society, *Songs from the Second Floor* is just the tip of the iceberg.

It would not be overstating the case to claim that Andersson has devoted his entire artistic project to the interrogation of the human condition and the reification of social life in the Swedish welfare state. Thus in line with the theme of this book, this chapter will present not only an overview of the works of an acclaimed filmmaker but also, more important, a singular perspective on the development of the welfare state that has garnered substantial public interest over the years.

Although hardly alone in defending the core vision behind the historical welfare project known as *Folkhemmet* (the people's home), Andersson has expanded on his personal conviction that the development has been guided by a too-narrow conception of life—in his films as well as in his commercials, writings, and numerous interviews. As he sees it, the politicians (both on the left and on the right) have measured life only in material terms, and the ideals of the early working-class movement—solidarity, civic spirit, and social equality—have withered away and left a void in the human mind and the social body: "With affluence came also greed and . . . human bonds, contacts, and friendship were exchanged for materialistic possessions."[5]

Lately, Roy Andersson's filmmaking has become the subject of international scholarly works, and *Songs from the Second Floor* in particular has been the focus of critical attention.[6] But as a whole, writing on the director tends to be more specific than general. It describes his style, themes, and major influences,[7] but does not map his trajectory as a filmmaker or the connections between his works and the larger cultural context on which they draw heavily. The aim of my article is, therefore, to analyze and contextualize the extensive cinematic critique of the social and existential ills of Swedish society that Andersson has crafted over the years. The overarching themes that unite his work are not in themselves novel—the alienation in modernity, the attendant loss of common humanity, and the corrosive influence of bourgeois capitalism and state bureaucracy[8]—but they have been updated through the director's application of iconoclastic perspectives, at the same time both painfully serious and acidly ironic. Further, as literary scholar Linda Hutcheon points out, irony is, like all other communication acts, largely culture-specific, relying on the presence of a common world of reference.[9] This is particularly true with regard to the director's broadsides against advanced cultural materialism that is inherently tied to the national discursive context.

In part, the limited focus on Andersson's filmmaking, even within the domestic research community,[10] is due to the fact that for a long time he was a complete outsider in Swedish cinema. *Songs from the Second Floor* was not only his international breakthrough film but also the comeback film he struggled to make for more than two decades. After the notorious fiasco with his second feature, *Giliap* (1975), Andersson, a headstrong perfectionist, was thrown out into the cold by the film industry. However, he managed to establish a highly successful alternative career in advertising, refining his style and building a reputation as a wronged visionary. He even started to shoot parts of the big-budget production *Songs from the Second Floor* by financing it from his own pocket before eventually receiving funding. Arguably, there is a romantic streak in the domestic image of Andersson—a charismatic maverick filmmaker if ever there was one—not least reinforced by his own irreverent and pretentious statements. Nevertheless, a contextualizing analysis of the drastic narrative about the welfare state that Andersson has presented calls for a dual focus, taking into account both his against-the-grain filmmaking and his profile as an unruly outsider. The question posed in this chapter's title, "Something Happened, but What?," primarily concerns the director's vision on the state of Swedish society, the thematic logic behind the depiction of the societal collapse in *Songs from the Second Floor*, as viewed against the cultural context from which it draws. But while this chapter maps the development of Andersson's critical perspective from his early features, it also highlights his history as a tenacious iconoclast who has framed and expanded his argument in the media. It argues that the director's cinematic critique of the welfare state as a beautiful but derailed project is rooted in the New Left of the 1960s and its dashed dream of a more humane and less materialistic society. I specifically stress the connection between his approach and the intellectual tradition of Critical Theory, which was a key intellectual influence of the nondogmatic left in Sweden. My main point is that he has persisted in raising the critical questions of yesteryear by regarding the state of modern society in relation to a radicalized artistic vision and a changing cultural context.

NATIONAL INNOCENCE LOST

When Roy Andersson's career began, cinema culture was blossoming in Europe. The 1960s saw the rise of a number of New Waves in various countries and the birth of auteur cinema, as prolific filmmakers such as Jean-Luc Godard, Michelangelo Antonioni, and Ingmar Bergman launched visual expressions and experimental narratives that changed the face of modern cinema.[11] The international success of Bergman contributed to the Swedish state's launching of the so-called film reform in order to further national film culture and the production of "artistically valuable film," inspired by similar European cultural-political projects. However, Sweden was (and is) a comparatively small nation, and the newly formed Swedish Film Institute (SFI) came to exert a far-reaching influence over national film production through a generous funding system. It also tried to stake out the future by founding the first national film school.[12] Although it is open to debate which films could be considered artistically valuable, SFI essentially privileged the production of aesthetically and intellectually sophisticated art cinema. One idea behind the national film school was even to cultivate talents with Ingmar Bergman as a specific role model.[13] However, this emphasis on a cinematic modernism *à la* Bergman provided fertile ground for conflict between the SFI management and many young filmmakers.

The late 1960s became a politically turbulent time in Swedish cinema, and renowned filmmaker Bo Widerberg's argumentative essay *The Vision in Swedish Film* (*Visionen i svensk film*; 1962) could be considered a precursor of things to come. In his book, Widerberg, then only a writer, mocked both the reverence for Bergman and the incapability of Swedish film to represent the lives of everyday people. Basically, he argued for a cinema capable of raising social awareness as well as elucidating the humdrum existence and materialist conditions of ordinary people.[14] Widerberg later expressed his ideal in his acclaimed feature debut, *The Pram* or *The Baby Carriage* (*Barnvagnen*; 1963), launching an impressionistic realism that became a source of inspiration for many young filmmakers—among them the film student Roy Andersson. Also, since this was the time of the leftist movement in Swedish society, many in the young generation (activists as well as filmmakers) were taking a stand against international capitalism and for socialism with a human face. Overall, the New Left of the 1960s expressed an idealistic belief in the possibility of a more humane society in which citizens would be able to more fully realize themselves—a belief inspired by Herbert Marcuse's nondogmatic, Marxist critique of modern industrial society in *One-Dimensional Man*.[15] Arguably, the expanding Swedish welfare project had eliminated many injustices of the old, class society, but now attention was directed to the drawbacks of progress, such as alienation, materialism, reification, and conformism. In fact, the expression "the Record Years," often used to describe the remarkable post–World War II economic expansion of the Swedish welfare state, was originally an ironic, left-wing characterization of the flipside of progress during the years 1968 to 1970. Thus the New Left's revolt had as much to do with the human world of thought as with materialistic conditions.[16]

A key film for the new political cinema was the documentary *The White Match* (*Den vita sporten*; 1968), made by Widerberg and students of SFI's school—among them Roy Andersson. The film covered a notorious Davis Cup tennis match between Sweden and the apartheid state Rhodesia resulting in clashes between the police and activists that finally forced the cancellation the event. Although it was a critical success, the film was marked by controversy and disputes, not least between the film collective and the cofinancer, SFI, which contributed to the conflict between the leftist film movement and the management of the Film Institute.[17]

Despite the controversies, Andersson made his debut under exceptional circumstances. To make a long story short, he was given the rare chance to step into Widerberg's shoes at the company Europa Film, which had lost the director to the prominent rival Svensk Filmindustri. In his first feature, *A Swedish Love Story*, Andersson not only worked with a big budget but also had an experienced crew, including members from the production of Widerberg's international art-film hit *Elvira Madigan* (1967). *A Swedish Love Story* became a big box-office success, earning enthusiastic reviews for its original depiction of the emptiness and materialism in contemporary Sweden; one critic specifically claimed that the film potentially clarified "what the current student protests were about."[18] Andersson was also hailed as one of the most promising talents in Swedish cinema: a perfectionist and original visionary, whose style was favorably compared to Czech director Miloš Forman's tragicomic gaze on the wider consequences of the ignorance and pettiness of ordinary people.

While boasting an artistic talent and a high level of self-confidence, Andersson cultivated a popular auteur persona as a down-to-earth and humorous person, distancing himself from what he saw as the stuck-up mentalities at SFI and the film school. An integral part of his personality was his working-class background in the industrial city Gothenburg, and he became known in the media as a filmmaker who combined a high, artistic ambition with a humble pathos and an anti-authoritarian streak. He particularly stressed his ambition to fight "the coerced servitude" of the working class to the bourgeois establishment in the name of social equality.[19] Andersson's proletarian background gave weight to his position as a socialist filmmaker, as he did not, like the majority of the New Left, come from a privileged, middle-class background. But unlike many young political filmmakers, he saw no incompatibility per se between radical art and broad entertainment, and he emphasized the importance of making sophisticated films for a wide audience.[20] One could say that Roy Andersson presented himself as both a radical auteur and a *Folkhems* filmmaker. *A Swedish Love Story* was indeed a different kind of film than the Marxist political films of the period, which attacked structural institutional oppression and capitalist exploitation.[21] Partly, Andersson worked in the same broad social critical tradition as Widerberg, investigating (in a less overtly polemical manner) the gap between *Folkhemmet* as a societal vision and a lived class reality. However, Andersson had a younger and more radical profile than Widerberg, who in the late 1960s was heavily criticized by the New Left for essentially conveying a Social Democratic—and a presumed reactionary—perspective on the social condition.[22] Nevertheless, as a filmmaker, Andersson made a strong connection between Swedish identity and the labor movement's historical project: while attacking the prevalent social mentality in the spirit of the New Left, he dramatized the development of *Folkhemmet* as an issue of broad concern.

A SWEDISH LOVE STORY

Thematically, *A Swedish Love Story* explores a state of existential crisis in the welfare state during the Record Years of the late 1960s. Although the narrative revolves around a tender love story between two teenagers, Annika and Pär, Andersson essentially tells a bigger, disillusioned story about their parents and relatives, who lead affluent lives that would have been unimaginable only a few decades earlier, but who, at the same time, are affected by growing alienation, conformism, and materialism. In fact, the film is rather deceptive in the sense that, through a teenage love story, it conveys a bitter critique of the social mentality in the modern *Folkhemmet*, with the beautiful cinematography contributing to the impression of a seemingly idyllic society. The dissonant tone is set from the start in the sequence when Pär's and Annika's families visit relatives at a nursing home. Making his way through a corridor, Pär's grandfather proudly brags to a nurse about how well-off his son is, but, at the same time, he communicates a feeling of ambivalence toward the affluence of modern life. Suddenly, he gets an encouraging pat on the back from a fellow patient: "You just wait until we get a Social Democratic government. Then the times will change," says the man, obviously suffering from senile dementia. This seemingly trivial line carries a profound irony: although the old class society has been firmly supplanted by the modern welfare society, something has gone wrong with the original vision of *Folkhemmet*.

The conflict between the two modes of life built up in the film can be described with the well-known concepts *Gemeinschaft* and *Gesellschaft*.

While Gemeinschaft principally concerns a rural collective community, Gesellschaft refers to the transition into a mass society where social interaction is marked by impersonality, rationality, and competition.[23] The concepts, which have both a nostalgic and a critical edge, are illustrative of how the film overall depicts a social change for the worse. The transformation is mirrored in Pär's parents, who, on the one hand, lead down-to-earth lives, and, on the other hand, are adopting materialist values and status mentality. This duality can be sensed in a scene where Pär's father installs fashionable but ever so impractical saloon doors in their home: a sly, ironic depiction of a working-class man struggling to adorn his home with showy kitsch. Furthermore, the film juxtaposes Pär's mother and father with Annikas's petty, bourgeois parents, who personify the darker side of Gesellschaft. Several scenes take place in the latter couple's downtown flat, exposing the emptiness and angst behind the supercilious façade that they show in public. Besides their relationship as husband and wife, Annika's parents have little in common, and the atmosphere between them is spiteful. To them, life is nothing but material possessions and social competition.

A Swedish Love Story's representation of life in the modern welfare state echoes Marcuse's analysis in One-Dimensional Man, which differed from conventional Marxist thinking in that it attributed a potential for change to the not-yet fully socialized young generation rather than to the working class. For Marcuse, the problem of the superstructure was the willful subordination of the mass to the capitalist industrial society due to the fruits of mass production, with affluence reducing the people's will to question the system. The welfare state, he argued, was repressive in the degree to which it promoted the satisfaction of needs, which require continuing the rat race of catching up with one's peers and enjoying freedom from using one's brain.[24] In A Swedish Love Story, Annika's father, John, a simpleminded refrigerator salesman, literally seems to be a one-dimensional man, ignorant of his own materialistic conformism. Roy Andersson has explained his fascination with the middle class and its uncertain, middle position in the social structure: "It always wants a little more than it ever gets and hence looks upon its failures with greater bitterness than the working class or upper class."[25] Much of the tragicomedy of John, a firm supporter of modern capitalism, lies precisely in his inability to live up to his own hollow ideals of success, as highlighted in a corporate party scene, where he is granted the humiliating "honor" of handing out awards to younger, more successful colleagues. Overall, the stilted party scene offers an acidic view of the banality of the new material-istic culture, as dressed-up salesmen with families gladly participate in the vacuous event, listening attentively to the managing director's insipid speech about a new refrigerator model.

The film's negative view of the new culture of the welfare state is emphasized through the ambivalent depiction of the teenage genera-tion, which collectively adopts the mentality of the adult world. This negative process of socialization, characterized by conformity and status thinking, hampers the innocent romance between Annika and Pär, who for a long time restrain their feelings due to social pressure and inner insecurities. Thus the young couple's ability to eventually overcome the repressive mentality has an important thematic func-tion: their blossoming love serves as an idealized, contrasting image of heightened and unrestrained life.

The film's finale is a culmination of the conflict between Gemein-schaft and Gesellschaft, portraying a crayfish party at the summer cot-tage of Pär's parents, at which Annika's family are guests. Traditionally viewed as an event of social equality—eating shellfish with the fingers makes refinement difficult—the crayfish party in Andersson's film becomes a veritable social battleground as the partygoers, under the influence of alcohol, lose their civility and inhibitions. The salesman John, in particular, loses his head after failing miserably to impress and outdo the host (whom he views as socially inferior), smashing all his fancy wine bottles and wandering off into the early morning mist. His conceited self-image has been shaken, and he vents his pent-up frustration and hopes that his daughter will have greater success in life than himself. "She shall be rich, rich, rich, rich . . . so she doesn't have to suck up to other bastards," he rants to himself, sobbing as he adds, "as I had to do." In a way, John's monologue reflects the fact that he is simultaneously the most simpleminded and clear-sighted person in the film, having grasped the underlying premises of the hollow, materialistic culture that he ignorantly embraces. The last image in *A Swedish Love Story* shows the salesman and the other partygoers who went looking for him, and who also got lost in the mist, marching home across a field, crestfallen and confused. Thus the film ends with a tragicomic tableau of a generation that has lost its way, both literally and figuratively, but that does not understand what has happened to the community or even that something has gone seriously wrong.

LIFE IN LIMBO

After the success of his debut film, Roy Andersson had big plans for a second film, with the working title *Two Brothers, One Sister* (*Två bröder, en syster*). But Europa Film pulled out of the production due to financial difficulties, and the project was never developed. In general, the 1970s became years of stagnation for Swedish film production, as SFI's big drive for art cinema proved less successful in the long run. While the film reform vitalized the climate for Swedish film for a short period, a handful of international successes could not compensate for the relentless downturn in the domestic market. Ultimately, this was largely due to the impact of television, but the problem ran deeper. The film school produced few talents of the caliber of Bergman or Widerberg, and a perception of a lack of quality and audience appeal began to spread within the industry.[26] According to Andersson, the so-called film crisis mirrored not only a deficiency in skill and creativity within the industry but also an overall lull in the social debate.[27]

Andersson's argument had poignancy, since the enthusiasm of 1968 had begun to wane by the mid-1970s. But it also reflected his increasingly irreverent stance, as he made a string of biting statements about the fundamental poverty and provincialism of Swedish cinema. As Colin Wilson points out in his classic study *The Outsider*, many modern artists have distinguished themselves by embracing an outsider status: a refusal of subjugation being one effective way to mark one's own originality and talent. Another characteristic outsider trait, according to Wilson, is the claim to be able to "see through the façade,"[28] and, in the case of Andersson, his lucidity extended to both cinema and politics. Although political radicalism had become a highly fashionable stance in the cultural scene of the 1970s, Andersson, in the spirit of the nondogmatic New Left of the 1960s, expressed doubts about the more dominant and doctrinaire revolutionary Marxist-Leninist movement, profiling himself as, in many ways, an iconoclastic filmmaker. Or, as he stated himself, "I really cannot compromise."[29]

The depth of Andersson's willfulness became apparent with his next project, *Giliap*. During the production (which dragged on for two years), rumors started to circulate about heated conflicts and creative crises, and when the film finally premiered it had dramatically exceeded its budget. Even worse, *Giliap* became a box-office fiasco and was savaged by the critics as pretentious and boring. Arguably, the film was an unexpected departure from *A Swedish Love Story*, in both style and tone. Far from the poetic impressionism and bittersweet irony of Andersson's debut film, *Giliap* was a gloomy and more overtly serious film, mostly shot in long takes from a distance to underscore the stagnancy and tediousness of everyday life. The director explained his new austere realism in terms of an ambition to cultivate an aesthetic of resistance to the intensified and intrinsically superficial experience of life that, according to him, had become characteristic of contemporary consumption society as well as modern cinema. In short, he was striving for a more radical synthesis of form and content, capable of concretizing the reification of social life and the deeper meaning hidden in humdrum existence. Basically, he wanted to show that "life is really so god-damn rich and grand, but the possibilities to enjoy the magnificent are so small."[30]

While Andersson himself saw *Giliap* as a development of politically committed cinema, his new stylized cinematography and defamiliarization technique were partly reminiscent of the aesthetics that the 1960s film generation had reacted against. Overall, the negative view of a supposedly bourgeois and elitist modernism, which had become dominant in the cultural debate of the 1970s,[31] was reflected in some of the reviews of *Giliap*. One critic claimed that the film was "almost reactionary,"[32] and another even compared it to "Bergman's 1940s cinema, with its vain trials of escape from the prisons of life."[33] But while clearly an anomaly in Swedish social-realist cinema (although hardly in contemporary European political film modernism),[34] Andersson's revised cinematic vision could be said to reflect a broader tendency in national film and literature toward pessimistic narratives about the possibility of social change in the wake of the political conflicts and economic crisis of the early 1970s.[35] As a bleak social comment, one may compare *Giliap* to, for example, the acclaimed writer Lars Gustafsson's trilogy *The Cracks in the Wall* (*Sprickorna i muren*; 1971–75) or Ulf Lundell's bestselling generational novel *The Sleep* (*Sömnen*; 1977)—both representing the mental climate of post-1968 Swedish welfare society as characterized by emptiness, lost ideals, and collective resignation.

The fact that Andersson had not only directed a spectacular flop but also made a name for himself within the film industry as a difficult perfectionist did not prevent him from sharpening his criticism of the mediocrity of Swedish cinema and the incompetence at the SFI—this at a time when he was even more dependent on funding. By the late 1970s, Swedish film production was in decline, and SFI had become a more or less obligatory partner, a development that affected the careers of many film workers. While the art-film institution made it possible for well-established directors such as Vilgot Sjöman to continue making films, despite poor reviews and disappointing box-office returns,[36] the small size of the national film industry and the concentration of power in the SFI became a serious problem for others. Although the management at SFI shifted, the doors of the art-film institution remained shut to Andersson and other unruly filmmakers such as Widerberg, who, despite his stature as a distinguished and popular auteur, was forced to turn to television. It was at this point that Roy Andersson truly became an outsider of Swedish cinema and not only by his own choice.

GILIAP

Giliap was a dramatically different film than *A Swedish Love Story*, in terms of its analysis of the state of society. Whereas Andersson's debut film investigated a shift from Gemeinschaft to Gesellschaft, emphasizing the polarization between genuine life and reified materialism, *Giliap* depicted a petrified world characterized by grayness. While partly a traditional, existential art film (burdened by somewhat overly pretentious dialogue), it nevertheless staked out the personal style—marked by realistic, poetic, and symbolic depictions of a society in limbo—to which Andersson's later work would consistently return: a world in a state of suspension between yesterday and tomorrow. *Giliap* takes place at Hotel Busarewski, an establishment past its prime where the anonymous title character, a young man nicknamed "Giliap," becomes a "waiter," both literally and figuratively; he is restlessly longing for a different life, yet is incapable of breaking free from his dull routines due to an inner passivity.

In terms of dramatic form, *Giliap* inverted the modernist art-film formula. The typical postwar European art film told a story about an estranged person who has lost all his essential contacts with the world and his own identity. Though clearly an abstract individual in this mold, agonizing over the emptiness of existence, the title character of *Giliap* was not the kind of upper-middle-class intellectual that one would find in the films of, for example, Bergman or Antonioni. Andersson anchored the drama of the human condition in the monotonous life of the common workingman, which meant his protagonist lacked the cultural and social capital typical of the heroes of 1960s art cinema.[37] Through a pondering character without the means to fully articulate his existential crisis, *Giliap* highlighted ordinary people's difficulty in thinking outside the conditions that confine their lives. At the same time, the film revised the conventions of 1960s leftist political drama by emphasizing the existential aspects of the alienation of the working class: without an emotional or intellectual language, the people working at the hotel are incapable of achieving community, and, consequently, they lead a collective life of alienation and passivity.

The film was, as mentioned, critically panned for being boring. But one can also say that it is characterized by an aesthetic of boredom, insofar as the subdued color scheme and stagnant narrative amplify the impression of listlessness. The notion of boredom, as a sense that the world has lost its meaning,[38] is reflected in the film's deliberate pacing. *Giliap* is built around scenes of routine work and feelings of emptiness, with the framing of the action in extended long shots emphasizing the characters' limited ability to affect their situation. Hotel Busarewski, a place where time seems to have been at a standstill for many years, is, of course, an allegory for the stagnation of the Swedish society, the people carrying on with their lives in a vacuum. The grumpy, wheelchair-bound restaurant steward is a key figure, struggling to maintain the illusion that Busarewski is the same distinguished establishment that it once was, but, as indicated by his outmoded manners and physical disability, he is hopelessly stuck in life. The steward's situation is viewed in a particularly tragicomic light in a scene where he meticulously prepares for a visit from the hotel management, but no one shows up, and he finds himself alone with his lifelong deception. Though it remains unclear what exactly has supplanted the old society, the negligence of the management gives a hint of the new spirit of the times. The society in *Giliap* is characterized by the loss of civic spirit, solidarity, and social equality—fundamental values of the culture of the welfare state. The word "solidarity" could be said to refer not only to the notion of unity and mutual responsibility but also to the ability to recognize oneself in the imperfection and weakness of others.[39] In the first scene in the film, a drunken customer gets thrown out of the hotel into the street. A couple of Salvationists sneak by and try not to look at the man rising from the wet cobblestones, indicating that even God's soldiers have lost the ability to show love for their fellow man. A rare glimpse of what is lacking is given in a scene when an impish old man accidentally spills soup on himself in the hotel restaurant. A long shot of the man standing in the dining hall, surrounded by people ever so gently cleaning his shirtsleeve, makes visible the otherwise absent human capacity for collective compassion.

This spontaneous display of solicitude is darkly echoed in a later scene, where the storeroom manager of the hotel ("the count," as he calls himself) burns a beggar with his cigarette during a night on the town, just to prove his social superiority. The count is a simpleminded person who tries to play what he believes to be the game of success in the new society, boasting to Giliap about his understanding of the fundamentals of life. Yet the count's petty, get-rich-quick schemes, "masterminding" thefts of food and goods from the hotel's storerooms, along with his vain attempts to make himself into someone important, cast an air of ridiculousness over his person, so that the character becomes a personification of Jean-Paul Sartre's existentialist concept of bad faith.[40] A typical expression of bad faith, according to Sartre, is to shun an authentic life by adapting to one's circumstances (like the old restaurant steward), but a person can also live in bad faith by subordinating oneself to false, transcendent values. Even more explicitly than the materialistic salesman in *A Swedish Love Story*, the count rejects the ideals of human love and social equality as relics of the past, and orders his life according to a homespun, every-man-for-himself philosophy. But *Giliap*, at the same time, paints a complicated picture of the protagonist, who also lives in bad faith. While remaining ambivalent about the camaraderie of the count, the title character consciously avoids forming bonds with other people. Pondering the inadequacy of life and living in the illusion that he one day will travel to faraway places, he withdraws from a beautiful and good-hearted colleague with whom he has fallen in love, thus suppressing his freedom and personality in favor of an *idée fixe*. Although in his later films Andersson would avoid romantic subplots and character-centered narratives, instead presenting panoramas of social life and attitudes in modern society, his focus on the common man's ignorance of his own negative values and his contribution to his own unhappiness would be central in his future work.

THE RADICAL TURN

After *Giliap*, Roy Andersson found himself out in the cold. However, since the beginning of his career, he had made commercials as a sideline, and, while vowing to make a comeback, he pursued what arguably would become *the* most prolific career in the history of Swedish film advertising: directing a string of widely popular commercials for high-profile customers such as the insurance company Trygg-Hansa and the national lottery Lotto. He rapidly gained a considerable reputation as an ingeniously funny as well as exceptionally quality-conscious maker of commercials, even spending more money on some ads than he was paid for making them. "Roy Andersson is Sweden's most successful director of commercials ever. No one has received as many prizes, domestic and foreign, as he has. He is a renowned international master in the genre, idiosyncratic and personal in a way that few others are," stated a newspaper feature in 1991.[41]

Arguably, Andersson's career in advertising is tied to the cultural transformations of Sweden during the 1980s, not only in the sense that the film advertising industry was booming at the time. A common view is that welfare society took an individualistic and materialistic turn during the decade. Not least, the yuppie phenomenon and the Swedish Employers Association's 1979 campaign "*Satsa på dig själv*" (Invest in yourself) have been regarded as signs of the changing times.[42] The shift was also marked by a broad affirmation of private consumption, everyday luxury, and "just having a good time"—values that ran counter to the presumed anticommercialism and moral puritanism of the 1970s. This tendency was reflected in Swedish cinema insofar as the production of art films was, to some extent, overshadowed by the increased output of light entertainment and genre films.[43] Also, SFI stepped down as an independent producer, and the funding system was revised so that it comprised not only artistically valuable films but also commercially successful ones.[44] Probably the most significant sign of the broad commercialization of the national media culture was the end of the public television monopoly in 1987, when the new, private television channel TV3 started to operate, airing commercials in Sweden for the first time in the nation's television history.

At the same time that Andersson (as a self-realized media entrepreneur and a director of popular commercials) reflected the ideals of success in the society of the 1980s, he strove hard to reconcile his contradictory role as a left-wing auteur and an advertising man, humorously sharing his blunt opinion on everything from the banality of the advertising industry to the necessity for a state-regulated market. Furthermore, Andersson profiled himself as a socially conscious maker of commercials, with an ironic distance from the generic message of happiness through consumption, a famous example being his Lotto films that tragicomically depicted frustrated players who missed the reading of the winning numbers. In interviews, he explicitly renounced "the sort of commercials that appeal only to 'winners'" and attach no importance to the "common man's struggle to get along in life."[45] In fact, he more or less used his work in advertising as an alternative artistic platform, developing his critical realism and launching the more experimental style of the complex image in 1985, which became a template for his filmmaking from then on. Andersson attributed to his refined tableau style, characterized by both heavy stylization and heightened ironies, a potential to clarify humanistic and political truths in more drastic and literal terms—the smallness and frailness of humanity becoming more apparent when contrasted against an abstract background of sterile rooms and standardized furniture.[46]

A watershed film for the director was his much talked about election film for the Social Democrats in 1985, *Why Should We Care about Each Other?* (*Varför ska vi bry oss om varandra*). The fact that Andersson, still a proclaimed radical socialist, closely associated himself with the labor party (at least for a time) can partly be viewed in the context of the changing political landscape. In 1976, the labor party was defeated in a general election for the first time in 44 years, and the 1970s was widely held to be the end of the *Folkhemmet* epoch and the beginning of the dismantling of the postwar welfare state model.[47] Although the Social Democrats later regained the government, the party (as well as the entire left) was faced with a strong new ideological contender in the form of neoliberalism, in European politics spearheaded by Margaret Thatcher, who famously declared that "there is no such thing as society." In interviews, Andersson stated that he had decided to side with the party in a time of crisis when socialism clearly stood against neoliberalism.[48] Drawing on the labor party's assertions that the parties of the right fundamentally threatened the welfare model with their promises of cuts to taxes and the public sector, *Why Should We Care about Each Other?* was crafted to provoke reflection about the outcome of neoliberal politics. Describing the message and the reception of the election film, one journalist wrote, "Bang! If the right seizes power, egoism will reign. Patients who can't pay for themselves will receive no care, children without money for school meals will be thrown out [of the lunchroom] . . . Bravo, the audience yells in one establishment. In another cinema, the spectators boo and throw candy wrappers at the screen."[49]

Overall, the late 1980s became a time of both great success and controversy for Andersson, who, to considerable acclaim, turned out increasingly offbeat commercials. But some customers rejected his works as too idiosyncratic, among them KF (Kooperativa Förbundet), the Swedish cooperative federation. While KF wanted to revamp its rather old-fashioned image to match the new consumer spirit of the 1980s, Andersson unabashedly poked fun at the dullness of the chain's image in his commercial, ironically portraying scenes of lugubrious everyday culinary life. The director firmly defended his concept by claiming that if he had represented KF as an exclusive brand, it would have been nothing less than a betrayal of the historical ideals of the labor movement. He argued that the chain, on the contrary, should take an active stand for the dignity and greatness of the common worker, regardless of his or her financial status.[50]

Andersson's most outlandish work during the period was the 1987 AIDS information film *Something Happened* (*Någonting har hänt*). In 1986, the Swedish National Board of Health and Welfare had engaged him to make a film about AIDS and safe sex to be screened for a youth audience. However, during the production, Andersson became convinced that the official account of the origins of HIV was a lie. As he saw it, the medical establishment had tried to cover up the truth with the story "that nature, suddenly, developed the disease down in the jungles of Africa," when, in fact, AIDS was the result of a technological accident in Western genetic laboratories.[51] Colored both by the dystopian atmosphere after the Chernobyl nuclear disaster and by the conspiracy culture after the assassination of Prime Minister

Olof Palme, *Something Happened* developed into a fierce critique of the scientific community. In a string of darkly comic scenes, rational science was portrayed as essentially simpleminded, Eurocentric, and antihumanist. The National Board of Health reacted strongly against Andersson's take on the subject and cancelled the project. The disagreement between the director and the client turned into a public controversy, where Andersson lambasted the authorities for trying to divert the public's attention from the real issue: the authoritarian rationality and the destructive capability of modern society.

As time went by, Roy Andersson grew increasingly alone in his fierce dedication to the conspiracy theory, but the much talked about *Something Happened* nevertheless paved the way for his return to cinematic filmmaking. His reputation as a wronged visionary had steadily grown since the mid-1970s, and eventually the Gothenburg International Film Festival gave him an opportunity to direct a short film as part of the relay film *90 minutes in the 90s* (*90 minuter 90-tal*). Andersson proudly stated that his ambition with *World of Glory* (*Härlig är jorden*; 1991) was to probe more deeply into the dark themes of the contested AIDS film.[52] Inspired by Polish director Krzysztof Kieślowski's *The Decalogue* (1989), his aim was to elucidate the general lack of humanity and higher moral ideals in contemporary society in relation to a source of national guilt: Sweden's appeasement politics toward Nazi Germany during the war.

WORLD OF GLORY

"Many people have said that the opening scene of *World of Glory* is the darkest they have ever seen," Andersson wrote apropos his own depiction of a genocide event in everyday suburbia.[53] In the shot, a crowd watches as naked men, women, and children are huddled like cattle in a closed truck parked in a gravel lot. "I don't want to!" a girl cries out in terror before she is forced into the truck. A tube, oozing smoke, is connected between the exhaust pipe of the vehicle and the compartment where the people are shut in. The vehicle starts up and drives slowly around in circles, while the onlookers watch indifferently.

To more fully grasp the drastic shift from the gloomy yet fragile drama of *Giliap* to the profound cultural pessimism of *World of Glory*, one may look at *Why Should We Care about Each Other?* In a series of drastically ironic vignettes, the election film describes a society devoid of solidarity. The first tableau depicts an overcrowded and run-down geriatric ward, into which a nurse wheels a new patient, but she just lets the bed roll on so that it crashes into another one. The whole situation seems absurd in its utter carelessness, but everyone acts as if nothing has happened. In a way, with the film Andersson found the fusion of form and content that he was aiming for with *Giliap*, while expanding his scope. His more stylized aesthetic milieus were, not least, characterized by a temporal vagueness, reminiscent of both 1950s *Folkhemmet* and 1980s Sweden, creating an impression of a past modernity with only the shell of the welfare state remaining. This made the message of the election film quite ambivalent. While obviously satirizing neoliberal society, its images of run-down institutions and public locales also lead to thoughts of a socialist state in decay, the sceneries having a distinct stamp of functionalism—an architectonic style not only associated with the historical welfare state project but also, at the time, increasingly criticized for being the manifestation of too instrumental a conception of human life.[54] Thus the film painted a darkly ironic image of a society derailed by the rampant antihumanism of both the state and the capital.

Andersson deepened his perspective in his second election film for the labor party in 1988, *Can We Care about Each Other?* (*Kan vi bry oss om varandra*), which depicted a dull, materialistic society drained of life. In the film, persons from different social classes speak straight into the camera about what they want most in life: one of them dreams about a sailboat, a second about a place to live, a third about lower taxes, a fourth about friends. Regardless of their dreams, they all seem listless and deeply alienated from the community. In this way, Andersson not only contrasts conflicting social attitudes—Gemeinschaft versus Gesellschaft, *homo collectivus* versus *homo economicus*—but also represents a radically dehumanized society without spirit. Thus one can say that the director, in a more explicit and categorical way, has focused on the disintegration of the welfare state project, his images of drab apartments and institutions inhabited by pale, predominantly middle-aged figures signaling the failure of the historical social vision that had once inspired them.

In the AIDS film *Something Happened*, Andersson bluntly posed the question of how modern society could truly combat the lethal disease if it had lost the spirit of life, as underscored in a scene of a sex education class. A teacher instructs the pupils on how to put condoms onto bizarre-looking rubber dummies, but without explaining what they are doing or why, only assuring the children that "this is very, very natural." The scene, which satirizes the authorities' inability to talk about not only the disease but also love and mutual caring, is followed by a series of downright shocking depictions of the inhumanity of modern rationality. In a tableau of a medical experiment in a concentration camp, Nazi soldiers drop blocks of ice into a basin where a Jewish man is standing, naked and shivering. The presence of doctors in white coats and a pile of corpses in the background reinforces the impression of a rationally executed inhumanity. In *Modernity and the Holocaust*, Zygmunt Bauman, another scholar working in the tradition of Critical Theory, argued that the Nazi genocide was an extreme consequence of the civilization process that emancipated the "desiderata of rationality from the interference of ethical norms and moral inhibitions."[55] In *Something Happened*, Andersson makes a similar, explicit parallel between the mentality behind the Holocaust and the mechanics of modern life, the motif of the sex education scene and the concentration camp tableau essentially being expressions of the same capability of modern society to drastically reduce human subjects to objects.

This bleak analysis was further sharpened in *World of Glory*. A reference to a well-known hymn (the Swedish version of "Fairest Lord Jesus"), the short film's title establishes a darkly ironic incongruity between an idealistic notion of the world and the world as portrayed in the film. The opening genocide scene sets the stage of a world drained of all moral and spiritual values. Among the indifferent onlookers of the gassing is a pale, middle-aged man, who turns out to be the main character of the film, which develops into a kind of trailer for his life, presenting various sides of his everyday existence in a string of tableaux. But although the character speaks directly and earnestly to the camera, he remains strangely aloof to the spectator, largely because the blankness of his face mirrors his inner world. The second scene shows the man sitting next to his mother's hospital bed: "I am very fond of her," he says, but his voice is flat, and when the old woman seeks his hand, he pushes it aside.

The man, a realtor, is an even more one-dimensional person than the petty, bourgeois salesman in *A Swedish Love Story*. "This is my bed," he says when he presents his home. "I eat breakfast in the kitchen and dinner too, mostly," he continues, unknowingly exposing his painfully hollow existence and instrumental view of life. When he shows his car in the street, all he says is this: "I am very pleased with it. I think it is good." While there is something tragicomic about the character, the spectator cannot help but view him in the grim light of the geno-cide, which may be a dream or a vision or even a haunting memory. *World of Glory* is a study of a man that is, at the same time, banal, horrific, and just one person in a crowd. A connection between the realtor's attitude and the social climate is made in a scene in which he shows an apartment to a young couple. "There are many people who want an apartment like this, especially young people. But they don't have any money. And if you don't have any money, you can't get an apartment," he curtly explains. The man's condescension toward the couple mirrors his indifference to the mass killing, making the film's perspective rather similar to Hannah Arendt's thesis on the banality of evil,[56] but, even more so, to the Norwegian-Swedish philosopher Harald Ofstad's provocative argument in *Our Contempt for Weakness* (*Vårt förakt för svaghet*). According to Ofstad, an intrinsic part of the Nazi ideology—social Darwinism—lived on in the modern democra-cies; while the welfare state is characterized by institutionalized care-taking, the system nevertheless fosters competition, admiration for the successful, and contempt for the weak.[57] In the same vein, *World of Glory* portrays both a materialistic culture and a moral blindness in modern society, grounded on the repression of its premises. As a reminder of the underlying capability of contemporary society, the gas truck can be discerned in the background of a street scene. And at night, the man, plagued by a nagging sense of guilt, stands wide awake in his bedroom, trying desperately to discern whether the harrowing screams he hears are imaginary or real. "You've got to get some sleep or you'll have a hard day tomorrow," says his wife, a line that hints at how modern, everyday life demands a numbness of the spirit.

A BLEAK PROPHECY

As a critical comment about Swedish society and the legacy of Nazism, *World of Glory* stood out as exceptionally unrelenting, even compared to prior dark allegories on the subject, such as P. C. Jersild's 1968 novel *The Pig Hunt* (*Grisjakten*), a satire about an overly rational bureaucrat in charge of a mission to exterminate all the pigs on Gotland, or Hans Alfredson's 1982 film *The Simple-Minded Murderer* (*Den enfaldige mördaren*), a metaphysical drama about the evil of a fascist capitalist in 1930s Sweden. In fact, Andersson's statement was drastic even in the context of the contemporary revisionist debate that was raging about the history of *Folkhemmet*, with the disclosure of the extent of the state's appeasement politics toward Nazi Germany, as well as its social engineering in terms of eugenics and compulsory sterilization contributing to a far-reaching deconstruction of the idea of *Folkhemmet* as a model society (see Ola Sigurdson's Chapter 1 on hygiene, health, and the Swedish ideals of modernity).[58] But while the debates categorically focused on the perceived dark side of the welfare state—even Gunnar and Alva Myrdal, two of the most revered Social Democratic figureheads, were ascribed a protofascist mentality—the majority of the critics focused their critical acumen on the historical burdens of guilt.[59] Thus even in the context of the heated debate, Andersson was among the very few to draw direct parallels between the national passivity during the war and the mentality of the contemporary welfare state.

The late 1980s and early 1990s also marked a new stage in Andersson's career insofar as he assumed the public role of an argumentative intellectual. This was partly a consequence of the controversy regarding the AIDS film and another idiosyncratic publicity campaign, *Successful Freezing of Mr. Moro* (*Lyckad nedfrysning av herr Moro*; 1992), a project commissioned by the County Council of Stockholm to increase interest in health-care education among young people in which Andersson raised critical questions about the existential values of contemporary society. While entertaining an intellectual profile in the same antiestablishment vein as many contemporary left-wing writers and artists, he distinguished himself by keeping a singular, old-school profile. The director not only emphasized the importance of traditional, Western humanist thought and dismissed the relativistic intellectual ideals of postmodernity (which had a considerable impact on the intellectual climate in the 1980s),[60] but he also cultivated a prophetic streak. Citing an eclectic range of modern thinkers, including Sartre, Bauman, philosopher Martin Buber, and political scientist Robert D. Putnam, he talked gravely about the deterioration of civic spirit and the need for holism as well as collective reflection on social values and spiritual goals. Arguably remaining more of a filmmaker with an intellectual idealism than an established social commentator, Andersson nevertheless carved out a niche for himself as, at the same time, a radical and an old-fashioned, moralistic critic of Swedish society. "A doomsday prophet? Thank heavens, in this era when the TV sofa seems to be associated with the highest form of artistic regeneration," one critic wrote.[61]

In 1995, Andersson published the scorching critical tract *Our Times' Fear of Seriousness* (*Vår tids rädsla för allvar*). While it is a work of great ambition and scope, the book can be described as a synthesis of his prior criticisms of the sad state of art and society—the lack of ideals of the powers that be, the antihumanism of rational modernity and modern capitalism, as well as the mediocrity and crass commercialism of the cinema. However, in the book, Andersson connected his various statements into a comprehensive and profoundly pessimistic analysis, more or less in line with the Critical Theory of Theodor Adorno and Max Horkheimer. The general thesis in Adorno and Horkheimer's *The Dialectic of Enlightenment*—the standardization of culture and the reification of all social forms in modern mass society[62]—is more or less echoed in *Our Times' Fear of Seriousness*, in which Andersson wrote about a nihilistic consensus mentality permeating all spheres of Swedish society and promoting the purging of serious thought.[63] In fact, he made direct parallels between Sweden, which in the early 1990s was in an economic recession and witnessing the rise of neo-Nazism, and Weimar Germany. He even symbolically associated his own filmmaking with *Entartete Kunst* (degenerate art), which was what the Nazi regime labeled the works of critical modernist artists such as Otto Dix and George Grosz, who, wrote Andersson, "with all imaginable visuality tried to open the eyes of people and warn them about the mounting catastrophe."[64]

While probably considered too idiosyncratic to generate serious debate, Andersson's tract nevertheless garnered critical acclaim and a cult following. It also contributed to his reputation as a visionary artist with the potential to create a film of great originality if only he were given the opportunity—an opinion expressed regularly in the media and not least by the director himself. Ever since the fiasco with *Giliap*, Andersson had talked far and wide about his spectacular plans for a new feature film, while at the same time lambasting the management of SFI and flaunting his unwillingness to compromise, most likely undermining his chances of securing financial support. Thus the news that Roy Andersson, after more than twenty years, had started the production of *Songs from the Second Floor*, initially paying out of his own pocket before being granted funding by SFI, made big headlines: "The Cinematic Genius from the 1970s Is Back," proclaimed a newspaper article in 1998.[65] Displaying absolute confidence, Andersson stated not only that he was making a film such as had never been seen before—meticulously shooting it over a period of several years—but also that it was an "important summary of the current state of the society and how we should proceed."[66] The director's stupendous ambition would surely have seemed absurd if it were not for the fact that *Songs from the Second Floor* not only won the Jury Prize at the Cannes Film Festival but also became an unlikely domestic box-office success, hailed by the critics as one of the greatest masterpieces of Swedish cinema. Commonly described by the media in terms of a personal redemption of the director—"a moral tale about the victory of willfulness over the will to compromise," one journalist wrote[67]—with the film's success, Roy Andersson finally became recognized as an artist of the stature that he himself, for a very long time, had claimed to be.

SONGS FROM THE SECOND FLOOR

Songs from the Second Floor, Andersson's grand statement about the condition of the welfare state, presents a dystopian panorama of a society that has ground to a halt. An early scene literally depicts how the old magic has lost its power: during a show, a magician fails to perform a routine act of sawing a man in half. Baffled, the magician looks at the wailing man in the box. In the film, the entire society is imbued with a dead-end atmosphere and paralyzed by apocalyptic phenomena: a procession of flagellants roams through the streets, just like during the plague years in medieval Europe, and the city is congested by a huge traffic jam of people literally stuck in life.

The sense of doom is driven by the fear of a financial crisis that bewilders the politicians. In *Our Times' Fear of Seriousness*, Andersson accused the Swedish politicians of showing the same mentality as the rulers of Weimar Germany, a "cadet logic" based on pure arbitrariness and shortsightedness, and due to their effeteness and wishful thinking that everything would go back to how it once was, he wrote, they compromised their principles and handed the future to the dangerous whims of fate.[68] In *Songs from the Second Floor*, the hidebound politicians put their trust in superstition, deciding to sacrifice the younger generation in the hope of appeasing the falling stocks. In a stunningly absurd tableau, the pillars of society—the government, the church, the union, and the royal family—gather by a gravel pit, banners flying in the wind. A crowd of thousands watches with reverence as a young girl is walked out on a plank over the chasm. As the queen strides forward and gives the girl a push to her death, a choir breaks into the hymn "Children of the Heavenly Father." However, the financial crisis is, in essence, the result of the politicians leaving the power to the ruthless forces of the market, and, at the end of the film, the heads of the market flee the country and the economic chaos they have caused. In a mass tableau, satirizing neoliberal individualism and the freedom of capital to move without any regard for social responsibilities, a horde of capitalists make their way through an airport terminal, pushing small mountains of suitcases and golf bags. But Andersson also delivers a broadside against the old capitalist structure and reactionary hierarchy that has prevailed in the welfare society. One scene depicts the hundredth birthday of one of the "wealthiest landowners in the country," a senile military general, who, when reverently congratulated by his colleagues, responds, "Send my regards to Göring," and raises his arm in a Sieg Heil salute.

The central character of *Songs from the Second Floor*, Kalle, is yet another one of Andersson's middle-class materialists living a life in bad faith: a down-on-his-luck salesman whose philosophy of life is to buy things that can be sold "with an extra zero added." Although not as heartless as the realtor in *World of Glory*, Kalle is nevertheless a complacent cog in a society that literally has turned into a Gesellschaft, building on the mindless exploitation of his fellow human beings. "Life is a market, it's as simple as that," says an unscrupulous business associate of Kalle's. Even the Christian message of love has come up for grabs, as Kalle's associate has hatched a plan to flog cheaply made crucifixes for "Jesus's two-thousandth birthday." As the height of irony, the plan fails, but not because of its tastelessness. Altruistic love has simply become passé. "How could I be so stupid as . . . to think you could make money on a crucified loser," sneers the businessman as he throws the worthless Jesus figures onto a scrap heap.

Songs from the Second Floor portrays a society permeated by the petty instinct of self-preservation. "One is only human," whines Kalle, "you can only do the best you can. Toil to put some food on the table and to have a little fun." But, although he is hiding in self-pity, he is literally haunted by ghosts from the past, among them a Jewish boy who was killed by the Nazis (symbolizing the national burden of guilt from the war) and the girl sacrificed by the establishment. Kalle tries to ignore the ghosts, but they keep pestering him, and the film culminates in the majestic closing scene where he stands alone in a desolate field outside the city. "I can't take it anymore," Kalle shouts at the ghosts approaching on a gravel road. But he cannot shake his guilty conscience; on the contrary, suddenly, a veritable army of ghosts rises from the field in front of him, signifying the vast moral debt he—and everybody else—has yet to face.

In the film, Andersson draws heavily on the poem "Stumble between Two Stars" (1937) by Cèsar Vallejo,[69] a Peruvian socialist poet who wrote about the vulnerability of the small man with great pathos. In a key scene at a mental hospital where one of Kalle's sons is being treated for depression, the young man, a poet, is comforted with lines from Vallejo's poem, one of which reads, "beloved is he who sits down." The poet cannot stop crying precisely because he "sat down," wrote about the life of humankind, and was struck by how badly everyone is treating each other. Andersson stages one of the hospital tableaux as a *pieta* in the Christian image tradition, depicting the poet surrounded by compassionate people, comforting him. "It's not dangerous to cry. You should cry when you are sad," says a fellow patient, while another inmate reminds him that Jesus was also tormented on the cross for being nice to other people.

Although *Songs from the Second Floor* oozes with irony, it shows no distance whatsoever from the Christian message of love. In fact, as a political moralist filmmaker, Andersson (privately an atheist) builds up a reverence for higher moral values that have been largely weakened in modernity. The director's criticism of a societal failure in a religious-existential sense is even more explicit in the film's thematic companion piece *You, the Living*. "Please dear Lord, forgive them," pleads a woman, kneeling in prayer in an assembly hall, while the other visitors sneak out the back. She continues, "Forgive those who think only of themselves. Forgive those who are greedy and cheap, those who cheat and deceive, those who get rich by paying lousy wages." Her preaching to deaf ears hints at a weak spot in the heart of modern society: that secularization has pushed aside the ethics of religion but without providing any compensating ethical framework.[70] A painful irony lies in the fact that the woman desperately confesses a collective guilt, while the society itself is not at all morally demanding. In the face of serious questions of conscience, people can simply withdraw.

While not as specifically focused on the disintegration of the welfare state as *Songs from the Second Floor*, *You, the Living*, in general terms, visualizes the experience of a modern age, where individualism and indifference overshadow human love. In a key scene, an aged psychiatrist complains of constantly having to "listen to patients who aren't satisfied with their lives, who want to have fun, who want me to help them with that." He explains, "They demand to be happy while at the same time they are egocentric, selfish, and ungenerous." People like that are impossible to help, claims the psychiatrist, who is not only too jaded but also too narrow-minded to reflect on the bigger causes and effects—nowadays, just prescribe pills, "the stronger the better." Ultimately, Andersson's films dramatize a curse of rational modern society: in a society that is bent on objectifying all spheres of the world, genuine life can only be found in the rare interruptions to the daily grind, as seen in the tableau in *Songs from the Second Floor* in which a man gets his finger stuck in a train door. While the majority of the commuters rush by on the platform, frowning at his misfortune, a handful of them have stopped to help him. Not knowing exactly what to do, they gawkily comfort and pat the man in a way that is both funny and moving, treating him with the same kind of tenderness that is conventionally reserved for children. The tableau emphasizes how humanity can be found in behaviors that are otherwise deemed ridiculous or contemptible in society; it is when Andersson's characters drop their public façade and expose their weakness and vulnerability that they display their flickering humanity. Thus it is in not only shocking scenes of cold rationality or indifference but also all-too-brief glimpses of solidarity and compassion that the director concentrates his critique of all that has gone wrong with the welfare society.

CONCLUSION: A BLAST FROM THE PAST

While *Songs from the Second Floor* established Roy Andersson as one of the prime figures of Swedish cinema of the 2000s, the director has remained an outsider, having less in common artistically and intellectually with younger, socially committed filmmakers such as Lukas Moodysson and Ruben Östlund (who was partly inspired by Andersson's work) than with old-school modernist European auteurs such as Michael Haneke and Béla Tarr—that is, the last believers in a cinema of a heroic statement, putting on display the existential and social ills of modern society and tracing the roots of these conditions in the universal human condition. Also, despite his remarkable comeback, Andersson had considerable difficulty securing funding for his next film, *You, the Living*, and he continued to take an antagonistic position in relation to the film establishment, accusing the decision makers at SFI of nepotism and incompetence before striking a decisive deal with the Franco-German television network Arte. In a way, one may consider Andersson's resurrected career to be as much the result of the dynamics of the European art-film market as of the national support for artistically valuable films.

Today, Andersson is perhaps the last living icon of 1960s Swedish art cinema (Bergman died in 2007, the year that *You, the Living* premiered), and, arguably, his public image has an added element of nostalgia, with his hearty personality, unassuming appearance, and moral ideals contributing to an image of a firm representative of a bygone era. But although Andersson's comeback coincided with a trend of nostalgia for the aesthetics and values of *Folkhemmet*—for example, both functionalist design and modern welfare state history have enjoyed a revival of attention in the national culture in recent years[71]—he has hardly softened his critique of Swedish society, past and present. While political parties on both the right and left have tried to reclaim and relaunch the concept of *Folkhemmet*, the director has maintained that although it is still a beautiful social vision, it has been seriously corrupted. Once siding with the Social Democrats in the 1980s, he has, like many other leftist intellectuals, been incensed by the party's gradual toning down of its traditional ideas of regulated capitalism and social equality.[72] Andersson, as categorical as ever, has even accused the labor party of contributing to the creation of the very kind of society that he depicted in the election film *Why*

Should We Care about Each Other?, as well as laying the ground for the success of the far-right nationalist party, the Sweden Democrats.[73] In 1995, he was writing on the supposedly prevailing attitude of nihilism and shortsightedness in a Swedish society stricken by an economic crisis and the rise of neo-Nazi violence, and he pointed out that the newspaper *Aftonbladet*, "the media flagship of the labor movement and the politics of solidarity, created the headline: 'You can profit from the currency crisis, too.' To be clear, the word 'you' was underlined in red."[74]

NOTES

1. J. Hoberman, "Suspended Animation" (2002), http://www.villagevoice.com/2002-07-02/film/suspended-animation (accessed January 31, 2013); and R. Ebert, "Songs from the Second Floor" (2002), http://www.rogerebert.suntimes.com/apps/pbcs.dll/article?AID=/20021101/REVIEWS/211010307/1023 (accessed March 18, 2014).
2. See Roy Andersson, *Vår tids rädsla för allvar* (Göteborg: Filmkonst, 1995).
3. Victor Shklovsky, *Theory of Prose* (Elmwood Park: Dalkey Archive, 1990).
4. See, for example, "De 25 bästa svenska filmerna," *FLM*, 17–18 (2012).
5. Berthil Åkerlund, *Insida: Svenska personligheter i intervju om drivkrafter och tro* (Uppsala: Cordia, 1992), 51.
6. Michael Lommel, "Die Erkaltung der Restwärme: Surreale Milleniumsbilder in Songs from the Second Floor," in *Surrealismus und Film: Von Fellini bis Lynch*, ed. Michael Lommel et al. (Bielefeld: Transcript, 2008); Dominique Russell, "The Ghost of the Second Floor," *Literature/Film Quarterly*, 36 (2008); Ursula Lindqvist, "Roy Andersson's Cinematic Poetry and the Spectre of César Vallejo," *Scandinavian Canadian Studies*, 19 (2010); Julianne Qiuling Ma Yang, *Towards a Cinema of Contemplation: Roy Andersson's Aesthetics and Ethics* (Dissertation, Hong Kong: University of Hong Kong, 2013).
7. See also Jan Holmberg, "Can We Bother about Each Other?," in *The Cinema of Scandinavia*, ed. Tytti Soila (London: Wallflower, 2005) and Dagmar Brunow, "The Language of the Complex Image: Roy Andersson's Political Aesthetics," *Journal of Scandinavian Cinema*, 1 (2011).
8. Peter Brunette, *Michael Haneke* (Chicago: University of Illinois Press, 2010), 1–2. See also John Orr, *Cinema and Modernity* (Oxford: Polity Press, 1993); András Bálint Kovács, *Screening Modernism: European Art Cinema, 1950–1980* (Chicago: University of Chicago Press, 2007); and James Naremore, *On Kubrick* (London: BFI, 2008).

9. Linda Hutcheon, *Irony's Edge: The Theory and Politics of Irony* (London: Routledge, 1995), 98.

10. For an excellent exception, see Peter Dahlén, Michael Forsman, and Klas Viklund, "Folkhemsdrömmen som sprack: Om den ironiska odramatiken i Roy Anderssons filmer," *Filmhäftet*, 1–2 (1990).

11. See Kovács, *Screening Modernism*.

12. Leif Furhammar, *Filmen i Sverige: En historia i tio kapitel och en fortsättning*. (Stockholm: Dialogos, 2003), 281–85.

13. Göran Gunér, "Filmskolan & Dramatiska institutet: Om Harry Schein och svensk filmutbildning," in *Citizen Schein*, ed. Lars Ilshammar, Pelle Snickars, and Per Vesterlund (Stockholm: Mediehistoriskt arkiv, 2010).

14. Bo Widerberg, *Visionen i svensk film* (Stockholm: Bonniers, 1962), 15.

15. Herbert Marcuse, *One-Dimensional Man: Studies in the Ideology of Advanced Industrial Society* (Boston: Beacon, 1991).

16. Kjell Östberg, *1968: När allting var i rörelse* (Stockholm: Prisma, 2002), 113, 122.

17. See Carl-Johan Malmberg, "Den vita sporten och den omöjliga neutraliteten," in *Svensk Filmografi 6: 1960–1969* (Stockholm: SFI, 1977).

18. "Säker debutfilm om tonårskärlek och vuxentristess" (review), *Dagens Nyheter*, April 25, 1970.

19. "En historia om Roy Andersson," *Chaplin*, 4 (1970).

20. "Okänd regissör får jättechans," *Dagens Nyheter*, March 11, 1969.

21. See Cecilia Mörner, *Vissa visioner: Tendenser i svensk biografdistribuerad fiktionsfilm 1967–1972* (Stockholm: Stockholm University, 2000).

22. Mariah Larsson, *Skenet som bedrog: Mai Zetterling och det svenska sextiotalet* (Lund: Sekel, 2006), 82–84.

23. Johan Asplund, *Essä om Gemeinschaft och Gesellschaft* (Göteborg: Korpen, 1991), 23, 63, 80.

24. Marcuse, *One-Dimensional Man*, 241.

25. "Kraschlandning för filmgeniet," *Arbetet*, February 25, 1989.

26. Furhammar, *Filmen i Sverige*, 323, 327–28.

27. *Filmkrönikan* (TV2, 1974 28/4).

28. Colin Wilson, *The Outsider* (London: Phoenix, 2001).

29. "Min nya film ska kännas i magen," *Expressen*, November 24, 1971.

30. "Det intressanta är 'det oviktiga,'" *Upsala Nya Tidning*, March 16, 1976.

31. Östberg, *1968*, 53.

32. "En dyster återkomst" (review), *Sydsvenska* Dagbladet, November 17, 1975.

33. "Halv framgång med Giliap" (review), *Dagens Nyheter*, November 17, 1975.

34. See David Bordwell, *Figures Traced in Light: On Cinematic Staging* (Berkeley: University of California Press, 2005), 157–58.

35. Peter Berglund, *Segrarnas sorgsna eftersmak: Om autencitetssträvan i Stig Larssons romaner* (Stockholm: Brutus Östlings bokförlag Symposion, 2004), 30–31.

36. See Lars Gustaf Andersson, "Den svenska konstfilmsinstitutionen," *Filmhäftet*, 1–2 (1995).

37. See Kovács, *Screening Modernism*, 65–69.

38. Lars Fr. H. Svendsen, *Långtråkighetens filosofi* (Stockholm: Natur and Kultur, 2003), 51, 156.

39. Sven-Eric Liedman, *Om Solidaritet: Att se sig själv i andra* (Stockholm: Bonniers, 1999), 55, 81.

40. Jean-Paul Sartre, *Being and Nothingness: An Essay on Phenomenological Ontology* (London: Routledge, 2000), 47–70.

41. "Behöll sin frihet i reklamfilmen," *Arbetet*, January 6, 1991.

42. Martin Wiklund, *I det modernas landskap: Historisk orientering och kritiska berättelser om det moderna Sverige mellan 1960 och 1990* (Stockholm: Brutus Östlings bokförlag Symposion, 2006), 320.

43. Ibid.

44. Furhammar, *Filmen i Sverige*, 253.

45. "Alla ropar på Roy," *Vi*, 48 (1988).

46. "Här kommer Roy," *Nöjesguiden*, 4 (1988).

47. See Göran Hägg, *Välfärdsåren: Svensk historia 1945–1986* (Stockholm: Wahlström & Widstrand, 2005) and Jenny Andersson, *När framtiden har hänt: Socialdemokratin och folkhemsnostalgin* (Stockholm: Ordfront, 2009).

48. "Tystnad—tagning," *Resumé*, 4 (1985).

49. "Oj, oj, vilket liv det blev Roy," *Aftonbladet*, April 16, 1985.

50. *Rekordmagazinet* (TV2, April 5 [1989]).

51. Ibid. It has later been claimed that the AIDS conspiracy theory has its origins in a disinformation campaign by the Soviet intelligence agency KGB and the East-German counterpart Stasi. For a critical review of Andersson's facts and his film, see Christoph Andersson, *Operation Norrsken: Om Stasi och Sverige under kalla kriget* (Stockholm: Norstedts, 2013).

52. "90-talet skildras av tio regissörer," *Arbetet*, February 2, 1990.

53. Andersson, *Vår tids rädsla*, 42.

54. See Hans Asplund, *Farväl till funktionalismen* (Stockholm: Atlantis, 1980).

55. Zygmunt Bauman, *Modernity and the Holocaust* (New York: Cornell University Press, 1989), 28.

56. Hannah Arendt, *Eichmann in Jerusalem: A Report on the Banality of Evil* (London: Penguin, 1994).

57. Harald Ofstad, *Vårt förakt för svaghet: Nazismens normer och värderingar—och våra egna* (Stockholm: Karneval, 2012), 213–14.

58. Yvonne Hirdman, *Att lägga livet till rätta: Studier i svensk folkhemspolitik* (Stockholm: Carlssons, 1989); Mia Pia Boëthius, *På heder och samvete:*

Sverige och andra världskriget (Stockholm: Norstedts, 1991); and Gunnar Broberg and Matthias Tydén, *Oönskade i folkhemmet: Rashygien och sterilisering i Sverige* (Stockholm: Gidlunds, 1991).

59. For an overview, see Conny Mithander, "Från mönsterland till monsterland: Folkhemska berättelse,'" in *Berättelse i förvandling: Berättande i ett intermedialt och tvärvetenskapligt perspektiv*, ed. Åke Bergvall, Yvonne Leffler and Conny Mithander (Karlstad: Karlstad University, 2000).

60. See Wiklund, *I det modernas landskap*, 285.

61. "Och här klipper Roy Andersson till" (review), *Aftonbladet*, August 24, 1995.

62. Theodor Adorno and Max Horkheimer, *Dialectic of Enlightenment: Philosophical Fragments* (Stanford: Stanford University Press, 2002).

63. Andersson, *Vår tids rädsla*, 11–12, 81–86.

64. Ibid., 72.

65. "Filmgeniet från 70-talet är tillbaka," *Sydsvenska* Dagbladet, May 3, 1998.

66. *The Greatness of the Small Man (Den lilla människans storhet)*, directed by Kjell Andersson and Bo Harringer (2000).

67. "Egensinnet segrade," *Göteborgs-Posten*, May 9, 2000.

68. Andersson, *Vår tids rädsla*, 83–84.

69. See Russell, "The Ghost of the Second Floor," and Lindqvist, "Roy Andersson's Cinematic Poetry."

70. See Zygmunt Bauman, *Postmodern Ethics* (Cambridge: Blackwell, 1993).

71. Andersson, *När framtiden har hänt*, 175.

72. Ibid., 88.

73. "Folkhemmets svanesång," *Filmhäftet*, 3 (2000).

74. Andersson, *Vår tids rädsla*, 87.

Chapter 5

Sex and Sin in a Multicultural Sweden

Andreas Johansson Heinö

Introduction

An examination of the Swedish soul must begin, I'm afraid, with sex.[1]

EVEN WELL INTO THE TWENTY-FIRST CENTURY, IT seems to be mandatory for an article on Sweden to give some attention to the myth of the "Swedish sin." The perception that there is a specific Swedish attitude in relation to sexuality has been reproduced in movies, literature, art, politics, and science for almost six decades. The idea of a free-minded, tolerant, and sexually progressive population was an essential part of the narrative of the Swedish welfare paradise. What happened to it?

In April 1955, *Time* magazine famously published an article titled "Sin and Sweden" about the Nordic country where, following the introduction of sexual education in public schools, the marginalization of the church, and the demise of Christian moral values, promiscuity among teens and premarital sex had become the norm. A decade later, when the sexual revolution had spread across America and parts of Western Europe, Sweden was perceived as the guiding light. In February 1968, United States Customs authorities seized copies of a new film by Swedish director Vilgot Sjöman, claiming it was obscene and pornographic material. Only after a decision by the United States Supreme Court in the spring of 1969 was *I Am Curious (Yellow)* released in American theaters, eventually becoming the most successful foreign film in US history (as measured by public attendance).

The title of Sjöman's movie, and its successor, *I Am Curious (Blue)*, obviously referred to the colors of the Swedish flag. In 1967, the very same year as *I Am Curious (Yellow)* premiered in Sweden, another soon-to-be famous Swedish intellectual, Carl Johan de Geer, used the flag for an art project: a painting of a burning Swedish flag with the equivalent of the "F-word" written across the yellow cross. De Geer's work still stands as a symbol of the antinationalist ideals that became articulated at that time. In the space of a few years, the meaning of words such as "patriotism," "national values," "fatherland," and "tradition" changed dramatically, for coming generations they symbolized old-fashioned, reactionary ideals reminiscent of a distant, premodern past, rather than being the keywords for good virtues that they had been up until the mid-1960s.

In the late 1960s, Sweden was still one of the most ethnically homogeneous countries in the developed world. Although European immigration had begun to increase during the decade, following the expanding Swedish industry's demand for foreign workers, Sweden had few ethnic minorities. The first generation of immigrants in the 1950s had quickly assimilated. Most of those arriving in the 1960s were expected to return home again. About 90 percent of the population belonged to the Protestant state church. The party system was one of the most stable in any democracy, and the Social Democratic Party—one of the strongest in the world—had remained in government for more than three decades. In the 1968 parliamentary election, it received more than 50 percent of the votes.

Change was about to come, however. The following decades would witness the emergence of a multicultural society, with Sweden, in fact, becoming one of Europe's more culturally diverse states. In 2012, 15 percent of Swedes were immigrants, and an additional 5 percent were children of immigrants. A large proportion of those who have arrived in recent decades are non-European. However, the basic premises for Swedish immigration politics have remained unchanged since the 1970s: cultural assimilation is voluntary for immigrants, citizenship is easy to obtain, and, although the debate on integration issues has intensified in recent years, there is still a consensus between the left and right concerning the ideals of cultural pluralism and a generous migration policy.

These changes have strengthened the self-image established in the 1960s of Sweden as an exceptionally open and tolerant country. In the political sphere, national symbols are seldom given much attention; on the contrary, nationalist rhetoric is often explicitly rejected as "un-Swedish behavior."

In one area, however, the limits of Swedish tolerance are increasingly being tested. Differing views on sexuality, gender equality, and family values are largely determined by cultural factors. Globally, there are significant variations among countries and among different cultural or religious groups within countries. At least partly as a result of immigration, conflicts related to different cultural values have become more common in Sweden. As in several other countries, these concern the limits of religious tolerance and the limits of freedom of expression. To a large extent, the debates are similar to those in other countries, containing pretty much the same arguments and the same examples. However, there is an additional twist to the Swedish case. Perhaps more than any other country, Sweden is still perceived to be the most "modern" nation in terms of gender equality and sexual freedom, as it is a frontrunner on many legal issues. Sweden is also a highly secularized country in terms of the values of the majority population, with few people in Sweden giving a high priority to religious and traditional moral values. But most important, while the actual values may vary even within the same cultural group, gender equality and sexual freedom make up important parts of the Swedish self-image. I would argue that these values have been transferred from ideology into national identity. This logically implies that a rejection of these values also implies a rejection of Swedishness.

But how does the self-image of "Swedish sin" relate to the self-image of "Swedish tolerance" today, after originally having been part of the same narrative? To what extent have narratives other than the ones representing a Swedish majority culture been established in the discourse on national identity in Sweden? Has the myth of Swedish sin really managed to survive the transition from a homogeneous secularized nation to a multicultural and multireligious society?

In this chapter, I try to answer these questions by studying the public debates on multiculturalism and sexual freedom from the 1960s to the present. I have primarily used two types of sources: debates in the national Parliament and opinion articles from major newspapers. The aim has been to find out whether, and in what way, there have been "clashes" between the "sin discourse" and the "tolerance discourse." Therefore, I have tried to find debates where a clash could be expected to appear by searching for issues such as honor culture, female genital mutilation, pornography, sexual education, gender roles, homosexuality, and so on.

1960s: The Beginnings

During the 1960s, immigration to Sweden reached higher levels than ever before. Immigration from the Nordic countries had been unregulated since the early 1950s, and during the first half of the 1960s, Sweden actively recruited immigrants from southern Europe to help meet the needs of the labor market. In contrast to Germany and several other expanding economies, Sweden did not introduce a guest-worker system, instead offering far-reaching social and economic rights to the immigrants from the start.

The 1960s saw the first debates in Sweden on how Swedish society should deal with the newcomers. On one side of the debate were those advocating assimilation. Sweden had traditionally tried, with varying degrees of success, to assimilate its national minorities—Sami, Roma, and Finns—and had almost no experience of coexisting with different ethnic or religious groups. The public schools had been a powerful instrument for forcing the minorities to learn Swedish, even if it meant oppressing minority languages. This policy was seldom accompanied by an excluding nationalist rhetoric, however. Instead, it was an integral part of the ideals of *Folkhemmet* (the people's home): equal citizens in a unified nation.

Advocates of cultural pluralism challenged the assimilation ideals, arguing that the state should not only allow immigrants to maintain their culture but also actively help them to do so. This should include public support of immigrant institutions, inclusion of minority languages in public education, and so on. Even though these two perspectives were opposites, the debate was not very polarized. This was a new topic for Swedish politicians to deal with, and the debate was characterized by a search for consensus, a deep trust in the advice of experts, and an openness to influences from abroad (in particular Canada).

In 1955, Sweden had already introduced mandatory sexual education in public schools. That decision followed the legalization of contraceptives in 1938 and the decriminalization of homosexuality between consenting adults in 1955. While public sales of condoms became common in the 1950s, it was the release of the contraceptive pill in 1964 that triggered the sexual revolution. Abortions were illegal, although the number of legal abortions increased during the 1960s following a less strict application of the rules.

At the end of the 1940s, the National Board of Cinema, originally created in 1911 to uphold public values and censor movies that were "brutalizing, arousing, or deceiving," ended its censorship of scenes showing nudity and drunkenness. The myth of Swedish sin was at least partly caused by the nudity in movies, such as Arne Mattsson's *One Summer of Happiness* in 1951 and Ingmar Bergman's *The Summer with Monika* in 1953.

While the Swedish sin narrative originated outside Sweden, formulated by non-Swedes, it soon became internalized among Swedes themselves to the extent that the self-image of a sexually open-minded country rapidly came to be a constituent part of Swedish identity. In 1967, the Swedish Institute, a state-sponsored institute responsible for the image of Sweden abroad, published a report (also released specifically for the US market) called "Society and Sex in Sweden." The aim of the report was basically to acknowledge the veracity of the myth and to explain the rationale behind it: free sexuality is "a natural consequence of an enlightened, modern, and democratic view on sex that has transcended old-time views on sin."[2]

In 1969, a government inquiry report surveying the sexual lives of the adult Swedish population was published, claiming to be the first of its sort in the world. The normative baseline was very clear. In the preface, it was stated that although some (sexual) rules were needed, there are too many rules today, and "sexual life in the Western world is a needlessly parsimonious reservoir of human joy."[3]

In the summer of 1969, American intellectual Susan Sontag published an essay about Sweden titled "A Letter from Sweden." Having lived in Sweden for two years, she praised the high living standard, the welfare state, and the Swedes' liberal views on sex. She described the public sex education: "In some city schools ninth graders are taken to visit birth-control centers to learn contraceptive techniques; condoms are sold in automatic vending machines on the streets and in men's rooms in restaurants and other public places. Sexual relations between teenagers are taken for granted and don't have to be hidden, even in conventional bourgeois families (I've read that 43 per cent of women are pregnant on their wedding day)."[4] Sontag also described the abundance of pornography: "Everything you can imagine is legal and easily available, at least in Stockholm. You can rent blue films by the hour or day, and cheaply, by calling one of a number of companies listed in the telephone directory; if you want a dildo, you can buy one at your nearest sex store."[5] She also noted how sexuality issues were covered in the media: "One of the biggest papers here, *Expressen*, carries a plain-spoken column written by a Danish couple that encourages people to experiment with different positions and preaches tolerance for erotic minorities; "Sten and Inge" have become household names in Sweden (as they are in Denmark), the Dr. Spock of the Scandinavian bedroom."[6] Most interestingly, Sontag finally reflected on the pride that the Swedes she met took in being Swedish: "Their high degree of national self-consciousness is partly what you would expect of a population with the highest per capita income in the world and a strong conviction of their country's moral superiority. The Swedes take evident pride in Sweden's uniqueness, its vanguard role on the international scene . . . Swedes . . . confidently await the inevitable movements of history that will lead other nations to imitate them. What happens in Sweden, more than one Swede has told me, happens five or ten or fifteen years later in some other advanced parts of the world."[7]

It is hard to find texts where the discourses on cultural diversity and sexuality actually overlap. During this period, they seem to be completely separate discourses, although joined together in a political rhetoric on tolerance, modernity, and openness. The debates on immigration rarely touched the subject of values, and the debates on sexual politics are completely within the framework of the homogeneous nation state. One of the few cases where these two discourses are almost connected is in a 1967 debate, which at least demonstrates an awareness that there may be a conflict between Swedish and minority values in terms of sexuality and gender equality. Per Gahrton, who was then a member of the Liberal People's Party (later to become an MEP for the Green Party), wrote, "We shall of course not apply our Swedish perspective to the family lives of the immigrants, to the extent that we would force or pressure them to adapt to the same type of "everyday life" as most Swedes have. Neither shall we deal with more intensity with the gender discrimination of immigrants than we do with Swedes—as long as it concerns adults. But I find it very hard to understand why we should deal less with the views and methods of immigrants when it comes to parenting."[8] Gahrton defended himself against claims that he was advocating an assimilationist policy: "There is definitely nothing particularly "Swedish" about religious neutrality in public schools, actions against traditional gender roles, or the fight against mistreatment of children and authoritarian parenting."[9] Two points can be made regarding the lack of open debate. The first is that the largest immigrant group in the 1960s came from Finland, a nation perceived to be fairly similar to Sweden in terms of secularism and modern values, although economically more backward. The other important immigrant groups were male workers from Yugoslavia, Greece, Italy, and Turkey, many of whom were expected to return home, rather than (as they did) stay and raise families with wives from their native countries.

The second important thing to note is that sexual and cultural minorities in the political rhetoric were perceived to be part of the same moment. Identity politics, although the term was rarely used in Sweden at this time, related to both categories. It was one struggle, rather than several, to break down the authoritative collective norms.[10] The same political slogans applied to both ethnic and sexual minorities, and, more important, it was the same older, reactionary generation that was perceived to be standing in the way of both the sexual and the cultural revolutions.

THE 1970s: MULTICULTURALISM AND SEXUAL RADICALISM

During the 1970s, sexual politics in Sweden became radicalized. In 1971, the ban on pornography was abolished. In 1975, abortions became free on demand, which basically meant that legalization harmonized with what had gradually become a de facto policy since the 1960s. At the end of the decade, the National Board of Health removed homosexuality from its list of diseases. In most aspects discussed, liberal views on sexuality prevailed. In 1977, a new curriculum for sexual education was launched, marking a change from a more biologically oriented education, aimed at teaching teens to avoid unwanted pregnancies, to a perspective that focused on sexual lust and praised the positive aspects of casual sex, rather than recommending abstention from it.

But in at least one area, the sex radicals went too far. In 1976, the Commission on Sexual Crimes presented a report that proposed a decriminalization of incestuous relations, a lower age limit for consenting sexual relations, and reduced punishment levels for rape and sexual abuses.[11] These radical proposals reflected the view that almost every form of sex is harmless in itself, and therefore that sexual relations should not be regulated. Negative aspects were attributed to old cultural beliefs and constraining norms in society, or to misunderstandings between the participants in the activity. Hence the state should be very restrictive in punishing people's sexual activities.

In some cases, this was also extended to include a remarkably tolerant view on pedophilia. In January 1973, the leading Swedish newspaper, *Dagens Nyheter*, published a much-debated article on the sexuality of children.[12] It was followed by another article early in 1980 in *Aftonbladet*, then the second-largest tabloid, which, under the title "Sex Is Nice for the Kids," argued that teachers in preschools should encourage and support sexual games between children.[13]

But the sex liberals also met critics. In 1975, Karin Söder, MP (later to become party leader) for the Centre Party, raised the issue of child pornography in the Swedish Parliament. The minister of justice, Lennart Geijer, replied that although he himself found pornographic images featuring children "tasteless," "it does not seem appropriate to intervene against pornography with a specific content, however repulsive it may seem."[14]

But the critics were gaining ground, and when the state report on sexual crimes was published, an attitude change had already occurred. Few of the proposals were turned into legislation.

In 1968, the Swedish Parliament had voted to restrict labor migration, a decision supported by both political blocs as well as the unions. Sweden did, however, maintain relatively generous asylum policies as well as comparatively liberal rules for family migration. Hence in the 1970s, Sweden continued to receive many new immigrants, while many of those who had arrived in the 1950s and 1960s remained and started to raise families. This meant that Sweden now had its first "second generation" of immigrants, and that the question of how to handle the education of immigrant children became more important. One effect was that immigrants increasingly came to be seen as "minorities" rather than as "temporary guests." The debate between advocates of assimilation and of cultural pluralism had ended with the latter group as winners. Hence in 1975, all parties in the parliament supported the new goals for the immigrant policy that was adopted. The goals were summed up in three keywords: equality, freedom of choice, and cooperation. Equality meant that immigrants should have the same rights as natives, which included the right to vote in regional and municipal elections. Freedom of choice meant the freedom to choose whether or not to assimilate. The choice not to assimilate was facilitated by state schools offering free education in minority languages. Cooperation, finally, meant that the state should mediate between the immigrant communities and the majority population.

These policy decisions were unique at the time (e.g., Sweden was the first country in the world to give voting rights to noncitizens), and they have often been used to illustrate a multicultural turn in Swedish immigrant policy. To some extent, such a turn had occurred. It definitely meant the end of the open assimilation ideals of the past. It also led to the state using considerable resources to support immigrant communities. But at the same time, the state remained ambiguous toward the idea of immigrant groups living separate lives. Barely anyone was advocating separate institutions for minority groups or even affirmative action. Instead, there was a lively debate on how the schools should guarantee that immigrant children learned both their mother tongue and Swedish.

In the 1970s, it also became apparent that some minority groups had very different values regarding sexuality and family life. A working group for sexuality and sexual relations (ASSI) was created. It included representatives of the National School Board, the Swedish Association for Sexuality Education, the major immigrant communities, and the National Board of Health. ASSI proposed mandatory immigrant and minority knowledge in the curriculum for teacher education. They also advocated the mandatory provision of information to immigrant parents regarding sexual education in schools. ASSI argued that it was important that all immigrant children obtain this education; otherwise, they would be "left at the mercy of commercial sexuality." ASSI also encouraged immigrant communities to create separate organizations for women, who should themselves take responsibility for their own emancipation.

This was a clear example of minority policy being influenced by the Swedish majority norm. A conflict of values was recognized, and the solution was to strengthen the Swedish values. Reading the comments from politicians at the time, it is almost impossible to find expressions of any kind of cultural relativism. It is not so hard to find them from experts and academics, however.

In the fall of 1979, a Swedish gynecologist claimed to have performed a circumcision procedure on several immigrant women. A member of the National Board of Health supported the doctor's actions: "When it comes to adults, we have to give them the freedom to make decisions about their own bodies. We cannot forbid a doctor to serve them professionally. There are more serious matters to attend to than preventing immigrant women from following a pattern that feels right and good for them."[15] The health minister agreed: "The circumcision of adult women may be right due to strong religious or social-psychological reasons . . . There is no Swedish law criminalizing circumcision. However, circumcision of little girls in their homes is abuse."[16] This led to a harsh debate with strong reactions from the public, and a partial retreat by the doctor, who claimed that the reporter had misunderstood him. Later the same year, the parliament, for the very first time, debated the issue of female circumcision (the term used at the time) in Sweden. Members of the Social Democratic and Communist opposition parties very strongly criticized the government and wanted the practice outlawed.[17]

It is interesting to note how all the critics in the debate referred to the standpoint of the Association of Immigrant Women. That immigrant women in Sweden themselves wanted circumcision to be criminalized seems to have been of huge importance. Several participants in the debate—all of them women—claimed to have learned about the issue from other immigrant women. A common rhetorical figure was that "this is not culture, it is torture." The responsible minister, Elisabet Holm, was very defensive. She agreed with the critics' view on the practice of circumcision, but she also referred to immigrant women: "I have also been contacted by immigrant women. They pleaded with me not to interfere with their manners and customs, as they believe that I am not in a position to understand the background. They also said that they have no understanding whatsoever of Swedish women's ways of living and thinking. The issue of circumcision is not so very simple. However, I firmly assert that there must be a limit to the tolerance of foreign cultural patterns. Child marriage and circumcision must be outside the boundary. It is my absolute firm belief."[18] All in all, the integration debate in the 1970s was strongly focused on how the natural assimilation pressure from the majority society could be limited. The perspective was most often that of the immigrants. What could the state do to guarantee real freedom of choice for them and their children, and how could minority children grow up to feel safe both within their own national identity and within the Swedish state? While issues of language were a focus, value conflicts were seldom directly addressed. Questions concerning family life, sexuality, and gender equality were rarely touched on. To some extent, this may have had to do with an underestimation of the actual cultural conflicts, but it was mostly due to the perspective that the Swedish majority had no right to dictate the values or cultural lifestyles of the immigrants. That is, Swedish values were deemed "better," but it was not as obvious that minorities should be judged according to the same criteria.

The same goes for the high-profile debates on sexuality. These debates were color blind—apart from a few cases where it was more or less clearly stated that the norms, and consequently also the behavior, of minorities were different. But that was considered more a matter of fact rather than a normative standpoint up for discussion.

THE 1980s: A RETREAT FROM RADICALISM

In the 1980s, the immigrant community in Sweden was transformed. Very few labor migrants arrived during this period; instead, there was an increase in refugee and family reunification migration. While non-European immigrants had been quite few until the mid-1970s, consisting mostly of political refugees from Latin America; in the 1980s, Sweden received large groups of migrants from all parts of the world, including Africa and the Middle East. For the first time in Swedish history, this also led to the creation of a substantial Swedish Muslim minority.

During this decade, anti-immigration movements also made their first appearance. In Malmö, the xenophobic Skåne Party entered the local parliament in 1985 with the slogan: "Remove Islam from Skåne." Three years later, the town of Sjöbo, a small municipality also in the Skåne region, organized a local referendum on whether to receive refugees. Across Sweden, small groups of militant racists and neo-Nazis also made the headlines on several occasions.

No major party, however, tried to exploit the growing xenophobic opinion. With that said, the 1980s clearly witnessed a turn away from multicultural ideals. In 1986, the government stated that freedom of choice for immigrants did not include the freedom to avoid the Swedish language or "basic values on which there is agreement in Sweden."[19] The same year also saw the introduction of a new policy called All of Sweden (*Hela Sverige*), which aimed to spread newly arrived refugees more evenly across the country in order to avoid a concentration of immigrants in the big cities.

With the arrival of the 1980s, the radical days of sexual liberalism were definitely over. In 1980, a ban on child pornography was introduced. A few years later, the discovery of the HIV virus changed attitudes toward casual sex and also led to the introduction of new legislation. In 1987, the parliament introduced the so-called Protection from Diseases Act. According to the new law, public arrangements were no longer allowed to be organized in a way that encouraged sexual activities. This was directly aimed at stopping male homosexuals from having casual sex with anonymous partners in places like public saunas. The law was to remain until 2004. Attitudes to public nudity also gradually changed, with fewer women bathing topless at public beaches.

Despite these changes in society, however, the myth of Swedish sin was still going strong. During that decade, it seemed to be mandatory for every major musician or movie star visiting Sweden to praise the beautiful and sexually available blonde Swedish women. Tourist books about Sweden at the time typically included pictures of topless women at the beach. In 1984, British director Colin Nutley, later to become one of Sweden's most successful film directors ever, arrived in Sweden to produce his first feature, a coproduced British-Swedish miniseries for television. The series, titled *Annika—A Love Story*, told the story of a young British male traveling to Sweden to live with a 15-year-old girl he met while she was in England on a language course. Nutley reproduced almost every part of the Swedish sin myth, including male and female teenagers naked in the sauna together, Annika's parents not objecting to their daughter having sex with her boyfriend, and, not least, how sensational the meeting with this strange culture was to the young British male.

In 1983, the National Board of Health and the Swedish Association for Sexuality Education financed the publication of a book for adults working in day-care centers, called *The Love Life of Children*.[20] The aim of the book was to help people working with young children handle questions concerning sexuality and the value conflicts that often arise between parents and teachers. While the book's authors were clearly influenced by the previous decades' liberal attitudes toward sex, almost exclusively focusing on the positive side of sexual games between children, they also dealt with difficult questions concerning pedophilia and how to identify children who were victims of sexual assault in their homes.

Most interesting is that the book directly discussed how to handle what the authors described as "cultural clashes." Based on their empirical studies of preschools in the early 1980s, the authors gave several authentic examples of everyday conflicts. Many of those typically related to immigrant parents objecting to male employees, in particular to males changing diapers and helping kids at the toilet. In one case, a group of Assyrian parents reacted strongly: "It was wrong for men to work with children, because that was women's business. They were bad role models."

Another example was a case of female teachers wearing bikinis in the playground in the summer. The immigrant mothers reacted strongly, calling the teachers "whores without morals." But what is interesting here is how the authors explained this reaction from the mothers: "In fact, they probably felt threatened because of the temptation that this near-nudity could mean for their men." This leads the authors to give the following advice: "The most important thing is not how you view nudity but that you are able to make a sharp distinction between moral conceptions in different cultures. This allows immigrants to feel safe within their own sphere. The message they hear is: we do not want to attract your husbands, it is just how we behave, and it does not have the same strong sexual connections for us that it has for you."[21] The perspective in the book is that it is natural that different cultures have different values. But at the same time, the authors also recognize the ability of cultures to change, and the current immigrant norms are repeatedly compared to older Swedish norms:

> There is often a sharp distinction between certain groups of immigrants and native Swedes. Family cohesion is important for some immigrant groups in a way that was meaningful in Sweden perhaps hundreds of years ago . . . The first thing immigrants see when they come to Sweden are examples of the "Swedish sin": females posed provocatively on

magazine covers, scantily clad and sexually challenging people on the streets, in films, and on TV showing what would never be shown in their home countries; divorces and stories about "easy living," perhaps stories about how their own countrymen have been degraded or about how kids have been "pulled down in the dirt." All this is very threatening for immigrants for whom family, relatives, cohesion, faith in God, obedience, and love for their relatives are central.[22]

The book was highly controversial on its release. Militant extreme right groups threatened the authors, who had to live under police protection. The Social Democratic health minister, Sten Andersson, had to defend the publication in a debate in the parliament: "It is a highly useful guide for parents who, often because of a previous bigoted and prejudiced view on sexuality, are at a loss and uncertain about their children's sexual games, the use of sexual words, and many awkward questions."[23] The debate about *The Love Life of Children* illustrates a more direct awareness in the 1980s that not all immigrants may approve of the Swedish perspective on sexuality and gender equality, and that this, in fact, does constitute a problem. In comparison with the 1970s, we see more examples of how the diverging lifestyles of minorities are framed as a problem for the host society. But since the majority culture also, to some extent, made a retreat from the more radical sexual liberalism of the 1970s, this clash never fully developed, and no politicians tried to capitalize on these issues.

THE 1990S: FEMINISM AND ANTIRACISM

In the early 1990s, anti-immigrant sentiment in Sweden was stronger than ever. A populist anti-immigration party entered the parliament in 1991 (only to be voted out in 1994). Several racist attacks occurred. But despite this, the established parties managed to maintain a consensus on a relatively liberal immigration policy. Again, immigration to Sweden reached new record levels, driven by large numbers of migrants arriving from the collapsing Yugoslavia and, during the latter part of the decade, attitudes toward immigration steadily became more positive.

An important feature of the debates in the 1990s was the emergence of racism as a central topic. Although racist incidents between natives and immigrants are documented at least as early as the 1970s, it was not until the 1990s that awareness of racism became an issue at all levels of society. An effect of this was a rediscovery of some dark chapters in Swedish modern history. That Sweden had been one of the countries in Europe, together with Norway and Germany, where sterilization laws were practiced most widely was not previously known to the general public. The official story had been that Sweden in the 1930s was a victim of the zeitgeist, but books published in the 1990s showed that Sweden's racist policy actually had internal causes, and was rationalized, by almost all major political actors, as necessary for the modernization of Sweden and the establishment of a universal welfare state. The 1990s also witnessed an increased focus on the historic treatment of the Sami and Roma people in Sweden, and on anti-Semitism, including a broad, state-sponsored campaign that included Holocaust information in schools.

Academic and media interest in questions concerning identity, ethnicity, and nationalism rose dramatically during these years. It is noteworthy that the perspective was very often critical of the existence of identity categories. Poststructuralist methods were popular, and Swedish identity was repeatedly "deconstructed," as was the whole concept of the nation-state. The use of words such as "multicultural" and "immigrant" was criticized as reflecting an essentialist view on identity categories. Instead, a more individualized perspective emerged. Immigrant policy was replaced by integration policy; immigrants were now to be treated as individuals, not as members of a collective, and so on.

In the field of sexual politics, the 1990s meant a large-scale comeback for feminism. Shortly before the 1994 election, a small group of high-profile feminist veterans of the 1970s women's movements threatened to start a "women's party" unless the major parties brought forward more female candidates. This eventually led to a majority of the Swedish parties adopting feminist programs and to more female candidates being elected.

The feminist turn also resulted in several new cases of legislation. In 1999, Sweden criminalized men who bought sex. It was still legal to be a prostitute, but illegal to buy services from one. In the same year, possession of child pornography was criminalized, and there were heated debates on violent pornography.

During the 1990s the concept of honor culture appeared in the Swedish debate for the first time. The first women reported to fall victim to honor killings were a 15-year-old girl from Iraq, killed by her brother and cousin, and a 26-year-old woman, also from Iraq, killed by her husband. Both murders occurred in 1996 but were not given much attention in the Swedish news. In 1999, another girl, a Swedish resident from Iraq, was killed by her father and her uncles, while in Iraq. However, at the time, few people were willing to recognize these crimes as honor killings. Few were, in fact, ready to accept the concept at all. Some considered it a racist concept. One of those who claimed that honor culture was a racist concept was the journalist Stieg Larsson, later to become known worldwide for his Millennium trilogy. In later years, those who rejected the "honor" terminology were criticized for cultural relativism. But this misrepresents the actual arguments made in the debate. The motivation for those who rejected the "honor" term was a concern that the use of a culturalist language would contribute to a sharp distinction between "us" and "them"—between natives and non-Swedes. Even though it may be argued that the result was, in fact, support for relativism, explicitly relativist arguments are not to be found in the actual debates that took place.

While honor culture was associated with Kurdish culture in particular, the 1990s also saw the rise of a new debate on Islam in Sweden. In the early 1990s, the xenophobic party New Democracy repeatedly used Islamophobic rhetoric. But the established parties were very careful. However, it did become more common to discuss the problems of integration of Muslim cultures in Sweden. For example, in 1997, the Centre Party put forward a motion in parliament on this problem: "We do indeed live in Sweden, but you are a Kurdish, Iranian, Turkish, Palestinian girl, and cannot be like Swedish girls. This is a common line in Muslim families with teenagers. Parents assume the customs of the old country. The teenagers compare [these] with the [customs of their] new [country] . . . The conflicts are there."[24] In 1992, Swedish music producer Billy Butt, an immigrant born in Kenya but of Indian heritage, was convicted of several rapes in Sweden. Butt confessed to having had sex with the girls, but denied any case of rape or abuse. He argued that the girls had slept with him in the hope that they would get a record contract. The only evidence against Butt was the witness statements of several of the alleged rape victims. Still, the leading newspaper *Expressen* launched a harsh campaign against Butt. In the media articles, the "ugly immigrant"—Butt's looks were clearly a long way from the beauty ideals in Sweden at the time—was contrasted with the beautiful blonde women that he was supposed to have raped. In the court, it was argued that "no cute girl would have sex with this man voluntarily."

The 1990s clearly mark a shift from the previous decades. Sexual freedom was problematized to a greater extent than perhaps ever before in Sweden. At the same time, gender equality came to be seen as a defining feature of Swedish identity. The law criminalizing men who pay prostitutes was described as very modern and progressive. At the same time, the potential clash between Swedish and immigrant cultures on issues of sexuality was given some attention, but that attention was still limited, not least due to a strong antiracist norm in the public debate.

THE 2000s: THE RETURN OF ASSIMILATION

Immigration to Sweden reached new record levels in the 2000s. The largest groups have come from countries such as Somalia, Iraq, and Afghanistan. While opinion has gradually shifted toward a more positive attitude to immigration, a minor anti-immigration party, the Sweden Democrats, has slowly grown, and in 2010 obtained enough votes to enter the parliament. But this party's arrival on the national scene has not influenced migration or integration policy. In fact, Sweden remains one of the few immigrant countries where leading politicians still have not officially rejected the ideals of multiculturalism. Following the introduction of stricter integration policies and the rejection of multiculturalist ideals by leading politicians in most Western European countries, this has made Sweden an outlier in the field of integration politics. In 2008, Sweden abolished its previous restrictions on labor migration and today has one of the most liberal migration policies in the world.

Issues relating to sexual politics routinely trigger much attention in the media. During the last decade, there have been several reforms, in particular concerning homosexuals. In 2002, same-sex couples were allowed to adopt children. In 2003, homosexuals and bisexuals were included in the law against hate crimes. Finally, in 2009, same-sex couples won the right to marry on the same terms as heterosexual couples. The annual Stockholm Pride festival has grown into one of the biggest public events in Sweden, regularly attracting political party leaders and other major public figures.

In January 2002, a young woman, born in Sweden to ethnic Kurdish immigrants from Turkey, was shot dead by her father. The victim, Fadime Sahindal, had been active in the campaign against honor
violence and, among other things, had been invited to speak in the
national parliament. The murder of Fadime Sahindal received enormous attention in Sweden. Her funeral was held in Uppsala Cathe-
dral, seat of the Swedish Archbishop, and was attended by members
of the government and the royal family. The murder almost on its
own turned the debate on honor culture upside down. In a debate in
the parliament, the minister responsible for integration, Mona Sahlin,
made the following statement: "The murder of Fadime Sahindal is an
example of the despicable actions young immigrant women may face
when their families do not agree to the surrounding society's norms.
To adapt to another country's values and internalize them is a difficult
process, but it is absolutely crucial to the future of Sweden."[25] Sahlin
went on to describe the social pressure on men from honor cultures
and how the Swedish society had to put even stronger pressure on
these families. Her policy solution was to "sharpen the introduction"
for newcomers, "with a clear focus on Swedish law and values." "In a
second debate, a week later, Sahlin repeated her position, now even
more strongly: There is obviously a problem, a very serious problem,
when people who live in Sweden do not share our society's fundamental values about the equal rights of men and women and the right of
every person to make their own life choices. The problem concerns the
whole of society, in all its sectors, and no one can shirk responsibility."[26] A member of the major center-right party, Lennart Fridén, went
even further, describing his meetings with several immigrants who had
claimed, "If I had known that I was not allowed to make decisions
affecting my own family, I would have gone to another country." Fridén's solution was harsh: "Already at the border one must be told that
there is only one law—the Swedish law . . . This means that these
people must be integrated intensively into Swedish society for them
to experience the pressure. If you live and work independently, the
relationship to the old country remains stronger than the relationship to the Swedish society. In a TV discussion there was talk about a
driver's license for immigrants. I think it is a good idea that you have
to show that you understand what you will face."[27] The honor murder
of Fadime Sahindal also led to an increase in research and in state

reports on the issue. In 2009, a major survey of high school students in the Stockholm area was published, with remarkable results. The report claimed that half of all children with both parents born outside Sweden lived in what was described as "virginity cultures." The figure for children with two parents born in Sweden was less than 1 percent. Within the "immigrant" category, there was a huge variation between children from the Middle East and other parts of the world.

The practice of female genital mutilation (the term now widely used, having completely replaced "female circumcision"), illegal since 1982, also raised concern. In 2006, Nyamko Sabuni, a member of the liberal People's Party and later to become minister for integration, suggested mandatory gynecological controls of all girls. A party colleague argued that, instead, controls should be restricted to girls in certain risk groups—that is, immigrants from East Africa. These proposals raised strong criticism and were never turned into actual policy proposals.

These examples can be described as a return of assimilation ideals. Although the term "assimilation" is seldom used in Sweden, a closer scrutiny of the integration discourse reveals that a central theme is the idea of helping immigrants adjust to Swedish values and behavior. Swedishness has become strongly connected to an idea of gender equality and individualism. According to political scientist Ann Towns, there is a dominant discourse that "equals Swedishness with gender equality and cultures within and from the Mediterranean-Middle East-North Africa with patriarchal violence."

The anti-immigrant party, the Sweden Democrats, has tried several times to exploit the cultural differences between natives and immigrants on gender equality and sexual freedom. In 2010, the party leader wrote a debate article containing an apology to the homosexual community, saying he was sorry about previous negative comments concerning homosexuality made by some of the party members. Instead, he claimed that the Sweden Democrats were the real friends of the homosexual community since they were the only ones who dared to deal with homophobia among immigrants: "It is also a clear indication of the strong concern that many homosexuals feel about mass immigration and the hatred of homosexuals which the growing Islamization brings. When the largest Muslim Youth League in Sweden invites the extreme cleric Sheik Abdullah Hakim Quick, who believes that homosexuals should be executed, as a speaker, we understand that gays would be looking for a defender of Western democratic values. There the Sweden Democrats fill a unique and vital role in society."[28] Along similar lines, the Sweden Democrats have also claimed several times to stand up for gender equality and connected this to Swedish values, when they have criticized the wearing of the Muslim veil and Muslim demands for separate hours in public swimming pools. The party has also connected group rapes to immigration, claiming that it is a non-Swedish practice.

But the idea that gender equality is a typical Swedish value, and that there is a dividing line between natives and immigrants on this issue, has been criticized. In 2006, the national association of Assyrians (claiming 10,000 members) protested against the portrayal of Assyrians as "woman-oppressing Sweden haters" and threatened to quit paying the mandatory television fee if public media did not change its portrayal of Assyrians.[29]

However, the strongest alternative perspective has been formulated by radical feminists. In 2005, a new political party emerged in Sweden, called the Feminist Initiative. It was created by Gudrun Schyman, former leader of the Left Party. The party failed to get into parliament in the 2006 and 2010 elections, receiving only about 0.5 percent of the votes. What is interesting to note is that they represented radical feminism combined with a strong antiracism component. The party, for example, does not use the concept of honor culture, since "it contributes to a false self-image."[30] The party has been criticized for not caring enough about the situation of immigrant women. In 2002, Schyman, while still leader of the Left Party, gave a speech that came to be known widely in Sweden as the "Taliban Speech." In it, she said, "The discrimination and the violations vary depending on where we are. But it is the same norm, the same structure, the same pattern being repeated in the Taliban's Afghanistan as here in Sweden."[31]

In the 2000s, the clash between Swedish and minority views on issues relating to sexual freedom has, for the first time, broken out fully. There is now a political party—in the spring of 2014 attracting about 9 percent of the voters in the opinion polls—that clearly politicizes the connection between Swedish identity and gender equality. Even though the Feminist Initiative is consistently criticized by other parties and the media, there has, nevertheless, been a shift in the mainstream as well.

The concept of honor culture is now widely used. The differing views on sexuality and gender equality are widely recognized and repeatedly discussed in politics. The Swedish Association for Sexual Education has even advocated the inclusion of a course on sexuality in the language and society course that immigrants are offered.

CONCLUSION

In the 1960s, sexual freedom and multicultural tolerance became important parts of the newly established narrative on modern Swedish identity. Sweden came to be associated with liberal views on sexuality and with generous and tolerant attitudes toward minorities and immigrants. For five decades now, these have been important features of the image of Sweden abroad and of the self-image of Swedes at home.

It was not until the beginning of the 2000s that the clash between these two ideals—the tolerance of minorities and the liberal attitude to sexuality—was fully realized. But an awareness of this potential clash can be traced back to the 1960s. Different aspects of the problem of immigrant groups holding diverging views on issues of sexual freedom and gender equality have been discussed for the last fifty years, concerning, for example, genital mutilation, LGBT parenting, and so on.

In contrast to what is often claimed in the contemporary debate, it is hard to find evidence of an open cultural relativism in earlier decades. That a "clash" has been avoided is not the result of Swedish politicians and intellectuals arguing that "it is their culture, let them do what they want." On the contrary, the majority norm has been upheld, and the issue of how to deal with minorities has mostly been seen as a question of when, and not whether, they will assimilate. It is only in the current decade, however, that political actors, including an anti-immigration nationalist party, have begun to exploit this clash. The effects of this change have yet to be seen.

NOTES

1. Jonathan Power, "In Search of the Swedish Soul," *Prospect Magazine*, July 2009.
2. *Society and Sex in Sweden* (Stockholm: Swedish Institute, 1967), 23.
3. *Om Sexuallivet i Sverige. Värderingar, normer, beteenden i sociologisk tolkning* (Statens offentliga utredningar 1969:2).

4. Susan Sontag, "A Letter from Sweden," *Ramparts Magazine*, July 1969, 31.
5. Ibid.
6. Ibid.
7. Ibid., 24.
8. Per Gahrton, "Var står David Schwarz?," *Aftonbladet*, July 24, 1967.
9. Ibid.
10. Ulf Bjereld and Marie Demker, *I Vattumannens tid: En bok om 1968 års uppror och dess betydelse idag* (Stockholm: Hjalmarsson & Högberg, 2005).
11. *Sexuella övergrepp: Förslag till en ny lydelse av brottsbalken om sedlighetsbrott avgivet av sexualbrottsutredningen* (Statens offentliga utredningar 1976:9).
12. Paul Frigyes, *Nyhetsflås och tidsanda. Svenska löpsedlar under ett sekel* (Carlsson: Stockholm, 2005).
13. "Sex är skönt för ungarna," *Aftonbladet*, February 3, 1980.
14. Lennart Geijer in the Swedish Parliament, February 20, 1975.
15. Sten Lundgren, "Svensk läkare erkänner: Omskärelse av kvinnor görs även här," *Vi*, 44 (1979), 9–11.
16. Press release from Minister of Health Elisabet Holm, November 20, 1979.
17. Debate in the Swedish Parliament, November 19, 1979.
18. Elisabet Holm in the Swedish Parliament, November 19, 1979.
19. Government proposition 1985/86:98, 20.
20. Gertrude Aigner and Erik Centerwall, *Barnens kärleksliv: Om kärlek, sexualitet och mötet med vuxenvärlden* (Stockholm: Prisma/RFSU, 1983).
21. Ibid., 54.
22. Ibid., 114.
23. Sten Andersson in the Swedish Parliament, May 20, 1985.
24. Parliamentary motion 1997/98: Sf615.
25. Mona Sahlin in the Swedish Parliament, February 7, 2002.
26. Mona Sahlin in the Swedish Parliament, February 13, 2002.
27. Lennart Fridén in the Swedish Parliament, February 13, 2002.
28. Jimmie Åkesson and Carina Herrstedt, "SD—ett parti för hbt-personer," *Aftonbladet*, March 30, 2010.
29. Ingrid Kyllerstedt, "10 000 hotar skolka från TV-licens," *Journalisten*, October 24, 2006.
30. Carl Emanuelsson, Stina Svensson and Sissela Nordling Blanco, "Därför använder vi inte hedersbegreppet," *Newsmill*, January 15, 2012, http://www.newsmill.se/artikel/2012/01/15/d-rf-r-anv-nder-vi-inte-hedersbegreppet (accessed March 28, 2013).
31. Speech at the Left Party Congress in Västerås, January 18, 2003, http://www.helgo.net/enar/politik/talibantalet.html.

CHAPTER 6

CHICK LIT AS HEALING AND SELF-HELP MANUAL?

YVONNE LEFFLER

CHICK LIT—TODAY'S BESTSELLING ROMANTIC NOVELS ABOUT STYLISH, career-driven, urban female protagonists in their twenties or thirties—addresses several issues of modern womanhood. The genre became popular in the late 1990s and is considered to be a subgenre of the romance novel, because the female protagonist's professional career, family, and friends are just as important to her as her romantic relationships. Marian Keyes's *Watermelon* (1995) features a protagonist who wrestles with how to be a mother in a modern world; Helen Fielding's *Bridget Jones's Diary* (1996) humorously describes a professional woman's negative self-image and its consequences when it comes to career and romantic relationships; and Candace Bushnell's *Sex and the City* (1996) is famous for its protagonist Carrie, her girlfriends, and their passion for shopping, but it also deals with many women's impossible dream about romantic love and well-being. In Swedish chick lit, by bestselling authors such as Kajsa Ingemarsson, Denise Rudberg, Elisabeth Andersson, and Martina Haag, the focus is even more on contemporary issues of womanhood and modern women's juggling of full-time jobs and family life. While these narratives are products of a specific Swedish context—its social structure and gender ideology—they also criticize and reevaluate different aspects of the Nordic welfare model.

Swedish chick lit is a remarkable example of how a popular Anglo-American genre has been adapted to Swedish audiences and has become part of a certain literary and political tradition. By Swedish writers, it is, as Jenny Björklund states, placed in a Swedish gender discourse promoting gender equality in relation to family, professional career, and personal life projects.[1] Gender issues and social realism have been prominent in Swedish literature since the mid-nineteenth century. Especially during the Modern Breakthrough in the 1880s, and one hundred years later, in the 1970s and 1980s, the focus on women's situations and emancipation brought Scandinavian literature to international recognition. In these periods, many women writers wanted to testify to their experiences as women in their own voices. The 1880s was a time of female breakthroughs, in terms of the number of women making careers as writers of fiction and as participants in the public debate on women's issues, and getting those issues onto the legislative agenda in order to ensure the implementation of laws. Also, in the 1970s and 1980s, many women writers took on women's emancipation when they recreated an old genre, the confessional novel. Several writers in the 1970s continued the documentaries of the 1960s, depicting the intimate sphere of unprivileged women's lives, while several women writers in the 1980s created rather ambivalent portrayals of modern womanhood when they demonstrated the discrepancy between rights fixed by law and actual social behavior.

Although chick lit is known as a popular genre promoting consumerism and a lifestyle in which romance, happiness, and economic status are important, most Swedish chick lit writers embrace a literary tradition of social realism and political engagement. Compared to Anglophone chick lit writers, the Swedish authors focus less on luxury weddings and shopping than on contemporary women's everyday struggles. Romantic love is less important than the heroine's ability to combine a decent family life with a successful professional career, something that requires an equal partner who is prepared to do his part of the housework at home. However, contrary to many of their Swedish predecessors in the 1970s and 1980s, their novels are not explicitly written to achieve social change and gender equality in the future. Instead, their works can be described as contemporary life narratives about how to cope with daily life as a woman and how to achieve personal fulfillment. Hence they reflect the increased individualization in Western society since the 1980s, where personal choice and the development of individual agency define the feminine identity. Therefore, the former Swedish Lutheran-based attitude that one ought to be of service to one's fellow beings and to put others' needs before one's own has been displaced by an individualistic approach to life. The overarching mission of life is now for the individual to form her own successful life journey. Swedish chick lit thus comprises narratives that explore the Swedish welfare society from a female viewpoint in order to expose contemporary women's personal experiences of everyday life in the modern welfare market. Dealing with the pragmatic and daily consequences of gender equality and the Swedish welfare ideology is a recurrently negotiated issue in Swedish chick lit.

Therefore, I aim to study Swedish chick lit as a source of sociocultural commentary. The purpose of this essay is to examine the differences between Anglophone and Swedish chick lit when it comes to ethical and social questions and ideas about happiness, well-being, and everyday life. I will examine how Swedish chick lit, on one hand, conforms to the Anglophone "chick lit formula" and, on the other hand, conveys both an ambiguous and rather different message. Although chick lit is famous for its focus on a stylish, professional, middle-class woman, her shopping, boyfriends, and sex, I reject these stereotypes and intend to redefine Swedish chick lit as a genre that teaches its female audience how to deal with much more serious matters, such as personal crises; family problems; and also various mental problems, such as depression and feelings of inferiority. It is not so much about how to achieve a glamorous romantic lifestyle, as it is about how to effectively apply necessary life strategies—that is, how to get on with ordinary everyday life as such. In that way, Swedish chick lit novels are part of today's self-help industry, using the "makeover" formula. At the same time, they rely on a long tradition of manuals of manners for women, dating back to the eighteenth century.

CHICK LIT AND WOMEN'S FICTION

Chick lit belongs to what is called women's fiction, an umbrella term for a wide-ranging collection of literary subgenres that, besides chick lit, also includes romance, romantic comedies, and female gothic. The term is used to refer to the type of popular fiction that targets female readers. When it is applied to novels, they are often considered to be stories about women and women's issues, written by women writers for women readers. Compared to most romance literature, chick lit is about a slightly older woman: a single, professional protagonist in her thirties, sometimes in her late twenties or early forties. The novels illustrate what happened after Cinderella was united with the prince and the difficulties she confronted when she was supposed to live happily ever after. Many narratives start when the heroine is dumped by Prince Charming and has to face new challenges as well as a variety of romantic, personal, and professional dilemmas. Still, most chick lit novels are structured according to the romance formula. They tell the story of the female character's meeting with a new and better man and the unfolding of their romantic relationship. They often contain what Pamela Regis calls the eight narrative elements of romance novels: "*a definition of society*, always corrupt, that the romance novel will reform; the *meeting* between the heroine and hero; an account of their *attraction* for each other; the *barrier* between them; *the point of ritual death*; the *recognition* that fells the barrier; the *declaration* of heroine and hero that they love each other; and their *betrothal.*"[2]

Nonetheless, chick lit distinguishes itself from the traditional romance novel in many ways. Most chick lit novels could be called "city girl books."[3] They are structured around an urban female protagonist and her middle-class aspirations and lifestyle; a protagonist who has a desire for upward mobility and, according to J. Knowles, is "seeking fulfillment in a romance-consumer-comedic vein."[4] To be more exact, chick lit novels are known for promoting a glamorous lifestyle. The stereotypical, chick lit protagonist in many Anglophone novels is urged to overspend in a consumer society in her quest for Mr. Right, all framed as a romantic comedy that makes light of rather serious personal dilemmas. One of the most striking examples is Sophie Kinsella's Shopaholic series (2001–10) about the irresponsible consumer Becky Bloomwood.

Still, in the plot of most chick lit novels, the female protagonist's quest for personal fulfillment is structured to instruct the protagonist— and thereby also the female reader of the novel—on how to deal with daily life. The protagonist's struggles are often narrated from her internal point of view in the form of a confession directed at the female reader. Many chick lit novels are composed as first-person narrations, journals, or private diaries, like Fielding's *Bridget Jones's Diary*. The composition of some novels is a mixture of novel and diary, like Haag's novels about Bella, such as *Underbar och älskad av alla* (Wonderful and Loved by Everybody; 2007), in which are embedded lists, letters, and various other texts by Bella. In those chick lit novels where the protagonist does not tell her story as a first-person narrator, the events are still depicted from her internal perspective. This internal perspective allows the reader to share the female protagonist's viewpoint and to participate in her life as an intimate friend. The protagonist confides her most private hopes, dreams, and frustrations. She turns to the addressee of her story—the female reader—for understanding and sympathy. Nothing is too trivial or too private to confide or confess. The reader of the novel thereby comes to feel close to the female protagonist, recognizing the message and identifying with her in a "that's me" manner. What happens to the protagonist also happens to the reader, at least in the reader's imagination.

Hence in chick lit, the girl-meets-boy story is replaced by the female protagonist's confession of a personal crisis; the romance formula is used to address women's setbacks, such as a woman's negative self-image and its consequences when it comes to romantic relationships. In that way, chick lit novels pass on a long tradition of instructional texts for women dating back to the eighteenth century and the emergence of conduct books and advice manuals. In those days, the manuals gave instructions on how to become a virtuous woman, a good wife and mother, a perfect child raiser, and an industrious housekeeper. Some of the manuals also included fictional examples to persuade female readers to model themselves on the characters and to duplicate their surroundings. These manuals, fictional conduct books, and novels of manners were often framed by an instructive introduction and a summing up in the form of an epilogue, where a well-meaning and experienced parental narrator—often a father or mother—explicitly lectured the female readers on how to become an exemplary "true" woman. The embedded fictional stories were used as persuasive examples, where the female reader was given the opportunity to explore various issues in an emotionally engaging fictional form via the female protagonist.[5]

FROM INNOCENT BRAT TO RESPONSIBLE WOMAN

What is it, then, that the female reader of chick lit should be instructed about? Contrary to the male action hero, the female protagonist's mission is not to fight external opponents or save the world from evil enemies. Instead, her task is to deal with personal failures and crises, uncertainty, and lack of self-esteem. As in the "bildungsroman," the story is structured around an individual and her dilemmas and mental growth. In some respects, the prototypical chick lit novel can be described as a coming-of-age or a "coming-of-consciousness" story, where the female protagonist's life is transformed in a fundamental way for the better.[6] When the narrative starts, the "chick" is presented as an aging teenager. She is obsessively worried about looks and weight, she is insecure, and she has an exaggerated belief in romantic relationships. When she is deserted by the man she thought was Mr. Right, she is unprepared and unable to juggle a new set of responsibilities in life. In many ways, she is a contemporary Madame Bovary, who has thrived on romance, happiness, glamorous women's magazines, commercials, and celebrity programs promoting an idealized worldview. Just like Emma Bovary, her romantic aspirations and dreams of a better life result in self-deception and misconceptions, and she is therefore ill-equipped to confront the harsh reality of life. Whatever event has developed unsuccessfully, such as her relationship with a man or her professional career, her sufferings are depicted as a direct result of her own wrongdoing. However, she never stops trying to improve things, a course that, for a start, is constantly met by a subsequent sense of disappointment. Contrary to Flaubert's novel, the main objective of the chick lit novel is to show readers how to overcome obstacles and how to improve. The aim of the events is to instruct the female protagonist—and the female reader—on how to go on with life and be happy. Unlike Emma Bovary, the chick lit protagonist is made to reevaluate her existence, all while she struggles to support herself and to find an alternative way of handling her life. On her long and painful quest for fulfillment and happiness, her romantic beliefs give rise to comic situations. The humorous and ironic tone is part of the instructional and persuasive rhetoric of the genre. For instance, in Kinsella's Shopaholic series, the hopeless shopper Becky regularly buys the *Financial Times* to look like a professional financial consultant in order to deceive those around her, while her personal finances are a catastrophe, with overdue bills and an overdrawn bank account. In Haag's Swedish novel *Underbar och älskad av alla*, the wannabe actress Bella starts off with an exaggerated idea of her talent and ability to perform. She confidently states, "It feels like the life I am living on earth is not the life I am intended to live."[7] To start her career as an actress, she pretends to have professional experience and talents she does not. When she is finally employed by the Royal Dramatic Theatre in Stockholm, she does everything she can to avoid being discovered, but eventually she is found out and immediately fired.

Chick lit is known to be a humorous and lighthearted genre. As Rocio Montoro claims, the positive emotional response and feel-good factor is vital to the success of chick lit.[8] The character of the heart-to-heart confession is balanced by the female protagonist's self-centered and ironic worldview. The protagonist mocks the stereotypical situations she finds herself immersed in, and her life strategy is to make light of the misadventures and misfortunes she suffers. Because of her self-reflective ironic attitude, the resolution of her struggles is that, in the end, she will become a stronger and wiser person. If she starts off as a heartbroken and emotional wreck, she will end up as a strong-minded and independent woman. Because of this formula, the reader can, right from the start, look forward to a happy ending; the female reader enjoys reading about the female character and her endeavors because, in the end, the protagonist will reach a higher understanding of the world. The message is: However deeply in trouble you are, there is always hope. In the end, you may set out to make your mark on the world, or at least to take control of your life. Eventually, your efforts will be rewarded in some way.

Thus a common trait of chick lit is the protagonist's painful self-deception and its comic depiction. Even though her efforts and ordeals may be exaggerated for comic effect, most readers probably flesh out the female protagonist according to her dramatic role—that is, her role as a fictional character in a chick lit story.[9] In one way or another, she also reminds the reader of a real-life woman she knows, or of the reader herself. Although the female protagonist's tribulations are depicted in a comic confessional style to encourage the reader to both recognize and smile at the situations depicted and thereby to identify with the protagonist's vulnerabilities, the story as such is there to convey a nagging feeling of an unsatisfying situation and serious women's issues. Even though the protagonist's efforts are described in a comical and exaggerated way, they are also depicted in a way that brings her close to the everyday reality of many women in the twenty-first century.

In many Swedish novels, the contemporary, realistic, almost documentary, character of the genre is stressed, while the comic effects are reduced. The Swedish protagonist does not indulge in the same frenetic shopping and jet-setting activities that many American characters do. Neither is her goal to find romantic love and to be rescued and supported by an alpha male, such as Mark Darcy in *Bridget Jones's Diary*. In Rudberg's novel *Väninnan* (The Girlfriend; 2000), the restrained Kristin lives a rather dull married life. Her marriage to David, a vain financier, is a catastrophe. He constantly bullies her, and he does everything he can to put her under his control and to make her behave in the way that the ideal wife of a young, well-to-do financier brat in Stockholm supposedly should. Kristin is not allowed to work more than part-time at an auction company, and her husband plans her housework, chooses her outfits, and directs her social life. She suffers from an inferiority complex because she has put on weight, and her oppressive husband has lost interest in her. Still, nobody but herself and her husband regard her weight as a significant problem. Other men pay her compliments, and her personal coach at the gym emphasizes the importance of eating nourishing food when she starts her new fitness program. When Kristin eventually realizes that she has a false self-image, she has a breakdown and goes through a series of crises. For a start, she tries to obey her husband, listen to his advice, and adapt to his whims and moods. Then when she takes up meeting her best girlfriend from school on the sly, she starts to reevaluate her married life and her husband's character. When she realizes that her husband has been cheating on her, the discovery, in combination with her inferiority complex, crushes her. However, like most Swedish characters, Kristin's way to a better life, autonomy, and fulfillment is through a professional career. Like most Swedish chick lit, Rudberg's novel manifests the Swedish policy of "statist individualism," an individual-based social policy.[10] It illustrates the impact of Lutheran tradition and the fundamental principle of Nordic societal structure, the highly valued virtues of diligence and work. Through work, citizens become part of society and can realize the idea of themselves as creative beings and contributors.[11] It also demonstrates the Swedish ideology of gender equality as a matter of granting women autonomy and employment. The first step on Kristin's path to self-improvement is starting to work full-time; like most Swedes, she has been brought up to be independent and to find a source of personal fulfillment in work. When she is in crisis, she clings to her work, and because she now pays more attention to her tasks at the reputable auction company, she is soon promoted to project manager by her employer, and she becomes her boss's personal assistant. Presently, she finds herself in full charge of the rest of the staff, the budget, and sales management.

As in the Anglophone tradition, the Swedish protagonists work within the middle-class domain. The protagonists are never manual workers, nurses, or teachers, but are urban professionals, often within media, design, business, or finance. They are journalists, writers, actresses, sales managers, businesswomen, entrepreneurs, or politicians whose careers shape their lives to a considerable extent. Most Swedish chick lit novels are centered on work life and career advancement rather than on romantic relations.[12] In Ingermarsson's *Små citroner gula* (Yesterday's News; 2004), Agnes's breakup from her unfaithful boyfriend is a move toward a successful professional life, as well as self-realization and happiness. After some struggles to find a new job, Agnes makes rapid advances in her career, going from waitress to the owner of a stylish gourmet restaurant in Stockholm. Whether or not she ends up being united with her new boyfriend is of less importance than her professional achievements.

Thus Swedish protagonists recover from unhappy relationships by turning their energy toward their professional careers. The reason they eventually triumph is because their professional merits are recognized. Both Kristin and Agnes have the strength to fight their depression because they concentrate on work, and it is because of their status at work that they manage to regain their self-esteem. Contrary to the presentation of Flaubert's Emma Bovary and most Anglo-American protagonists, they do not seek fulfillment in men but rather in work. They overcome their ordeals because of their workaholic attitude. They manifest the same ideal as Stieg Larsson's heroine and victimized avenger Lisbeth Salander in the Millennium trilogy (2005–10); they fight their personal shortcomings by becoming outstanding professional women. Their quest for personal fulfillment is their search for professional triumph and personal rehabilitation. Because they form and pursue their personal project, they may live happily ever after. Many Swedish protagonists would agree with Maria in Andersson's *På andra sidan*

Venus (On the Other Side of Venus; 2006) when she happily declares, "I rather like being a singleton. Sex is absolutely overrated and I can wholeheartedly concentrate on my career."[13] The established myth of Swedish sin, a specific liberal attitude toward sex, is not confirmed in Swedish chick lit novels—quite the contrary; compared to many Anglophone heroines, the Swedish protagonists are fairly chaste or at least very little occupied by sexual relations or fantasies.

The Curing Crises

A successful professional life and recognition at work is the road to high self-esteem and fulfillment for Kristin, Agnes, and most Swedish protagonists. Problems and triumphs at work, and relations and conflicts with colleagues are vital to the plotline. Andersson's novels about three career-driven girlfriends—*På andra sidan Venus* and *Här och nu* (Here and Now; 2007)—can be categorized as advice manuals on how to be a successful career woman. The girlfriends' problems at work, their advancements and setbacks, and their relationships with colleagues and persons in charge are described in detail. When things are not going well at work, they meet, not to confess their latest love affairs, but to support and coach each other every time one of them faces new challenges at work. The advice and the strategies they suggest are presented in such a way that the reader of the novel can benefit from them too. Consequently, most Swedish chick lit novels could be categorized as "working-girl novels." Although the female protagonist's romantic relationship is often secondary to her professional life, some of her problems are caused by her involvement with an impossible man and the emotional consequences of that relationship. However, the best way for a Swedish protagonist to recover from a breakdown and depression is to face new work challenges and professional advancement. Her therapist, par excellence, is a wise and supportive work coach.

However, although the female protagonist is a working girl, she is often an emotionally insecure girl, "a pubertal monster," as the female protagonist is called in Rudberg's *Åse* (2008).[14] She is a girl who has focused too much on her professional occupation and her social responsibilities. In Ingermarsson's *Bara vanligt vatten* (Just Ordinary Water; 2009), the popular celebrity writer Stella acts like a self-possessed businesswoman. Nevertheless, behind her cool exterior, there is a vulnerable little girl whose life falls to pieces when she discovers a leak in her newly renovated bathroom. She immediately finds herself in crisis; her fashionable flat is turned into something of a construction zone as a renovation crew takes it over. When she tries to work in her study, she cannot concentrate and is unable to finish the novel she is working on; meanwhile, her publisher is constantly nagging her about submitting her manuscript. At the same time, she is feeling increasingly terrorized by a devoted fan, and, adding to it all, one day she surprises her boyfriend in bed with another man. In spite of this, she has no one but her dumped boyfriend to turn to when her pursuing fan threatens her. After a turbulent night, she ironically sums up her current situation: "Just what she needed right now. A flat turned upside down, an unwritten novel, comforting sex with her gay ex, a stalker, and a moody craftsman. What a party kit!"[15]

In chick lit, the road to maturation and self-knowledge is rocky; before the female protagonist can improve and progress, she must break down and suffer. Most narratives are centered on the protagonist's shortcomings: her pain and mental disarray. Her distress often makes her seriously ill, but she does not succumb to a fatal disease such as cancer, ALS (amyotrophic lateral sclerosis, or Lou Gehrig's Disease), or AIDS, nor to chronic conditions such as allergies, diabetes, migraines, or rheumatism. Instead, her development into a strong-minded woman takes place as she faces existential and emotional challenges. In those few cases where she requires medical treatment, her condition is always caused by her emotional problems and mood disorder.

Some Anglophone novels are constructed as fictional pathographies—that is, as literary narratives that describe personal experiences of illness and treatment.[16] Such a novel can, as Stephanie Harzewski writes, be looked upon "as an intermediary between the success story and the mental illness narrative."[17] Keyes's novels *Rachel's Holiday* (2007) and *Anybody Out There?* (2009) are two illustrative examples. In *Rachel's Holiday*, the protagonist's anxiety and lack of confidence result in an eating disorder and drug addiction. After an almost fatal overdose, she is put into a treatment clinic specializing in the rehabilitation of drug addicts. Most of the novel describes her cringeworthy embarrassments at the clinic, and how she participates in endless group therapy sessions and eventually learns to recognize and handle

her problems. She realizes that her therapist is right when she characterizes her as "a person with a distorted, warped value system. With so
little sense of who she is that she affects a different accent with different
people."[18] *Anybody Out There?* depicts another mental problem. When
Anna is severely injured in a car accident, in which her husband is killed,
she has to go through the stages of mourning. At first, she does not
accept her husband's death, and she immerses herself in memories and
tries to reach him in different ways. Most of the novel describes her time
as a physically broken and emotionally shattered patient, first in her
parents' home in Dublin, then in her apartment in New York. After the
first phase of denial, she is struck by the fact that her husband is dead,
and she goes through a series of earth-shattering revelations before she is
reconciled with her new knowledge and situation.

Both of Keyes's novels present the protagonist's emotional and mental problems, her psychological dilemmas, and her time as a patient
in treatment. They describe a physically ill and an emotionally trau-
matized protagonist whose quest for love is subordinate to her quest
for healing and mental well-being. The accounts of romantic rendez-
vous are secondary to the detailed depictions of mental treatments,
personal coaching, and pep-talking sessions, together with self-help
instructions and behavioral guidelines. *Anybody Out There?* is not a
novel about romance—that is, Anna's meeting with a new mate after
the death of her first one—but about her loss, anguish, and grief. Not
until the very end, in the concluding epilogue, is it implied that she
might, in due course, start a new relationship with another man. In
Rachel's Holiday, it is not until Rachel has been drug-free for a year and
is studying to become a psychologist that she is ready to be reunited
with her ex-boyfriend, Luke. Accordingly, she has to recover from her
breakdown and to start a new and independent life before she is ready
to get together with a man. In these two novels, the female protagonists' romantic relationships are hardly described at all. Their meetings
with new men are just hinted at as a confirmation of their maturity
and recovery. So there are no accounts of romantic love and boy-
meets-girl relationships according to the romance formula. Instead,
the novels are constructed according to the formula of a pathography,
a patient's painful recovery from a serious illness or disease.

In Swedish chick lit novels, the protagonist's sufferings are primarily related to external circumstances, and her rehabilitation is seldom

dependent on medical treatment. If she becomes ill, it is because of her emotional stress and is related to her social situation. In Rudberg's *Jenny S* (2005), the protagonist's separation from her partner means she has to leave her job at a bank, as well as her hometown, family, and friends. During this emotionally traumatic period, she suffers painful migraine attacks, but they are solely depicted as physical symptoms of her mental strain. However, her new and interesting job in Stockholm, her attractive employer, and his welcoming friends turn Jenny's new life into a professional and social success. When she returns to her hometown to see her ex-boyfriend, she is a self-confident, stylish woman who dares to confront her past failures.

Contrary to most Anglo-American characters, the Swedish protagonist's breakdown is often caused by her struggles to balance family life with a demanding career; in other words, the novels depict a situation most Swedish women recognize and one that is constantly referred to in Swedish media. Most Swedish protagonists are slightly older than the Anglo-American singletons, and several of them are mothers to a couple of children. Unlike the Anglophone protagonists, they do not worry obsessively about their looks, nor are they pursuing an unrealistic dream of catching a wealthy, good-looking Prince Charming. Instead, they are constantly torn between their responsibilities at home and their duties at work and between caring for others and investing in their own personal careers or life projects. They manifest the modern emancipated woman's struggle in the Nordic welfare state, where men and women are officially equal but where women still do most of the housework. They express the cultural confusion surrounding motherhood and career as well as womanhood and a high-level professional position. In Ingemarsson's *Den ryske vännen* (The Russian Friend; 2005), Kathy, Minister of Foreign Development, feels perpetually guilty because she has to rely heavily on her husband's help to keep things functioning at home. In Ingemarsson's *Inte enklare än så* (Not Easier than That; 2003), Annika is facing the same difficulties. Her job as an executive at an IT company requires her full commitment. As her husband works as a freelance writer, he spends more time at home with their children and, accordingly, does most of the housework. Both Kathy's and Annika's husbands are portrayed as the kind of considerate mates that most Anglophone protagonists dream about and with whom, if they are fortunate enough, they are

united at the very end of the story. In the Swedish novels, these caring husbands instead pose a problem for the female protagonists.
Their constant loyalty enhances the female protagonists' inner conflict, which manifests as a continuous juggling that precipitates an
identity crisis. During the course of events, the protagonist therefore
often meets another, more exciting, man at work, often the "impossible man." If her main conflict at the beginning of the novel is how
to balance her time and responsibilities at home and at work, she soon
confronts another dilemma: Should she give in to her attraction to
an intriguing but unpredictable man, or should she stick to her reli-
able, trustworthy, but somewhat dull husband at home? The choice
is not easy, but the protagonist is eventually brought to understand
the true value of a dependable and thoughtful partner. He is the man
she needs if she is to live a fulfilled life as a modern Swedish woman
who wants to combine a happy family life and a stimulating but time-
consuming professional career. In those cases when the protagonist
does not recognize her needs in time, she finds herself in deep crisis,
as in Ingemarsson's *På det fjärde ska det ske* (It Will Happen on the
Fourth; 2002), where the restless and pubertal Paula's self-indulgent
behavior finally prompts her caring and loving boyfriend to leave her.

The external persona of the Swedish protagonist is often a professionally successful but exhausted woman, who struggles to combine being a caring mother, a sexy woman, and a professional winner.
Although Paula in *På det fjärde ska det ske* is a competent globetrotter,
and Stella in *Bara vanligt vatten* is a media celebrity, they are both
examples of women who, on the surface, have grown up too fast.
They skillfully handle their external affairs, such as job, legal, and
social duties in society. Professionally, they successfully outdo most
men. Their problem is, however, that they do not recognize their
emotional wants and do not know how to retain their femininity.
These female protagonists express many Swedish women's perpetual
inner conflict—how to balance family life and professional career and
how to be a hardworking, assertive climber and still be perceived as
attractive and feminine. When the Swedish protagonist is attracted
to another man, it is because he, as a male, verifies her femininity
and sex appeal. Through his attention, she becomes aware of her
emotional needs and her romantic dream. Although she eventually chooses to leave him and return to her boyfriend or husband at

home, as Annika in *Inte enklare än så* and Marie in *Den ryske vännen* do, her emotional suffering confirms her femininity and emotional development. The trials and emotional conflicts she has to cope with humanize her and make her worthy of the reader's understanding and empathy. Her ability to overcome her ordeals results in an emotionally satisfying, life-affirming, and optimistic ending. She becomes a true postmodern heroine because she is able to help herself mobilize her inner emotional—and female—strength.

CHICK LIT NOVELS AS SELF-HELP MANUALS

There are many similarities between chick lit, women's fictional conduct books published in the eighteenth and nineteenth centuries, and today's women's magazines and self-help manuals. The references to female concerns and a female sexual identity are used to connote feelings of intimacy and closeness; the intention is to create a relationship between the female protagonist and the female reader, as well as to communicate a sense of positive resolution and girl power. The packaging of chick lit, such as the layout of the book covers, confirms that the books deal with subjects that are important in women's lives: romantic love, marriage, family, professional career, infidelity, children, divorce, friendship, weight issues, and aging. The novels are often marketed with glossy covers in rosy, pastel colors—preferably pink—and sometimes with golden details and text. The cover text is often in curved letterforms to embody a female identity, a personal style referring to handwriting and to heart-to-heart talks between girlfriends. Pictures of stylish women in stiletto heels, or trendy women in everyday situations, are part of the prototypical chick lit cover.[19]

The references to stylish women's magazines and consumer culture are, however, less common on Swedish covers. A female hand carrying a plastic bag of yellow lemons decorates the front cover of the paperback edition of Ingemarsson's *Små citroner gula*.[20] A blurred, black-and-white photo of a rushing woman in a white dress facing a man in a dark suit is featured on the hard-copy cover of Ingermarsson's *Inte enklare än så*.[21] An intimate photo of the female author, together with a personal presentation in the blurb or on the back of the inside flap, adds to the confidential image on Haag's novels, for instance *I en annan del av Bromma* (In Another Part of Bromma; 2008).[22] These frequent photos and bios of the writers at the back are there to establish a bond between the female writer and her female protagonist, as well as between the writer and her female reader. They invite the reader to join the female community of the novel and the authentic world it is referring to. Although it is a fictional story, the message is that it is about authentic women's matters, and the photos of the writer and the presentation in the blurb often stress the documentary character of the novel. Even though it is not an autobiographical novel, it is, at least, a novel written by a recognizable and well-known female writer who knows what she is writing about and who wants to share her "tried-and-true" experiences with all those women who happen to be in the same situation and who recognize the problems the female protagonist faces.

The bond between author and reader is even more stressed when the female author is well-known as a writer of personal autobiographical columns and self-help books. Writers such as Keyes, Haag, and Ingemarsson are known to their audiences as columnists in women's magazines. Many of them also publish collections of their instructional feature articles in books targeted to a female readership. Some of Keyes's popular feature articles are collected in *Under the Duvet* (2001) and *Further Under the Duvet* (2005), and they are structured with headlines such as "Mind, Body, Spirit . . . and Shoes," "Friends and Family," and "All Grown Up." Swedish chick lit writers combine the same genres and publication models. Both Ingemarsson and Haag republish their feature articles in various collections, such as Ingemarsson's *Kajsas värld* (The World of Kajsa; 2006) and Haag's *Martinakoden* (Martina's Code; 2006). The latter consists of Haag's intimate and self-ironic columns, formerly published in women's magazines, where her life as a writer, actress, and mother of young children is described to strengthen the bond between her, her female protagonists, and the female readers of her columns and novels. In *Kajsas värld*, Ingemarsson writes to her female readers in the first person, and on the front cover is a closeup photo of the writer posing in a low-cut, pink top, while on the back cover is a more traditional photo of a serious professional writer dressed in black. The front covers are like those of typical women's magazines that are jam-packed with headlines such as "How to Become a Real Woman: 10 Hot Tips!" and "Help Yourself to the Life of Your Dreams!" The layout and the typography of the headlines refer to well-known Swedish women's magazines, such as *Damernas värld* (Women's World), where Ingermarsson publishes her feature articles. References to women's magazines are also obvious as her feature articles in *Kajsas värld* are sorted under headlines such as "Body and Soul," "She and He," and "Family and Leisure." The articles can, accordingly, be described as a combination of personal confession and instructional advice given by an experienced woman who has achieved a good life the hard way.

Hence just as Keyes's, Ingemarsson's, and Haag's novels relate to the confidential tone of their columns, their novels are constructed as fictional stories about the same kind of unfortunate and struggling female protagonist as the reader meets in their columns. Their novels are very much fictional examples of those instructions and advice that are launched in today's women's magazines, coaching literature, and self-help manuals. The close relationship between chick lit and women's magazines in the Anglophone countries has been stressed, for instance, by Caroline Smith.[23] Much the same could be said about Swedish chick lit, although the references to designer clothes, makeup advice, and fashionable furnishings to encourage certain consumer behavior are not as obvious as in the Anglo-American novels. Instead, Swedish chick lit novels are noticeably centered on how to balance family life and a professional career. They very much become self-help manuals in their own right, providing the readers with an alternative instructional guide on how to understand who they are and what they want, encouraging the female readers to reflect on personal development and well-being.

One of the most popular Swedish authors of self-help books targeted to female readers is Mia Törnblom, who has published her concept in books such as *Självkänsla nu! Din personliga coach visar hur* (Self-Esteem Now! Your Personal Coach Demonstrates How; 2005). Her method is to find a balance between what she calls self-confidence (i.e., confidence in one's ability to produce) and self-esteem (i.e., knowledge of one's own value as a woman).[24] Much the same message is proclaimed by Ingemarsson in her feature articles, advice manuals, and novels. Initially, her female protagonists demonstrate a juvenile outlook on life, like, for instance, the egocentric Paula in *På det fjärde ska det ske.* She is unable to hang on to anything and is constantly on the move, always leaving her loving and caring boyfriend behind, always expecting him to wait for her until she returns. Like Paula, most chick lit protagonists initially look on themselves as victims and frequently compare themselves to others to confirm that perception. They are eager to behave according to the behavioral code for successful and fashionable urban, middle-class women. At the start, they feel inferior in some way; they are not pleased with their private or professional lives. They want to improve their lives, as well as themselves as women.

The protagonist's low self-esteem and negative self-image are even more accentuated when, or if, she is dumped by her partner. In Rudberg's *Jenny S*, the female protagonist dresses the way she thinks her boyfriend wants her to and the way she did when they first met at school. She is proven wrong when he starts dating her best girlfriend, whose personal style is quite the opposite of Jenny's. Suddenly, her world falls apart and she has to reconsider her life to be able to recover from her breakdown. To be able to live a more independent life, Jenny starts to follow the advice prescribed in the latest coaching manuals. Following their step-by-step instructions, she starts to list different goals in order to regain control of her life and to understand who she is and what she wants.[25] She adopts a self-imposed discipline based on the premise that an individual's defense against inner storms is to organize her time.[26] To reduce stress and recover, most Swedish female protagonists immerse themselves in physical activities, exercise, and fitness programs, and here they act on the behavioral guidelines of today's fitness industry. In Ingemarsson's *Bara vanligt vatten*, Stella escapes the chaotic situation in her water-damaged flat by occupying her mind with something totally different: riding. In doing so, she achieves what the manuals advocate, by "living in the present." In Rudberg's *Åse*, the protagonist tries to pull through by focusing on the present and playing tennis, whereby she manages to "affirm and confirm herself," to quote Mia Törnblom's self-help instructions.[27]

Today's chick lit also refers to 200-year-old advice manuals for women, where the female protagonist was to be brought up to be a virtuous wife and exemplary mother by means of cautionary or ideal examples. The instructional guidelines and their fictional examples from the eighteenth and nineteenth centuries advocated a complementary gender system, according to which a woman should submit herself to the patriarchal order—that is, obey her father, husband, and God.[28] Today's chick lit promotes another ideal, an independent and self-assured woman, a man's equal. The female character is to become the perfect, well-to-do, middle-class woman marketed by today's self-help industry and its two ethical standards, Protestant self-discipline and the kind of self-fashioning promoted by capitalism and consumer culture.[29] The message is: You can transform and improve yourself and your life if you just try hard enough. The protagonist's development confirms the importance of self-esteem and a confident appearance, as well as the idea that anyone can improve and achieve success. The ultimate proof of the female protagonist's triumph and that she has finally reached her goal is when she recognizes her needs and desires. That is, among other things, she will never again approve of a man who does not appreciate her the way she is.

However, in the Swedish chick lit novel, the protagonist's recovery is very much directly related to her work life, and the self-help instructions are very much coaching literature for career-driven women. The world of work in Swedish chick lit is neither, as in most Anglophone novels, window dressing nor a backdrop to the business of finding love.[30] In Swedish chick lit, a full-time occupation and a successful career are the keys to self-fulfillment, self-worth, and happiness. If the female protagonist is to heal and improve, she has to have a rewarding professional life; she confirms the innate Swedish idea that it is necessary for a woman to have a life of her own outside the private emotional sphere. Her work is necessary for her quest for self-definition, and the message is explicit: a woman has to deal with her personal problems, have a career, and become reconciled with her former mistakes and failures before she can find love and be united with a suitable mate. To be united in a romantic relationship with an equal and caring Mr. Right, who recognizes and accepts her professional advancement, is the ultimate confirmation of mental growth and future well-being in Swedish chick lit.

WOMEN'S LIBERATION AND A ROOM OF ONE'S OWN

As mentioned before, chick lit is often accused of promoting the consumer culture advocated by women's magazines and makeover programs and of touting middle-class aspirations and lifestyle. It has been claimed to reinforce gendered stereotypes and to embrace exaggerated consumerism. However, to refer to the Swedish left-wing journalist Göran Greider's analysis of the genre, the most forbidden sometimes reflects the truth.[31] Chick lit is a genre that, in many ways, validates women's experiences. Contrary to most other popular genres, maleness is underrepresented in chick lit novels.[32] In their own way, chick lit novels describe the contemporary "truth" about women's issues and women's daily lives. They give a quasi-faithful representation of certain female values and beliefs that may invite the readers to recognize and sympathize with those real-life values and so also with the female protagonists. Protagonists, such as the British Bridget Jones and the Swedish Agnes in *Små citroner gula*, become icons of a certain kind of femininity, a constructed point of identification for many female readers. The success often lies in the "that's me" phenomenon, whereby Bridget Jones and Agnes become regarded not only as fictional characters but as representatives of today's everywoman. Chick lit has an authenticity that many contemporary readers miss in women's fiction of the past; thereby, they sense that it tells something about themselves and where they are in life right now.[33]

In that way, chick lit reflects and reveals the society that produces it, reproducing the dominant ideology of a certain time and a certain culture. Sympathizing with the female protagonist allows the reader to try out, in her imagination, a recognizable but still different woman's life. In *Reading Women*, Nanci Milone Hill admits to being addicted to women's fiction because it allows her to seek out another life: "Through these novels I have been a Southern belle, a hip young CEO, a woman dealing with cancer or the loss of a loved one, and a woman besieged by friendship. Women's fiction speaks to me because it delves into the topics that are important in my own life—intimate relationships, friendship, overcoming loss—and it also offers hope for the future."[34] According to Rocio Montoro's survey, many female readers find therapeutic qualities in chick lit.[35] The Swedish scholar Cecilia Pettersson's work on bibliotherapy and her study on sick-listed women's rehabilitation programs also proves the importance of chick lit stories. According to Pettersson's investigation, many burnt-out women on sick leave use chick lit as therapy, and they stress both the relaxing and the recreating potential of the genre.[36] This emotionally satisfying reaction is probably connected to an optimistic ending, and most readers seem to agree about how a chick lit novel should unfold and conclude; they expect and want a happy ending to the female protagonist's struggles. The positive emotional response and feel-good factor is vital to the success of the genre. As Lauren Baratz-Logsted writes in her defense of chick lit, the novels do not solve world crises—the conflict in Iraq or the riddle of cancer—but they narrate about life as such, about friendship, love, and death.[37]

Several of the writers of the short stories in *This Is Chick-Lit* (2006) confirm that what makes the genre of special value is the way it provides an entertaining story that also helps the reader to come to terms with her own everyday life and to think in a new way. The writers stress that their characters demonstrate how people think and behave, and that they verify and validate women's experiences in a way that is emancipating. According to chick lit author Deanna Carlyle, the novels are a space for women outside the restrictions, demands, and oppression of the patriarchy. Stephanie Harzewski claims that the genre is a combination of romance and the novel of manners, and Cathy Yardley states that the narratives are women's "bildungsromanen," novels that depict women's way to higher maturity.[38]

In one sense, chick lit novels are entertaining, self-help novels that instruct women on how to behave and how to get on with life. In today's society, failure is a taboo. Therefore, modern popular fiction is full of recipes for how to be successful, but not for how to come to terms with failure, according to Richard Sennett.[39] Chick lit illustrates how to succeed, maybe not how to cope with failures but how to overcome them. In an emotionally engaging fictional form, they show what to do to improve and how to become a self-assured and independent woman. The chick is always a role model for women's emancipation and liberation, which confirms women's ability to transform and to make their mark on the world if only they try. Like most heroic stories, the story is structured around one individual, and the rest of the characters and plot lines are subordinate to her quest. The protagonist is struggling to recover from her loss in a way that results in change and improvement. In that way, the stories may work as emotional and cognitive training, where the narrative makes the reader try out the different scenarios and situations in her own imagination. The representation may invite the reader of the novel to look, within the frame of the fictional story, for different ways out of the problems the protagonist finds herself in, which may result in the reader of the novel mentally, cognitively, and emotionally preparing herself to confront, interpret, and handle similar situations in real life—that is, to deal, more or less directly, with the vicissitudes of her own life.[40] As the Swedish literary scholar Maria Nilson declares, many interesting questions are asked without being given any conclusive answer as to how to improve and live one's life. Some novels demonstrate, however, as she maintains, that it is possible to live life in many different ways and that this awareness is part of the process of becoming a grown-up woman.[41] That life can look different to women in different age groups is a message stressed in Ingemarsson's novels, where she works with several parallel plotlines and female protagonists; an example is *Lyckans hjul* (Wheel of Fortune; 2007), where she depicts the lives of four women of different ages and situations.

How persuasive and engaging the message is and how well it is received by the female reader depends on the story and the narration. Chick lit is characterized both by a certain plotline and by a specific narrative technique. The rhetorical devices used are similar to those in the literary tradition that preceded it, former instructional advice manuals and romances targeted to female readers. The story is presented in a way that is intended to stir emotions; viewpoint, mood, and style are used to invite the female reader to recognize and sympathize with those real-life values the female protagonist represents. To share the protagonist's internal perspective on the events depicted is to imagine what it might be like to be in the same situation. The female protagonist's viewpoint is used to make the events feel true and authentic. Through this, the narrative form is used to establish a close bond between the protagonist and the reader of the novel; it makes the reader both recognize and explore the protagonist. The subjective, intimate tone and voice of the narrator creates a sense of authentic presence; the female protagonist, narrator, or focalizer becomes a subject to identify with—a close friend rather than a fictional character.

The comedic and self-ironic tone of chick lit novels also adds to the attractiveness of the genre, which is thereby also challenging, rather than simply deploying, the ideologies transmitted by conduct manuals, women's magazines, and self-help books.[42] The depiction of the female protagonist's deficiencies and failures is such that it makes the female reader indulge in giddy self-recognition, but at the same time feel a bit superior as she is able to recognize the protagonist's flaws. The reader is thus both made to laugh at the protagonist's shortcomings and to enjoy being a bit more mature, according to Nilson.[43]

It is important that the reader stay slightly ahead of the protagonist and therefore to be able to predict the coming events before the protagonist. For instance, in Rudberg's *Jenny S*, the reader knows that Jenny's husband is unfaithful to her before Jenny does. In Ingemarsson's *Bara vanligt vatten*, the reader figures out which man is worth paying attention to long before the female protagonist does. In this way, it is possible to find therapeutic values in chick lit; it may provide the reader with an emotional catharsis because of this combination of a superior perspective and an enjoyable mixture of tears and laughter, frustration and success, as well as internal and external perspective. The reader is made to both recognize herself in the protagonist and feel a bit superior: to identify with her and to giggle at her without feeling guilty. To chuckle at your best friend's failures is not OK, but to laugh at a fictional character's mistakes is all right. Chick lit novels may therefore make the reader feel that she is not alone in her feelings of insufficiency and deficiency, at the same time as she is helped to learn how to deal with them.

Haag's novel *Underbar och älskad av alla* is an illustrative example of a comical protagonist and her failures. Bella is so preoccupied with her own talent and so eagerly searching for professional fulfillment that she subscribes to all coaching instructions and self-help advice that comes her way. However, her exaggerated embracement of the coaching values turns out to be a mistake and results in her failure. Instead, she has to recognize her own personal needs. As in most chick lit, the focus is on the protagonist's personal choice and development, and thus the novel confirms what Hilary Radner claims to be the tenets of today's feminine identity.[44] Nevertheless, Bella is still able to recover, to maintain her belief in her own talent, and to create her alternative instructional guide to a successful life.

It must be stressed that the attraction of chick lit is its emotionally satisfying and optimistic message. Chick lit novels are stories about the female protagonist's progress and final triumph, about how she improves because of her failures and how she comes to terms with her everyday life. Like today's makeover programs, chick lit has a socio-emotional function; it confirms that it is always possible to make a change and to improve, at least if you want to badly enough and are capable of facing and dealing with your problems. Both makeover programs and chick lit novels are about persons who have failed and are in crisis and, therefore, first have to admit to and confess their disappointment and failures before they can find help and a coach. Just like the protagonist in a makeover program, the female protagonist in a chick lit novel has to admit her failure in order to gain control over it. Her sufferings and efforts can then be rewarded. Because she is willing to subject herself to the recommended treatment—self-help instructions or makeover programs—she will attain the anticipated improvement and transformation. In the makeover programs, it can be a more attractive appearance, better personal finances, a stylish new home, rewarding work, a satisfying sex life, or enjoyable leisure time. In chick lit, it is personal fulfillment, and in Swedish chick lit especially, autonomy and self-esteem. With the female protagonist's transformation, chick lit validates the same message that is disseminated in various media channels: it is possible for a woman who has been unsuccessful to change her life for the better in every sense, if she just makes up her mind to go through with her project.

However much chick lit verifies the self-help ideology, it also expresses today's ideas about a lack of purpose or a sense of pointlessness, a sense of what Émile Durkheim in 1897 named "anomie," a discrepancy between external expectations and the accessible resources to carry them out.[45] The novels manifest what Zygmunt Bauman calls "fluid modernity," a state without norms, where the individual does not have any norms or authorities to cling to but has to invent and carry through with her own life project.[46] Chick lit is very much about a discrepancy between ideals and reality, dreams and actual possibilities, and how the female character is made to reevaluate her life and to create a new important female project. In today's chick lit, "to be" has become "to make"; internal qualities have been replaced by external actions. In romantic fiction and novels of manners of the past, the heroine had to prove her virtue and goodness; whatever happened, she remained a good example of female virtues. Today's chick lit expresses another message: the perfect female protagonist acts, and through this she is able to improve and to transform into something better. It is thus not enough to be; a person has to advance, and she must— sometimes assisted by a personal coach—invent and construct her own success and happiness. As in old romance literature, it is based on the idea of an innate emotional justice, but in today's chick lit, it is a story about an authentic modern woman, not a born heroine who has to remain a heroine, but a true woman, loveable but flawed, who has to work at coping with life.

Therefore, today's chick lit tells a story that may nourish many female readers' dreams about change, improvement, and happiness and, at the same time, encourages them to improve themselves and their lives. The chick lit story demonstrates that it is possible for a woman, once she is ready to act, to achieve ultimate success and to become a self-made heroine with a valuable life project. In Swedish chick lit, the valuable life project always includes a successful professional career. In order to achieve that, the Swedish heroine must become an emotionally mature and self-confident woman who recognizes her own needs. She also requires a caring mate with whom she can share family life on equal terms. In that way, Swedish chick lit very much confirms the fundamental principle of Nordic societal structure, the highly valued virtues of work and employment. Moreover, Swedish chick lit also shows how a successful woman can realize the idea of gender equality and emancipation, both among colleagues at work and as a mother and wife at home.

NOTES

1. Jenny Björklund, "Mer än makor och mödrar: svensk chick lit och den skandinaviska välfärdsmodellen," in *Chick lit—brokiga läsningar och didaktiska utmaningar*, ed. Maria Nilson and Helene Ehriander (Stockholm: Liber 2013), 72.

2. Pamela Regis, *A Natural History of the Romance Novel* (Philadelphia: University of Pennsylvania Press, 2003), 14.

3. Cf. Cathy Yardley, *Will Write for Shoes: How to Write a Chick Lit Novel* (New York: Thomas Dunne, 2006).

4. J. Knowles, "Editorial," *Diegesis: Journal of the Association for Research in Popular Fictions* (Special Issue on Chick Lit), 8 (2004), 2.

5. For more about the tradition of conduct books and manuals of manners, see Gunlög Kolbe, *Om konsten att konstruera en kvinna. Retoriska strategier i 1800-talets rådgivare och i Marie Sophie Schwartz' romaner* (Göteborg: Göteborgs universitet, 2001). On the connection between chick lit and today's advice manuals, see Stephanie Harzewski, "Tradition and Displacement in the New Novel of Manners," in *Chick Lit: The New Woman's Fiction*, ed. Suzanne Ferriss and Mallory Young (New York: Routledge, 2006), 29–46.

6. Yardley, *Will Write for Shoes*, 4–5.

7. Martina Haag, *Underbar och älskad av alla* (*och på jobbet går det också jätte-bra*) [*Wonderful and Loved by Everybody*] (Stockholm: Piratförlaget, 2005), 43.

8. Rocio Montoro, *Chick Lit: The Stylistics of Cappuccino Fiction* (London: Continuum, 2012), 170.

9. Regarding dramatic role, see Jonathan Culpeper, *Language and Characterization: People in Plays and Other Texts* (Harlow: Longman, 2001), 86–87.

10. Lars Trädgårdh, "Statist Individualism: On the Culturality of the Nordic Welfare State," in *The Cultural Construction of Norden*, ed. Øystein Sørensen and Bo Stråth (Oslo: Scandinavian University Press, 1997), 255–85.

11. Henrik Stenius, "The Good Life Is a Life of Conformity: The Impact of Lutheran Tradition on Nordic Political Culture," in *The Cultural Construction of Norden*, ed. Øystein Sørensen and Bo Stråth (Oslo: Scandinavian University Press, 1997), 164–65.

12. See Björklund, "Mer än makor och mödrar," 71–91.

13. Elisabeth Andersson, *På andra sidan Venus* [*On the Other Side of Venus*] (Stockholm: Kalla Kulor Förlag, 2006), 56.

14. Denise Rudberg, *Åse: Roman* (Stockholm: Bonniers, 2008), 77.

15. Kajsa Ingemarsson, *Bara vanligt vatten* [*Just Ordinary Water*] (Stockholm: Norstedts, 2009), 351.

16. Regarding pathographies, see Katarina Bernhardsson, *Litterära besvär, Skildringar av sjukdom i samtida svensk prosa* (Stockholm: Ellerström, 2010), 290.

17. Stephanie Harzewski, *Chick Lit and Postfeminism* (Charlottesville: University of Virginia Press, 2011), 137.

18. Marian Keyes, *Rachel's Holiday* (New York: Avon, 2002), 413.

19. About Anglophone chick lit covers, see Montoro, *Chick Lit*, 17–57.

20. See cover of Kajsa Ingemarsson, *Små citroner gula* [*Yesterday's News*] (Stockholm: Bokförlaget Forum, 2004).

21. See Kajsa Ingemarsson, *Inte enklare än så* [*Not Easier than That*] (Stockholm: Bokförlaget Forum, 2003).

22. Martina Haag, *I en annan del av Bromma* [*In Another District of Bromma*] (Stockholm: Piratförlaget, 2008).

23. Caroline Smith, *Cosmopolitan Culture and Consumerism in Chick Lit* (New York: Routledge, 2007).

24. Mia Törnblom, *Självkänsla nu! Din personliga coach visar hur* [*Self-Esteem Now! Your Personal Coach Demonstrates How*] (Stockholm: Månpocket, 2005).

25. Cf. Törnblom, *Självkänsla nu!*, 143–53.

26. Cf. Richard Sennett, *The Corrosion of Character: The Personal Consequences of Work in the New Capitalism* (New York: W. W. Norton, 1998), 100–101.

27. Törnblom, *Självkänsla nu!*, 53, 67.

28. Kolbe, *Om konsten att konstruera en kvinna*, 34, 73, 169–72, et passim.
29. Regarding how these standards refer to Protestant and capitalist values, see Sennett's discussion of Max Weber, "The Protestant Ethic and the Spirit of Capitalism," in Sennett, *The Corrosion of Character*, 102–6.
30. About the secondary status of the world of work in Anglophone chick lit, see Juliette Wells, "Mothers of Chick Lit? Women Writers, Readers, and Literary History," in *Chick Lit: The New Woman's Fiction*, ed. Suzanne Ferriss and Mallory Young (New York: Routledge, 2006), 54–59.
31. Göran Greider, "Det mest förljugna," *Aftonbladet*, August 6, 2007.
32. Montoro, *Chick Lit*, 115.
33. Cf. Suzanne Ferriss and Mallory Young, "Introduction," in *Chick Lit: The New Woman's Fiction*, ed. Suzanne Ferriss and Mallory Young (New York: Routledge, 2006), 3–5.
34. Nanci Milone Hill, *Reading Women: A Book Club Guide for Women's Fiction* (Santa Barbara, CA: Libraries Unlimited, 2012), xi.
35. Montoro, *Chick Lit*, 183.
36. Cecilia Pettersson, "Mellan självbekräftelse och självförglömmelse. Om terapeutisk läsning," in *Läsning. RJ:s årsbok 2013/2014* (Göteborg: Makadam, 2013), 151–52.
37. Lauren Baraatz-Logsted, "Introduction," in *This Is Chick Lit*, ed. Lauren Baratz-Logsted (Dallas, TX: Benbella, 2006), 4.
38. Deanna Carlyle, "Dead Men Don't Eat Quiche," 101; Stephanie Harzewski, "Tradition and Displacement," 29–46; Yardley, *Will Write for Shoes*, 4–5.
39. Sennett, *The Corrosion of Character*, 118.
40. Cf. Brian Boyd, *On the Origin of Stories: Evolution, Cognition, and Fiction* (Cambridge, MA: Belknap Press of Harvard University, 2009).
41. Maria Nilson, *Chick Lit. Från glamour till vardagsrealism* (Lund: BTJ förlag, 2008), 83, 154.
42. Cf. Caroline Smith, *Cosmopolitan Culture*, 16.
43. Maria Nilson, *Chick Lit*, 22,149.
44. Hilary Radner, *Neo-feminism: Girly Films, Chick Films and Consumer Culture* (London: Routledge, 2011), 6.
45. Èmile Durkheim, *On Suicide* (London: Penguin, 2006).
46. Zygmunt Bauman, *Liquid Modernity* (Cambridge: Polity, 2000).

Bibliography

"90-talet skildras av tio regissörer." *Arbetet*, February 2, 1990.

Adorno, Theodor, and Max Horkheimer. *Dialectic of Enlightenment: Philosophical Fragments*. Stanford: Stanford University Press, 2002.

Aigner, Gertrude, and Erik Centerwall. *Barnens kärleksliv: Om kärlek, sexualitet och mötet med vuxenvärlden*. Stockholm: Prisma/RFSU, 1983.

Åkerbäck, Peter. "Scientologi-kyrkan." In Ingvar Svanberg and David Westerlund (eds.), *Religion i Sverige*. Stockholm: Dialogos Förlag, 2008.

Åkerlund, Berthil. *Insida: Svenska personligheter i intervju om drivkrafter och tro*. Uppsala: Cordia, 1992.

Åkesson, Jimmie, and Carina Herrstedt. "SD–ett parti för hbt-personer." *Aftonbladet*, March 30, 2010.

"Alla ropar på Roy." *Vi*, 48, 1988.

Alwall, Jonas. "Scientologerna och samhället: Dialog eller konflikt?" In Carl-Gustav Carlsson and Liselotte Frisk (eds.), *Gudars och gudinnors återkomst: Studier i nyreligiositet*. Umeå: Institutionen för religionsvetenskap, Umeå Universitet, 2000, 99–116.

Ambjörnsson, Ronny. *Mitt förnamn är Ronny*. Stockholm: Bonniers, 1998.

Andersson, Christoph. *Operation Norrsken: Om Stasi och Sverige under kalla kriget*. Stockholm: Norstedts, 2013.

Andersson, Daniel, and Åke Sander (eds.). *Det mångreligiösa Sverige—ett landskap i förändring*. Lund: Studentlitteratur, 2005.

Andersson, Elisabeth. *Här och nu [Here and Now]*. Stockholm: Kalla Kulor Förlag, 2007.

———. *På andra sidan Venus [On the Other Side of Venus]*. Stockholm: Kalla Kulor Förlag, 2006.

Andersson, Jenny. *När framtiden har hänt: Socialdemokratin och folkhemsnostalgin*. Stockholm: Ordfront, 2009.

Andersson, Lars Gustaf. "Den svenska konstfilmsinstitutionen." *Filmhäftet*, 1–2, 1995, 4–14.

Andersson, Roy. *Vår tids rädsla för allvar*. Göteborg: Filmkonst, 1995.

Andersson, Roy, Kalle Boman, and István Borbás (eds.). *Lyckad nedfrysning av herr Moro*. Stockholm: Gidlunds, 1992.

Arendt, Hannah. *Eichmann in Jerusalem: A Report on the Banality of Evil.* London: Penguin, 1994.

Arweck, Elisabeth. *Researching New Religious Movements: Responses and Redefinitions.* London: Routledge, 2006.

Asplund, Hans. *Farväl till funktionalismen.* Stockholm: Atlantis, 1980.

Asplund, Johan. *Essä om Gemeinschaft och Gesellschaft.* Göteborg: Korpen, 1991.

Baraatz-Logsted, Lauren. "Introduction." In Laurem Baratz-Logsted (ed.), *This Is Chick Lit.* Dallas, TX: Benbella, 2006, 1–6.

———. "Shell Game." In Elizabeth Merrick (ed.), *This is Not Chick Lit: Original Stories by America's Best Women Writers.* New York: Random House, 2006: 119–42.

Bauman, Zygmunt. *Intimations of Postmodernity.* London: Routledge, 1992.

———. *Liquid Modernity.* Cambridge: Polity, 2000.

———. *Modernity and Ambivalence.* London: Polity, 1991.

———. *Modernity and the Holocaust.* New York: Cornell University Press, 1989.

———. *Postmodern Ethics.* Cambridge: Blackwell, 1993.

Beckman, Vanna. "Offentlighetsprincipen exploateras." *Läkartidningen,* 104:39, 2007, 2769–70.

"Behöll sin frihet i reklamfilmen," *Arbetet,* January 6, 1991.

Benjamin, Walter. "On the Concept of History." In *Selected Writings: 1938–1940.* Cambridge, MA: Belknap Press of Harvard University, 2003, 389–400.

Berglund, Peter. *Segrarnas sorgsna eftersmak: Om autencitetssträvan i Stig Larssons romancer.* Stockholm: Brutus Östlings bokförlag Symposion, 2004.

Bernhardsson, Katarina. *Litterära besvär, Skildringar av sjukdom i samtida svensk prosa.* Stockholm: Ellerström, 2010.

Bjereld, Ulf, and Marie Demker. *I Vattumannens tid: En bok om 1968 års uppror och dess betydelse idag.* Stockholm: Hjalmarson and Högberg, 2005.

———. *Kampen om kunskapen: Informationssamhällets politiska skiljelinjer.* Stockholm: Hjalmarson and Högberg, 2008.

Björklund, Jenny. "Mer än makor och mördrar: svensk chick lit och den skandinaviska välfärdsmodellen." In Maria Nilson and Helene Ehriander (eds.), *Chick lit–brokiga läsningar och didaktiska utmaningar.* Stockholm: Liber, 2013, 71–91.

Boëthius, Mia Pia. *På heder och samvete: Sverige och andra världskriget.* Stockholm: Norstedts, 1991.

Bogdan, Henrik. "The Church of Scientology in Sweden." In James R. Lewis (ed.), *Scientology.* Oxford: Oxford University Press, 2009, 335–44.

Bondevik, Hilde, and Knut Stene-Johansen. *Sykdom som litteratur: 13 utvalgte diagnose.* Oslo: Unipub, 2011.

Bordwell, David. *Figures Traced in Light: On Cinematic Staging*. Berkeley: University of California Press, 2005.

Boréus, Kristina. *Högervåg: Nyliberalismen och kampen om språket i svensk debatt 1969–1989*. Stockholm: Tiden, 1994.

Boyd, Brian. *On the Origin of Stories: Evolution, Cognition, and Fiction*. Cambridge, MA: Belknap Press of Harvard University, 2009.

Broberg, Gunnar, and Matthias Tydén. *Oönskade i folkhemmet: Rashygien och sterilisering i Sverige*. Stockholm: Gidlunds, 1991.

Bromley, David G., and Anson Shupe. *Anti-Cult Movements in Cross-Cultural Perspective*. New York: Garland, 1994.

———. *Strange Gods: The Great American Cult Scare*. Boston: Beacon, 1981.

Brunette, Peter. *Michael Haneke*. Chicago: University of Illinois Press, 2010.

Brunow, Dagmar. "The Language of the Complex Image: Roy Andersson's Political Aesthetics." *Journal of Scandinavian Cinema*, 1, 2011, 83–86.

Carlyle, Deanna. "Dead Men Don't Eat Quiche." In Elizabeth Merrick (ed.), *This Is Not Chick Lit: Original Stories by America's Best Women Writers*. New York: Random House, 2006: 101–18.

Childs, Marquis. *Sweden: The Middle Way*. New Haven: Yale University Press, 1936.

Church of Scientology in Sweden homepage. http://www.scientologikyrkanisverige.info/ (accessed August 5, 2008).

Clow, Barbara. "Who's Afraid of Susan Sontag? Or, the Myths and Metaphors of Cancer Reconsidered." *Social History of Medicine*, 14:2, 2001, 293–312.

Culpeper, Jonathan. *Language and Characterization: People in Plays and Other Texts*. Harlow: Lonman, 2001.

Dahlén, Peter, Michael Forsman, and Klas Viklund. "Folkhemsdrömmen som sprack: Om den ironiska odramatiken i Roy Anderssons filmer." *Filmhäftet*, 1–2, 1990.

"De 25 bästa svenska filmerna." *FLM*, 17–18, 2012.

Demker, Marie. "Positiv attityd till invandring trots mobilisering av invandringsmotstånd." In Lennart Weibull, Henrik Oscarsson, and Annika Bergström (eds.), *I framtidens skugga*, SOM-report no 42. Gothenburg: University of Gothenburg, 2012.

———. "Racism, Xenophobia and Opposition to Immigration in Sweden." In Stefan Dahlberg, Henrik Oscarsson, and Lena Wängnerud (eds.), *Stepping Stones: Research on Political Representation, Voting Behavior and Quality of Government*. Göteborg: Department of Political Science, University of Gothenburg, 2013.

"Det intressanta är 'det oviktiga.'" *Upsala Nya Tidning*, March 16, 1976.

Douglas, Mary. *Purity and Danger: An Analysis of the Conception of Pollution and Taboo.* London: Routledge, 2002.

Durkheim, Èmile. *On Suicide.* London: Penguin, 2006.

Ebert, R. "Songs from the Second Floor." (2002). http://www.rogerebert.suntimes .com/apps/pbcs.dll/article?AID=/20021101/REVIEWS/211010307/1023 (accessed January 31, 2013).

"Egensinnet segrade." *Göteborgs-Posten*, May 9, 2000.

Elinder, Leif. "Dyslexi, DAMP och Aspergers syndrome–Friska sjukförklaras i diagnostiskt samhälle." *Läkartidningen*, 94:39, 1997, 3391–93.

Emanuelsson, Carl, Stina Svensson, and Sissela Nordling Blanco. "Därför använder vi inte hedersbegreppet" (2012). http://www.newsmill.se/artikel/ 2012/01/15/d-rf-r-anv-nder-vi-inte-hedersbegreppet (accessed March 28, 2013).

"En dyster återkomst" (review). *Sydsvenska* Dagbladet, November 17, 1975.

"En historia om Roy Andersson." *Chaplin*, 4 (1970).

Esping-Andersen, Gösta. "Jämlikhet, effektivitet och makt." In Per Thullberg and Kjell Österberg (eds.), *Den svenska modellen.* Lund: Studentlitteratur, 1994.

Evans, Natalie. "'A Racist Spectacle': Swedish Culture Minister Slammed for 'Black Face' Cake" (2012). http://www.mirror.co.uk/news/world-news/ swedish-minister-of-culture-slammed-for-racist-797906 (accessed January 3, 2013).

Ferriss, Suzanne, and Mallory Young. "Introduction." In Suzanne Ferriss and Mallory Young (eds.), *Chick Lit: The New Woman's Fiction.* New York: Routledge, 2006, 1–16.

"Filmgeniet från 70-talet är tillbaka." *Sydsvenska* Dagbladet, May 3, 1998.

Filmkrönikan. Sweden: Sveriges Television, TV2, April 28, 1974.

"Folkhemmets svanesång." *Filmhäftet*, 3, 2000.

Föreningen rädda individen homepage. http://www.fri-sverige.se (accessed August 11, 2014).

Frigyes, Paul. *Nyhetsflås och tidsanda. Svenska löpsedlar under ett sekel.* Stockholm: Carlssons, 2005.

Frisk, Liselotte. *Nyreligiositet i Sverige: Ett religionsvetenskapligt perspektiv.* Nora: Nya Doxa, 1998.

Frykman, Jonas, and Orvar Löfgren. "På väg–bilder av kultur och klass." In Jonas Frykman and Orvar Löfgren (eds.), *Modärna tider: Vision och vardag i folkhemmet.* Lund: Liber förlag, 1985, 33–139.

Furhammar, Leif. *Filmen i Sverige: En historia i tio kapitel och en fortsättning.* Stockholm: Dialogos, 2003.

Gahrton, Per. "Var står David Schwarz?" *Aftonbladet*, July 24, 1967.

Gillberg, Christopher, and Sophie Ekman. "Skolan knäcker 120 000 barn." *Dagens Nyheter*, March 20, 1997.

Gillespie, Karin. "Trash Talk." In Elizabeth Merrick (ed.), *This Is Not Chick Lit: Original Stories by America's Best Women Writers*. New York: Random House, 2006, 187–96.

Gornall, Jonathan. "Hyperactivity in Children: The Gillberg Affair." *British Medical Journal*, 335 (2007), 370–73.

Greider, Göran. "Det mest förljugna." *Aftonbladet*, August 6, 2007.

Gunér, Göran. "Filmskolan and Dramatiska institutet: Om Harry Schein och svensk filmutbildning." In Lars Ilshammar, Pelle Snickars and Per Vesterlund (eds.), *Citizen Schein*. Stockholm: Mediehistoriskt arkiv, 2010, 190–207.

Haag, Martina. *I en annan del av Bromma* [*In Another Part of Bromma*]. Stockholm: Piratförlaget, 2008.

———. *Underbar och älskad av alla (och på jobbet går det också jättebra)* [*Wonderful and Loved by Everybody*]. Stockholm: Piratförlaget, 2005.

Hadenius, Stig. *Svensk politik under 1900-talet: Konflikt och samförstånd*, 4th ed. Stockholm: Tiden Athena, 1996.

Hägg, Göran. *Välfärdsåren: Svensk historia 1945–1986*. Stockholm: Wahlström and Widstrand, 2005.

"Halv framgång med Giliap" (review). *Dagens Nyheter*, November 17, 1975.

Hanegraaff, Wouter J. "Forbidden Knowledge: Anti-Esoteric Polemics and Academic Research." *Aries*, 5:2 (2005), 225–54.

"Här kommer Roy." *Nöjesguiden*, 4, 1988.

Harzewski, Stephanie. *Chick Lit and Postfeminism*. Charlottesville: University of Virginia Press, 2011.

———. "Tradition and Displacement in the New Novel of Manners." In Suzanne Ferriss and Mallory Young (eds.), *Chick Lit: The New Woman's Fiction*. New York: Routledge, 2006, 29–46.

Hill, Nanci Milone. *Reading Women: A Book Club Guide for Women's Fiction*. Santa Barbara, CA: Libraries Unlimited, 2012.

Hirdman, Yvonne. *Att lägga livet till rätta: Studier i svensk folkhemspolitik*. Stockholm: Carlssons, 1989.

Hoberman, J. "Suspended Animation" (2002). http://www.villagevoice.com/2002-07-02/film/suspended-animation/ (accessed January 31, 2013).

Holmberg, Jan. "Can We Bother about Each Other?" In Tytti Soila (ed.), *The Cinema of Scandinavia*. London: Wallflower, 2005.

Hutcheon, Linda. *Irony's Edge: The Theory and Politics of Irony*. London: Routledge, 1995.

Ingelstam, Lars. *Framtidstron och den svenska modellen*, Tema T Rapport 15. Linköping: Universitetet i Linköping, 1988.

Ingemarsson, Kajsa. *Bara vanligt vatten* [*Just Ordinary Water*]. Stockholm: Norstedts, 2009.

————. *Den ryske vännen* [*The Russian Friend*]. Stockholm: Bokförlaget Forum, 2005.

————. *Inte enklare än så* [*Not Easier than That*]. Stockholm: Bokförlaget Forum, 2003.

————. *Kajsas värld* [*Kajsa's World*]. Stockholm: Bokförlaget Forum, 2006.

————. *Lyckans hjul* [*Wheel of Fortune*]. Stockholm: Norstedts, 2007.

————. *På det fjärde ska det ske* [*It Will Happen on the Fourth*]. Stockholm: Bokförlaget Forum, 2002.

————. *Små citroner gula* [*Yesterday's News*]. Stockholm: Bokförlaget Forum, 2004.

————. *Små citroner gula*. Stockholm: Månpocket, 2006.

Inglehart, Ronald, and Christian Welzel. *Modernization, Cultural Change, and Democracy: The Human Development Sequence*. Cambridge: Cambridge University Press, 2005.

Johannisson, Karin. "Politisk anatomi." In *Kroppens tunna skal: Sex essäer om kropp, historia och kultur*. Stockholm: Bokförlaget Pan, 1998, 221–257.

Johansson Heinö, Andreas. *Vi gillar olika? Hur den svenska likhetsnormen hindrar integrationen*. Stockholm: Timbro, 2012.

Jörberg, Lennart. "Svensk ekonomi under 100 år." In Bo Södersten (ed.), *Svensk ekonomi*, 3rd ed. Stockholm: Rabén and Sjögren, 1984, 17–50.

Kardemark, Wilhelm. *När livet tar rätt form: Om människosyn i svenska hälsotidskrifter 1910–13 och 2009*. Diss. Göteborg: Institutionen för litteratur, idéhistoria och religion, 2013.

Kärfve, Eva. *Härnspöken—DAMP och hotet mot folkhälsan*. Stockholm: Brutus Östlings bokförlag Symposion, 2000.

Keyes, Marian. *Anybody out There?* London: Michael Joseph, 2006.

————. *Further under the Duvet*. London: Michael Joseph, 2005.

————. *Rachel's Holiday*. New York: Avon, 2002.

————. *Under the Duvet: Postcards from the Bed*. London: Michael Joseph, 2001.

Knowles, J. "Editorial," *Diegesis: Journal of the Association for Research in Popular Fiction*. Special Issue on Chick Lit, 8 (2004), 3–4.

Kolbe, Gunlög. *Om konsten att konstruera en kvinna. Retoriska strategier i 1800-talets rådgivare och i Marie Sophie Schwartz' romaner*. Göteborg: Göteborgs Universitet, 2001.

Kommitén för mänskliga rättigheter homepage. http://www.kmr.nu/ (accessed January 3, 2013).

Kovács, András Bálint. *Screening Modernism: European Art Cinema, 1950–1980*. Chicago: University of Chicago Press, 2007.

"Kraschlandning för filmgeniet." *Arbetet*, February 25, 1989.

Kyllerstedt, Ingrid. "10 000 hotar skolka från television-licens." *Journalisten*, October 24, 2006.

Larsson, Mariah. *Skenet som bedrog: Mai Zetterling och det svenska sextiotalet.* Lund: Sekel, 2006.

Lehman, Stephanie. "How to Be a Millionaire." In Elizabeth Merrick (ed.), *This Is Not Chick Lit: Original Stories by America's Best Women Writers.* New York: Random House, 2006, 235–46.

Lewin, Leif. *"Bråka inte!" Om vår tids demokratisyn.* Stockholm: SNS Förlag, 1998.

Liedman, Sven-Eric. *Om Solidaritet: Att se sig själv i andra.* Stockholm: Bonniers, 1999.

Lindqvist, Mats. "Ingenjör Fredriksson i framtidslandet." In Jonas Frykman and Orvar Löfgren (eds.), *Modärna tider: Vision och vardag i folkhemmet.* Lund: Liber förlag, 1985.

Lindqvist, Ursula. "Roy Andersson's Cinematic Poetry and the Spectre of César Vallejo." *Scandinavian Canadian Studies*, 19, 2010.

Lommel, Michael. "Die Erkaltung der Restwärme: Surreale Milleniumsbilder in Songs from the Second Floor." In Michael Lommel et al (eds.), *Surrealismus und Film: Von Fellini bis Lync.* Bielefeld: Transcript, 2008.

Malmberg, Carl-Johan. "Den vita sporten och den omöjliga neutraliteten." In *Svensk Filmografi 6: 1960–1969.* Stockholm: SFI, 1977.

Marcuse, Herbert. *One-Dimensional Man: Studies in the Ideology of Advanced Industrial Society.* Boston: Beacon, 1991.

Melton, J. Gordon. *The Church of Scientology.* N.p.: Signature Books, 2000.

Mieszkowski, Katharine. "Scientology's War on Psychiatry" (2005). http://www .salon.com/2005/07/01/sci_psy/ (accessed January 8, 2013).

"Min nya film ska kännas i magen." *Expressen*, November 24, 1971.

Mithander, Conny. "Från mönsterland till monsterland: Folkhemska berättelser." In Åke Bergvall, Yvonne Leffler, and Conny Mithander (eds.), *Berättelse i förvandling: Berättande i ett intermedialt och tvärvetenskapligt perspektiv.* Karlstad: Karlstad University, 2000.

Montoro, Rocio. *Chick Lit: The Stylistics of Cappuccino Fiction.* London: Continuum, 2012.

Mörner, Cecilia. *Vissa visioner: Tendenser i svensk biografdistribuerad fiktionsfilm 1967–1972.* Stockholm: Stockholm University, 2000.

Myrdal, Alva, and Gunnar Myrdal. *Kris i befolkningsfrågan.* Stockholm: Albert Bonniers förlag, 1934.

Myrdal, Gunnar. *An American Dilemma: The Negro Problem and Modern Democracy*, Vol. 1. New York: Harper and Brothers, 1944.

———. "A Worried America." *Current*, 202, April 1978.

————. *Hur styrs landet?* Stockholm: Rabén and Sjögren, 1982.

————. "Socialpolitikens dilemma II." *Spektrum*, 2:4, 1932.

Naremore, James. *On Kubrick.* London: BFI, 2008.

Niemi, Mikael. *Popular Music.* Trans. by Laurie Thompson. London: Flamingo, 2003.

Nilson, Maria. *Chick lit. Från glamour till vardagsrealism.* Lund: BTJ förlag, 2008.

Nilsson, Lennart. "Svenska folket, den offentliga sektorn och välfärdsstaten." In Sören Holmberg and Lennart Weibull (eds.), *Lyckan kommer, Lyckan går.* SOM-report no 36. Gothenburg: University of Gothenburg, 2005, 53–66.

Nordström, Ludvig. *Lort-Sverige,* 3rd ed. Stockholm: Kooperativa förbundets bokförlag, 1938.

Nylund, Karl-Erik. *Att leka med elden: Sekternas värld,* 2nd ed. Stockholm: Sellin and Partner Bok och Idé AB, 2004.

"Och här klipper Roy Andersson till" (review). *Aftonbladet,* August 24, 1995.

Ofstad, Harald. *Vårt förakt för svaghet: Nazismens normer och värderingar–och våra egna.* Stockholm: Karneval, 2012.

"Oj, oj, vilket liv det blev Roy." *Aftonbladet,* April 16, 1985.

"Okänd regissör får jättechans." *Dagens Nyheter,* March 11, 1969.

Olofsson, Gunnar. "'Den stränge fadern och den goda modern': Sociologiska perspektiv på den moderna staten." In Ulf Himmelstrand and Göran Svensson (eds.), *Sverige—vardag och struktur: Sociologer beskriver det svenska samhället,* 2nd ed. Stockholm: Norstedts, 1993, 585–615.

Om Sexuallivet i Sverige. Värderingar, normer, beteenden i sociologisk tolkning. Statens offentliga utredningar 1969:2.

Orr, John. *Cinema and Modernity.* Oxford: Polity, 1993.

Oscarsson, Henrik, and Sören Holmberg. *Nya svenska väljare.* Stockholm: Norstedts Juridik, 2013.

Östberg, Kjell. *1968: När allting var i rörelse.* Stockholm: Prisma, 2002.

Pedersen, Mette. *Not One of Us: National Identity versus Islam–A Comparative Discourse Analysis of the Danish People's Party, the Party for Freedom and the Sweden Democrats.* MA thesis. Aalborg: Aalborg University, 2011.

Pettersson, Cecilia. "Mellan självberättelse och självförglömmande. Om terapeutisk läsning." *Läsning. RJ:s Årsbok 1013/2014.* Göteborg: Makadam, 2013, 148–56.

Power, Jonathan. "In Search of the Swedish Soul." *Prospect Magazine,* July 2009.

Qvarsell, Roger. "Mellan familj, arbetsgivare och stat: En idéhistorisk essä om det sociala ansvarets organisering under två århundraden." In Erik Amnå (ed.), *Medmänsklighet att hyra? Åtta forskare om ideell verksamhet.* Örebro: Libris, 1995, 9–18.

Radio Sweden. "Library Removes 'Lilla hjärtat' Books" (2012). http://sverigesradio.se/sida/gruppsida.aspx?programid=2054&grupp=3578&artikel=5387600 (accessed January 3 2013).

Radner, Hilary. *Neofeminism: Girly Films, Chick Films and Consumer Culture*. London: Routledge, 2011.

Regis, Pamela. *A Natural History of the Romance Novel*. Philadelphia: University of Pennsylvania Press, 2003.

Rekordmagazinet. Sweden: TV2, April 5, 1989.

Ricoeur, Paul. *The Rule of Metaphor*. Trans. by Robert Czerny. London: Routledge, Kegan and Paul, 1978.

Rothstein, Bo. *Den korporativa staten: Intresseorganisationer och statsförvaltning i svensk politik*. Stockholm: Norstedts, 1992.

Rothstein, Mikael. "'His name was Xenu. He used renegades . . .': Aspects of Scientology's Founding Myth." In James R. Lewis (ed.), *Scientology*. Oxford: Oxford University Press, 2009, 365–87.

Rudberg, Denise. *Åse: Roman*. Stockholm: Bonniers, 2008.

——. *Jenny S*. Stockholm: Bonniers, 2005.

——. *Väninnan* [*The Girlfriend*]. Stockholm: Fischer, 2000.

Runcis, Maija. *Steriliseringar i folkhemmet*. Stockholm: Ordfront, 1998.

Russell, Dominique. "The Ghost of the Second Floor." *Literature/Film Quarterly*, 36, 2008.

"Säker debutfilm om tonårskärlek och vuxentristess" (review). *Dagens Nyheter*, April 25, 1970.

Sartre, Jean-Paul. *Being and Nothingness: An Essay on Phenomenological Ontology*. London: Routledge, 2000.

Sennett, Richard. *The Corrosion of Character: The Personal Consequences of Work in the New Capitalism*. New York: W. W. Norton, 1998.

"Sex är skönt för ungarna." *Aftonbladet*, February 3, 1980.

Sexuella övergrepp: Förslag till en ny lydelse av brottsbalken om sedlighetsbrott avgivet av sexualbrottsutredningen. Statens offentliga utredningar 1976:9.

Shklovsky, Victor. *Theory of Prose*. Elmwood Park: Dalkey Archive, 1990.

Showalter, Gena. "Every Girl's Dream." In Suzanne Ferriss and Mallory Young (eds.), *Chick Lit: The New Woman's Fiction*. New York: Routledge, 2006, 211–25.

Sigurdson, Ola. *Den lyckliga filosofin: Etik och politik hos Hägerström, Tingsten, makarna Myrdal och Hedenius*. Stockholm: Brutus Östlings bokförlag Symposion, 2000.

Siplin, Karen. "Nice Jewis Boy." In Elizabeth Merrick (ed.), *This Is Not Chick Lit: Original Stories by America's Best Women Writers*. New York: Random House, 2006, 87–100.

Smith, Caroline J. *Cosmopolitan Culture and Consumerism in Chick Lit*. New York: Routledge, 2007: 20–44.

Society and Sex in Sweden. Stockholm: Swedish Institute, 1967.

Sontag, Susan. *Illness as Metaphor and AIDS and Its Metaphors*. New York: Picador, 1990.

Sörlin, Sverker. "Utopin i verkligheten: Ludvig Nordström och det moderna Sverige." In Ronny Ambjörnsson (ed.), *I framtidens tjänst: Ur folkhemmets idéhistoria*. Stockholm: Gidlunds, 1986.

Ståhl, Bo R., and Bertil Persson. *Kulter, Sekter, Samfund: en studie av religiösa minoriteter i Sverige*. Stockholm: Proprius Förlag, 1971.

Statens offentliga utredningar (Statens offentliga utredningar 1998:113). *I God Tro—Samhället och nyandligheten*. Socialdepartementet, Betänkande av Krisstödsutredningen, Statens offentliga utredningar, September 1998.

Stenius, Henrik. "The Good Life is a Life of Conformity: The Impact of Lutheran Tradition on Nordic Political Culture." In Øystein Sørensen and Bo Stråth (eds.), *The Cultural Construction of Norden*. Oslo: Scandinavian University Press, 1997, 161–71.

Svendsen, Lars Fr. H. *Långtråkighetens filosofi*. Stockholm: Natur and Kultur, 2003.

Swedish National Election Studies homepage. http://www.valforskning.pol.gu.se/english/ (accessed January 3, 2013).

Therborn, Göran. "Hur det hela började: När och varför det moderna Sverige blev vad det blev." In Ulf Himmelstrand and Göran Svensson (eds.), *Sverige—vardag och struktur*, 2nd ed. Stockholm: Norstedts, 1993, 25–53.

Thullberg, Per, and Kjell Östberg (eds.). *Den svenska modellen*. Lund: Studentlitteratur, 1994.

Törnblom, Mia. *Självkänsla nu! Din personliga coach visar hur*[*Self-Esteem Now! Your Personal Coach Demonstrates How*]. Stockholm: Månpocket, 2005.

Trädgårdh, Lars. "Statist Individualism: On the Culturality of the Nordic Welfare State." In Øystein Sørensen and Bo Stråth (eds.), *The Cultural Construction of Norden*. Oslo: Scandinavian University Press, 1997, 253–85.

"Tystnad–tagning." *Resumé*, 4, 1985.

Uddhammar, Emil. *Partierna och den stora staten: En analys av statsteorier och svensk politik under 1900-talet*. Stockholm: City University Press, 1993.

Urban, Hugh B. *The Church of Scientology: A History of a New Religion*. Princeton, NJ: Princeton University Press, 2011.

Wells, Juliette. "Mothers of Chick Lit? Women Writers, Readers, and Literary History." In Suzanne Ferriss and Mallory Young (eds.), *Chick Lit: The New Woman's Fiction*. New York: Routledge, 2006.

Widerberg, Bo. *Visionen i svensk film*. Stockholm: Bonniers, 1962.

Wiklund, Martin. *I det modernas landskap: Historisk orientering och kritiska berättelser om det moderna Sverige mellan 1960 och 1990*. Stockholm: Brutus Östlings bokförlag Symposion, 2006.

Williamson, Kevin D., "Why Sweden Stinks." In *A Politically Incorrect Guide to Socialism*. Washington, DC: Regnery, 2011.

Wilson, Colin. *The Outsider*. London: Phoenix, 2001.

Yang, Julianne Qiuling Ma. *Towards a Cinema of Contemplation: Roy Andersson's Aesthetics and Ethics*. Diss. Hong Kong: University of Hong Kong, 2013.

Yardley, Cathy. *Will Write for Shoes: How to Write a Chick Lit Novel*. New York: Thomas Dunne, 2006.

NOTES ON CONTRIBUTORS

Henrik Bogdan is an associate professor in the history of religions at the University of Gothenburg. He is the author of *Western Esotericism and Rituals of Initiation* (State University of New York Press, 2007) and coeditor of numerous collections, including *Aleister Crowley and Western Esotericism* (Oxford University Press, 2012), *Occultism in a Global Perspective* (Acumen, 2013), *Handbook of Freemasonry* (Brill Academic, 2014), and *Sexuality and New Religious Movements* (forthcoming). Bogdan is the book review editor of *Aries: Journal for the Study of Western Esotericism*, an associate editor of *The Pomegranate: The International Journal of Pagan Studies*, and a board member of the European Society for the Study of Western Esotericism (ESSWE).

Daniel Brodén is a researcher in film studies at the University of Gothenburg. Brodén's main research interests are the media culture and cultural history of the Swedish welfare state. He recently coedited a book on cinema and modernism (with Kristoffer Noheden), *I gränslandet* (Gidlunds, 2013) [In the Borderland]. His dissertation *Folkhemmets skuggbilder* (2008) [Dark Shadows of the Welfare State], a comprehensive study on the domestic crime film genre, was awarded the nonfiction book of the year award by The Swedish Crime Writers Academy.

Marie Demker is a professor of political science at the University of Gothenburg. She is the author of more than 15 books and anthologies, among them *Colonial Power and National Identity, Pierre Mendès France and the History of French Decolonisation* (Santérus, 2008), and several book chapters and articles on political parties in Europe. She recurrently publishes chronicles and is an active commentator on politics in Swedish media.

Andreas Johansson Heinö is a researcher in political science at the University of Gothenburg and a senior fellow at the liberal think tank Timbro in Stockholm. He is an expert on multiculturalism and Swedish national identity and also the author of *Hur mycket mångfald tål demokratin?* (Gleerups, 2009) [How much diversity can democracy sustain?] and *Gillar vi olika?* (Timbro, 2012) [Do we really like it different?].

Yvonne Leffler is a professor of comparative literature at the University of Gothenburg. Her main areas of research and publications are in the field of Scandinavian nineteenth-century literature and contemporary popular fiction. She has published several books, including *Horror as Pleasure: The Aesthetics of Horror Fiction* (Almqvist & Wiksell, 2000) and articles about Gothic fiction, nineteenth-century novels, and popular fiction in postmodern society. Besides working with "Fiction and Health," she is currently directing a research project on the transcultural dissemination and reception of Swedish literature in the nineteenth century.

Ola Sigurdson is a professor of systematic theology and the director of the Centre for Culture and Health at the University of Gothenburg. He has held visiting scholarships in Uppsala, Sweden; Cambridge, England; and Princeton, New Jersey. The author of more than 15 books and anthologies, among them *Theology and Marxism in Eagleton and Žižek* (Palgrave Macmillan, 2012) and *Heavenly Bodies* (forthcoming), he is also active as a cultural journalist and commentator in Swedish media.

INDEX OF NAMES